PRAISE FOR *DRAFT DAY*

An instant national bestseller

"Draft day can make or break your team for years to come. This is essential reading for anyone who wants to understand how teambuilding in hockey really works."

JOHN DAVIDSON, President of Hockey Operations for the Columbus Blue Jackets

"Doug MacLean may have a reputation for bluntness, but that's just the beginning when it comes to my friend and longtime Sportsnet coworker. The truth is, he's as honest in life as he is at work, whether that's on the air, in the boardroom, or behind an NHL bench. Like the man, his book holds no punches. *Draft Day* gets right to the point and is the most entertaining and insightful book you'll read this year."

NICK KYPREOS, cohost of *Real Kyper & Bourne*, author of *Undrafted*, and Stanley Cup champion

"Come for the great storytelling from Doug MacLean and Scott Morrison, stick around for the revealing NHL draft tales, especially the incredible Eric Lindros trade story you won't find anywhere else."

BOB McKENZIE, TSN draft expert and NHL insider

"Doug MacLean did some amazing wheeling and dealing to make me the number one overall pick in 2002. In *Draft Day*, he tells the story behind that draft and others like it to show all the thought and work that goes into building teams."

RICK NASH, former Columbus Blue Jackets star and Maurice "Rocket" Richard Trophy winner

"The draft is the most franchise-altering night on the NHL schedule, and Doug gives a real behind-the-scenes look. *Draft Day* is an insightful read for hockey fans."

ELLIOTTE FRIEDMAN, broadcaster for *Hockey Night in Canada* and cohost of *32 Thoughts: The Podcast*

"Doug MacLean is a hockey lifer and an entertaining storyteller. You'll enjoy this book."

GERARD GALLANT, NHL coach and former player

"[A] worthy read on a lot of levels. . . . As MacLean's book makes clear, in the world of pro sports, sometimes the line between being immortalized and being unemployed is probably finer than we'd like to think."

Toronto Star

DRAFT DAY

HOW HOCKEY TEAMS PICK WINNERS
OR GET LEFT BEHIND

DOUG MacLEAN
WITH SCOTT MORRISON

PUBLISHED BY SIMON & SCHUSTER

NEW YORK   LONDON   TORONTO   SYDNEY   NEW DELHI

SIMON &
SCHUSTER
CANADA

A Division of Simon & Schuster, LLC
166 King Street East, Suite 300
Toronto, Ontario M5A 1J3

This Simon & Schuster Canada edition October 2024

SIMON & SCHUSTER CANADA and colophon are
registered trademarks of Simon & Schuster, LLC

Simon & Schuster: Celebrating 100 Years of Publishing in 2024

For information about special discounts for bulk purchases, please contact Simon &
Schuster Special Sales at 1-800-268-3216 or CustomerService@simonandschuster.ca.

Interior design by Alexis Minieri

Manufactured in the United States of America

1   3   5   7   9   10   8   6   4   2

Library and Archives Canada Cataloguing in Publication

Title: Draft day : how hockey teams pick winners or
get left behind / Doug MacLean with Scott
Morrison.
Names: MacLean, Doug, 1954- author. | Morrison, Scott, 1958- author.
Description: Simon & Schuster Canada edition. | Includes
index. | Previously published in 2023.
Identifiers: Canadiana 20240355865 | ISBN 9781982149963 (softcover)
Subjects: LCSH: Hockey players—Selection and
appointment. | LCSH: National Hockey League.
Classification: LCC GV847.45 .M33 2024 | DDC 796.962/64—dc23

ISBN 978-1-9821-4996-3
ISBN 978-1-9821-4994-9 (hardcover)
ISBN 978-1-9821-4995-6 (ebook)

To my parents, Fran and Jim, my loving and supporting wife, Jill, incredible kids, Clark and MacKenzie, and so many friends in and out of the game—I could never have had this life in the NHL without you. Thank you is not enough.

CONTENTS

PREFACE

I WILL NEVER FORGET THE FINAL FEW WEEKS OF THE 2003–04 SEASON. IT MIGHT have been the time when I truly understood the mental tug-of-war a National Hockey League general manager, especially the GM of a struggling, still relatively new expansion franchise, goes through. It was the fourth of my ten seasons as president and GM of the Columbus Blue Jackets.

Midway through the previous season, I was sitting in my office after a tough home loss to the Nashville Predators when the phone rang. It was my owner, Mr. John H. McConnell, telling me I had to fire my head coach, Dave King. I asked him who was going to coach. He said, "You are!" So now I am the head coach, the third title on my business card along with president and GM, and one title too many. Maybe two.

The local media was convinced I fired Dave because I wanted to coach. That wasn't the case. Obviously, I couldn't tell anyone the real reason, that it was my owner's idea. At one point after I had taken over from King, we got within six points of a playoff spot. I thought, this is looking good, all things considered. Even the media was saying the old Florida Panthers coach was back. Well, it went south pretty quickly. The next season, 2003–04, during the thirty-seven games I was behind the bench, we won a grand total of nine games. On January 1, I promoted my old friend and assistant coach Gerard Gallant to take over.

During the forty-five games after Gerard took over, we won sixteen games. It was still a good move promoting him because I didn't need to be working three jobs and the record wasn't his fault. Gerard went on to become a very good coach. But the season was another immense struggle and disappointment.

I remember in March we lost eight straight games and it was pure torture. Seven years on the job, I was fearing I might not survive myself. On March 21, we were in Vancouver. That night our two stars, Rick Nash and Nikolai Zherdev, both put on an unbelievable show. We had an amazing game and finally won, 5–4. And I felt great. We had ended the losing streak, stopped the bleeding, and our two stars, the future of the franchise, were phenomenal. For a moment or two, the present didn't feel so bleak because the future looked bright. Even the *Hockey News* had written in its prospects issue that Columbus was in great shape moving forward. They devoted a cover to the "Rick and Nic Show." According to the media experts, we were on the verge of taking big steps. We were experiencing pain, but those two draft picks—Nash and Zherdev—were going to lead us to the promised land, or so we hoped.

After that game, the team returned home to Columbus and mercifully we only had seven more games to finish the season. But the emotions truly were mixed. On one hand we wanted the season to end because of all the losing and we were out of the playoffs. On the other hand, we couldn't wait for the next one to begin. I stayed out west to do some scouting and a few nights later at home we beat Minnesota 2–0, then Anaheim 3–1, for a modest three-game winning streak. I remember being excited about the wins. I was on the road scouting with Dale Tallon, who was an assistant GM with the Chicago Blackhawks at the time. After one of those wins, Dale asked me what I was so excited about and I said, "We finally won some effing games." The Hawks struggled that season, too, but while we were winning, they were losing or tying games. But Dale was just as happy as me.

How does that work?

That's when I fully understood the conundrum every GM experiences: You have to win to survive, but some seasons losing is not a bad thing; it's actually the best thing. The key, I suppose, is finding a way to lose and survive and not be accused of tanking!

Before that game in Vancouver, we were holding the fourth overall pick of the draft (prior to the dreaded draft lottery being held, of course). That draft was a big one because it included Alexander Ovechkin and Evgeni Malkin, both potential franchise players. Winning that game dropped us to fifth in the lottery ranking at the time with the Washington Capitals moving into the fourth spot. So, by winning, we were effectively losing.

When it came time for the lottery, Pittsburgh had finished last, a point behind Chicago and Washington and four points behind us. Washington won the lottery and Ovechkin and we all know how that turned out, with Ovi becoming one of the greatest scorers ever and the Caps eventually winning a Stanley Cup years later. Pittsburgh fell to second and got Malkin. They won the lottery the next year (more about that later) and got Sidney Crosby and three Stanley Cup victories. We also know how it ultimately turned out for me in Columbus!

It's funny, but during the 2022–23 season Montreal Canadiens GM Kent Hughes was having the same feelings I had years earlier. The Habs were having growing pains and a lot of injuries. They lost a lot but also had moments when they played well and won because of their good, young talent and coach Martin St. Louis. One day Hughes was asked, with the generational player Connor Bedard in the 2023 draft, if winning too often was a bad thing.

"I said to Marty [coach Martin St. Louis], we've gotten to a point where the wins are good only to a certain point and the losses are bad only to a certain point," referencing the balance between culture building, developing your young players, and improving the draft lottery odds.

After that 2004 draft lottery we stayed in the four spot, which was very frustrating. The draft that year was in Raleigh and, incredibly, it got worse for us. The feeling going in was that after the first two picks (Ovechkin and Malkin), the drop-off in talent was drastic. The next couple of prospects were defenseman Cam Barker with Medicine Hat, and winger Andrew Ladd with the Calgary Hitmen. Our scouts were not sold on Barker. We liked Ladd and watched him a lot, but my chief scout, Don Boyd, and the staff weren't sold on him. Wayne Smith, our scout in Quebec, loved left winger Alexandre Picard, who was with Lewiston of the Quebec league, and desperately wanted him. He was being compared to Patrice Bergeron, a former second-round pick of the Boston Bruins, who turned out to be a great player. The scouts told me I could move back from number four to as deep as number eight, get a second-round pick tossed in the deal, and still get Picard.

We made a decision as a staff and decided to trade down. Jimmy Rutherford, the GM of the Carolina Hurricanes at the time, called me at the table a few minutes before the draft and asked if I would consider moving the fourth pick. The draft was in his city and he wanted to make a splash. He owned the eighth pick. Well, we had made the decision we would move, so we made the deal, flipping from four to eight and getting an additional second-round pick in the 2004 draft. Our staff was elated we made the trade, confident we would still get Picard at eight and have that extra pick.

With the third pick Chicago took Barker and Jimmy took Ladd at number four. Blake Wheeler, a big right winger, went fifth to Phoenix, goaltender Al Montoya went to the New York Rangers, and Florida took winger Rostislav Olesz seventh.

With the eighth selection Columbus selected Picard. I remember after we made the pick Tim Murray, who was scouting with Anaheim at the time, walked by our table on his way to making the ninth overall pick and said, "Man, you got a player. What a great selection. We wanted him." We left Raleigh after the draft on a high. Were we ever wrong.

Ovechkin and Malkin became superstars, as expected. Barker had an average career, with injuries and contract hassles getting in the way. Ladd played 1001 NHL games and was pretty darn good. Picard played 67 games. I wish Timmy and the Ducks had gotten Picard. He had trouble keeping up with the pace of the game and just wasn't good enough.

And it was a disastrous draft overall for us. It got worse as both our second-round picks—right winger Adam Pieneault from Boston College at forty-six overall and defenseman Kyle Wharton from Ottawa at fifty-nine—played a total of three NHL games. We drafted a goalie, Dan LaCosta from Owen Sound, who played four NHL games. Then our next five picks never played in the NHL. Our final pick, in the ninth round, defenseman Grant Clitsome out of Nepean, played 205 games. Go figure. That's the draft.

With respect to scout Wayne Smith, he was offered a promotion and a job with the Bruins after the draft and went on to help them win a Stanley Cup. He was a good scout, and we had lots of good scouts, but that's the imperfect science of the draft.

I still haven't gotten over the excitement we felt watching Nash and Zherdev perform their magic in that Vancouver win, and then the sick feeling in my stomach seeing the Capitals get a generational player in Ovechkin. The lottery has not been a friend to the Blue Jackets. The wins down the stretch that year felt great, but they ultimately didn't do us any favors. And then we didn't do ourselves any favors with our selections.

As my good friend Brian Burke said to me when I got the job in Columbus: "It's simple, Doug; just make sure you finish last every year until you get stars." We never quite figured that out. We were bad enough, finished low enough, but never had any lottery luck. In 2001, our second draft, we were picking eighth. What were we doing picking eighth? We had seventy-one points and our owner was unbelievably excited. But eighth! That was the year Ilya Kovalchuk went first to Atlanta and Jason Spezza went second to Ottawa. We got goaltender Pascal Leclaire at eight, a decent pick, but he only played 173 NHL games. And he certainly wasn't a Kovalchuk or Spezza.

Aside from finishing last every year and hoping you have lottery luck, winning at the draft means having the right pieces in the front office. Ken Holland has been a great friend for many years.

He spent thirty-six years in the Detroit Red Wings organization—two as a goalie, the rest in management. He started his management career as an amateur scout in Western Canada, hired by GM Jim Devellano. We were in the organization together for four years. Ken worked his way up, eventually becoming chief scout, goaltending coach, and then assistant GM in 1994, replacing me when I was let go and eventually landed in Florida. We spent a lot of time together either scouting in Western Canada or across Europe.

Two years after Ken replaced me, teams were calling the Red Wings asking for permission to talk to him about becoming their GM. Detroit realized they had a gem, and after the Wings won the Stanley Cup in 1997 they made Kenny the GM. For the next twenty-two years he remained GM and executive vice president. During that time, he won the Stanley Cup another three times—in 1998, 2002, and 2008—with just five players a part of all four championships. He won the President's Trophy four times, the Central Division ten times, and the Red Wings won five regular-season conference titles. They also had a streak of twenty-five consecutive playoff appearances, the last nineteen with Holland as GM.

In fall 2021, he was inducted into the Hockey Hall of Fame as a builder. A pretty impressive résumé, to say the least. When Ken talks, hockey people listen. And not just because he is a great guy. It was during his induction speech that Ken summed up what makes teams winners and champions: "Scouting is the lifeblood of a successful team!"

He then went on to thank some of the best scouts in the business, who worked with him in Detroit, the likes of Mark Howe, Joe McDonnell, Hakan Andersson, Archie Henderson, Glenn

Merkosky, Jiri Fischer, and the late Dan Belisle. Some of these scouts helped build the Red Wings into a championship organization. Some were pro scouts, some amateur. It takes a team to win on the ice and it takes a team to win off the ice.

By the way, of those five players who won all four Stanley Cups, three were drafted by the Red Wings—Nicklas Lidstrom, a Hall of Famer, in the third round, 53rd overall; Darren McCarty in the second round, 46th overall; Tomas Holmstrom in the tenth round, 257th overall. Scouting is the lifeblood of a successful team!

Holland was a five-foot-eight goaltender, who was selected 188th overall by the Toronto Maple Leafs in 1975. He played nine professional seasons with the Red Wings and Hartford Whalers organizations, playing just four NHL games (three with Detroit, one with Hartford) before he was let go by the Wings but soon offered that scouting job by Devellano. So, not all picks work out, at least on the ice!

And since May 7, 2019, he has been the president of hockey operations and GM of the Edmonton Oilers, an organization that prior to his arrival had seen both sides of the draft—a lot of years with high picks and no results, not even playoff appearances. For three straight years they drafted first overall: 2010 Taylor Hall, 2011 Ryan Nugent-Hopkins, 2012 Nail Yakupov. Still nothing. In 2013, they drafted defenseman Darnell Nurse seventh overall. The next year, center Leon Draisaitl third overall. And then they had the really big draft lottery win and things started to look up. In 2015, they got generational player Connor McDavid first overall. Even so, there have been struggles, although the last few seasons the Oilers have taken major steps forward. It's just another example of how fickle and how important the draft is.

In the eighties, when the Oilers were a dynasty, winning the Stanley Cup four times in five years, they were draft wizards under GM Glen Sather and chief scout Barry Fraser, who passed in 2022. They drafted the likes of Mark Messier, Kevin Lowe, Grant Fuhr, Paul Coffey, Jari Kurri, and Glenn Anderson, all future Hall of Famers. And, of course, they were gifted the un-drafted Wayne Gretzky (more about that later). But it shows how unpredictable the draft can be, from feast in the eighties to not exactly famine but not being able to make it work for a lot of years afterward.

All of those picks were made before Ken arrived, but even though it took time, those picks became the lifeblood of a successful team.

Being an NHL GM is an incredible experience on so many levels and the draft week is truly a highlight because, as Ken said, you know what it means in achieving success. It's a week leading up to two days of great anticipation and excitement and pressure. It's a week during which you can make things happen for your franchise. Or not.

It's absolutely true that those days might be the most impor-tant for an NHL team and the GM. Yes, you can bolster your team through trades and free-agent signings, but draft day is criti-cal. For the young players it's when dreams begin, and for the clubs it's when foundations are laid. Good and bad. It can be a franchise-changing day (which is what GMs dream about). And it's not just the first round that can alter the fortunes. Think about the Boston Bruins—they got Patrice Bergeron in the second round, forty-fifth overall in 2003; Brad Marchand in the third round, seventy-first overall in 2006; David Pastrnak in the first round, twenty-fifth overall in 2014. Greatness can be found anywhere.

Not that it's so easy. In 2015, the Bruins had three consecutive picks in the first round: numbers thirteen, fourteen, and fifteen. It was supposed to be the draft, under GM Don Sweeney, that would set up the Bruins for the future. First, they selected defenseman Jakub Zboril from Saint John. He has been okay. Then they took winger Jake DeBrusk from Swift Current, whom I like a lot. Finally, they took winger Zachary Senyshyn from Sault Ste. Marie. He played fourteen games for the Bruins. The next three picks were center Mathew Barzal, winger Kyle Connor, and defenseman Thomas Chabot, who was playing with Zboril in Saint John. Swap in those three and it would have been the draft for the ages for the Bruins. But that's the way it goes.

Some of the brightest minds in the game don't always get it right. Even can't-miss prospects sometimes do miss. Remember, you're trying to predict what an eighteen-year-old kid is going to be like at the next level, maybe a year away, or several years away. And there is so much to consider, from skills to attitude, hockey sense to common sense.

And with the arrival of the salary cap for the 2005–06 season, in many ways the draft became even more important, because of the need for good, young, cheap talent to stock and build the roster.

The world of the NHL is ever changing. Consider the 2016 draft in which a Ping-Pong ball helped change the fortunes of the Toronto Maple Leafs. But that draft is further evidence of changing times, how the salary cap and the latest collective bargaining agreement offer new challenges to teams. Look at the top picks in that draft. Auston Matthews is still with the Leafs. Patrik Laine went second to Winnipeg but eventually was traded to Columbus for number three overall, Pierre-Luc Dubois. Number four, Jesse

Puljujärvi, was traded to Carolina. Number five, Olli Juolevi, was traded by Vancouver and was with Florida, Detroit, then Anaheim. Number six, Matthew Tkachuk, was traded by Calgary because he wanted out. Number eight, Alexander Nylander, was traded by Buffalo. Number nine, Mikhail Sergachev, was a bad trade by Montreal. Number ten, Tyson Jost, also was traded, as was number eleven, Logan Brown. Of the top eleven picks, only Matthews and number seven, Clayton Keller (Arizona), stuck with their draft teams. It was a combination of contract disputes, players wanting out, bad trades, and some ordinary picks that created all the movement. It's very unusual that you have a draft like that, especially when it was considered a top draft going in.

As you will see in the pages ahead, a lot of work goes into a draft, from the GM to the scouts, and a lot of factors go into how it all plays out, from smarts and good sense to good luck and fate determined by a bloody lottery Ping-Pong ball. I will share insights of what happens behind the scenes leading up to the draft, from assembling a scouting staff to preparing a draft list. We'll look at the best and worst drafts, some historically amazing drafts, involving some of the shrewdest GMs and scouts, the likes of Sam Pollock and Bill Torrey, and one draft that might have cost me $30 million personally!

You will learn there is no shortcut to a good draft, no secret recipe, that it's an imperfect science. It's all about putting together a good team off the ice, using all the resources available, from eyeballs to analytics. It's an art, and a hard one to master. And it's about lessons that can help you in life, whether you work in sports or not. Draft day: when lives are changed, futures are decided, and champions are born.

INTRODUCTION

THE 2022 DRAFT

MONTREAL IS ONE OF MY FAVORITE CITIES. BUT WHEN IT COMES TO HOCKEY IT'S TRULY a special place. Back in the day, a game at the old Montreal Forum, at the corner of Atwater Avenue and Rue Ste-Catherine, was an unbelievable experience, win or lose. It was the home of the storied Montreal Canadiens. There was so much history, the Stanley Cup championships and superstars of the game. And, according to lore, even ghosts.

I was lucky enough to play two seasons myself at the Forum with the Montreal Junior Canadiens back in the early seventies. Our dressing room was next to the Canadiens room. We played our home games on Sunday, so we were given passes to watch the big team play on Saturday nights. Often the ushers would get us lower bowl seats that weren't being used. What an amazing experience. And it was just as thrilling going back as a rival coach and GM.

In the first seventeen years the NHL had the annual entry draft, starting in 1963, it was held either in Montreal hotels, most often the Queen Elizabeth, or at the league offices—and it was always private. The first time it was opened to the public and the prospects was in 1980 at the Forum. That was a special event, with the Canadiens owning the first overall pick. When they chose a big center named Doug Wickenheiser, and not local Montreal junior star Denis Savard, well, cue the controversy.

In 2022, there was another historic draft in Montreal, this time at the Bell Centre, the Canadiens' new home after the old Forum shuttered in 1996. This draft was special in so many ways, too. Because of Covid, it was the first time in three years that the NHL was able to gather again, after two virtual drafts. Montreal is always a special destination, and the new building has a great vibe to it. But because of everything that had happened in the world, it truly felt like a celebration to have everyone together again. There was a palpable excitement and anticipation, more so than in previous years. And once again the Canadiens had the first overall pick. The Bell Centre was packed and noisy for the occasion. It promised to be an exciting show.

It was the sixth time the Canadiens drafted first overall (all of them taking place in Montreal), the most of any franchise, but also the first time they had drafted first on merit, because they had finished dead last. Two first overall picks, Guy Lafleur and the late Wickenheiser, were acquired by trades. Two others (Michel Plasse and Réjean Houle) involved territorial rights. And then there was Garry Monahan, the first pick in 1963, the first-ever draft, when teams were allowed to select players who weren't on the six teams' sponsored lists or signed to C forms. The talent pool wasn't deep.

The lottery for the 2022 draft, which gave Montreal the first pick, occurred on May 10, the same day the late Lafleur scored his famous playoff goal in 1979 to beat Don Cherry and the Boston Bruins. Luck? Karma? Ghosts of the old Forum?

"You hope as an organization that you don't pick number one overall too often," said Canadiens GM Kent Hughes, at the time only months on the job. "But when you're in that situation, it's pretty special."

The draft, after all, is key to every team's future and what transpired on this night was going to have a profound impact on the franchise.

It was also the first time that the team with the first overall pick was drafting in its home city since the Maple Leafs drafted Wendel Clark first overall in 1985 in Toronto. And like that draft, there was considerable debate right up to selection time as to who would go first.

For most of the year leading up to 2022, Kingston Frontenacs center Shane Wright was considered the consensus first overall. He was ranked number one by Central Scouting, but his stock seemingly dropped over time. I think it was a case of Wright, who had gained exceptional status as a fifteen-year-old to play in the Ontario Hockey League (OHL), might have been under the microscope for too long. Scouts were searching for flaws, and other players stepped up their game. Hard to say.

Wright had thirty-two goals and ninety-four points in sixty-three games, which is not bad. I have to believe that the pandemic, which disrupted two seasons, may have affected his development. "This year was nowhere near my best," said Wright. "Not even close." Still, his development could change dramatically.

Even Dan Marr, the director of Central Scouting, acknowledged it was going to be an unpredictable draft. And it was. "The first three teams that pick in the draft could get the number one player in the draft," said Marr. "It's that tight and close." He probably would have extended that to the top four teams had he known how truly unpredictable it would become.

The draft week started on a high note with Colorado Avalanche GM Joe Sakic being named winner of the Jim Gregory General Manager of the Year Award, just a few weeks after he became only the third person in NHL history (after Milt Schmidt with Boston and Serge Savard with Montreal) to win a Stanley Cup as a player and GM with the same team. And it was the thirty-fifth anniversary of when Quebec selected Joe fifteenth overall.

Sadly, the hockey world was stunned and saddened on the morning of the 2022 draft, waking up to the news of the sudden passing of popular San Jose Sharks scout and seventeen-year NHL veteran Bryan Marchment at the age of fifty-three. Marchment was taken one spot behind Sakic by Winnipeg in the 1987 draft. A very sad moment and a reminder of how small and close the hockey world is and how precious life is.

The arena was electric that night and almost full, which doesn't happen in every city. But it always does in Montreal. The night started with a video montage of the top prospects, and when Wright hit the screen the crowd roared. It continued, of course, with the tradition of the fans booing commissioner Gary Bettman, although there was respectful quiet when he introduced Guy Lafleur's son Martin and Mike Bossy's daughter Tanya. Lafleur and Bossy had passed away a week apart a few months prior. Both were heroes in Quebec, of course, and superstars in the NHL, and both had their drafts in Montreal. It was a wonderful, emotional tribute, with the crowd chanting, "Guy, Guy, Guy."

As Bettman noted, so many "careers began on nights like this at the NHL draft in Montreal."

Another nice touch by the Canadiens was having coach Martin St. Louis address the crowd to the familiar strains of "Olé, Olé, Olé." St. Louis had the great line that after forty-seven years he was finally attending his first draft. He was, of course, undrafted and yet still is a Hall of Famer. The stuff of dreams and a reminder of how unpredictable the draft process can be, that some years future stars slip through the cracks.

When Kent Hughes and his entourage went to the podium there was a different stir in the arena. The crowd seemed primed and ready for Wright to be announced. They were chanting his name and there were several fans wearing Habs sweaters with Wright's name on the back. Some held signs: "Make the Wright choice."

Then Hughes announced the first overall pick: big winger Juraj Slafkovsky. It was the highest a Slovak had ever been drafted, beating Marian Gaborik, who went third in 2000. The interest in Slafkovsky grew in the months leading up to the draft, his best season ever. He played with TPS Turku, in Finland's top pro league. He had a great Olympics, where he was named MVP, and a terrific World Championship.

"I don't think I even heard my name called," said Slafkovsky. "I just heard 'Slovakia' and then I was like shocked and then I didn't even listen anymore. I was like shaking and I had goose bumps."

The reaction in the building, well, that was a new one for me. There was a mix of cheers, some groans, and a few boos. Time will tell if the Habs made the right choice, but that's the draft.

After that first pick, the buzz picked up again when New Jersey Devils selected Slovakian defenseman Simon Nemec, at number two overall. They needed a d-man more than a center. That was just the second time two players from the same European country were drafted one-two. (The others? Russians Alex Ovechkin and Evgeni Malkin, first and second in 2004.) In fact, a record three Slovakia-born players went in the first round, with the Habs later taking winger Filip Mesar at twenty-six.

The Arizona Coyotes had the third pick and selected center Logan Cooley from the USA Hockey National Development Team program. Cooley grew up in Pittsburgh and played in the Little Penguins program, which was spearheaded by Sidney Crosby three years after his draft.

Wright was still available. There were whispers that he could potentially fall as deep as number seven. Wow. What a night for Wright, from first to who knows when. But he didn't have to wait much longer—he was selected fourth overall by the Seattle Kraken. While he was no doubt disappointed about not being taken first overall, and humbled to fall to four, there was a sentiment among some hockey folks that Seattle might ultimately be a better fit for him. A smart, polite kid, Wright said all the right things afterward, even when he was accused of casting a glare at the Canadiens draft table on his way to the podium. He insisted he didn't.

"Obviously you want to go first," he told reporters. "That's definitely something that every guy wants. You picture your name being called first and walking on that stage and putting on that jersey, especially with the draft being in Montreal. It's definitely going to put a chip on my shoulder for sure and give me a little more motivation.

"I think teams take the best guy they feel is a fit. They take the best player that they think is going to fit their franchise. So, at the end of the day, it's not my decision. You want to be picked as high as possible, but it's not my choice.

"I got drafted into the NHL. I achieved the lifelong dream of being drafted to an amazing team in Seattle with a great future ahead. I wouldn't say it's relief; I would say more excitement. I'm more proud and just honored to be drafted."

Devils GM Tom Fitzgerald admitted it was a good draft but also a tough one to rank.

"I called this draft unique because of the unpredictability of it and where kids would go," he said. "For us, it was really hard putting that list together and trying to figure out which kid has the highest upside from the viewings that we had from different leagues, different international events. This may have been one of the hardest drafts to predict when it comes to which player you felt had the highest upside."

It's interesting, but not too long after the draft a video was released of Wright and his father, Simon, sitting in the stands, waiting as Shane was passed over three times. Simon turned to Shane and said, "I know it's easy to say, it's not when you go, it's what you do. It's never been about when. Where and what you do."

When Wright's name was finally announced by Kraken GM Ron Francis—himself a fourth overall pick—father and son hugged and Simon repeated: "It's not when; it's where and what you do."

Truer words. Obviously, it's an honor to go first, but going fourth is pretty darn good, too. From that moment on, it is what Simon said, it's what you do.

On Twitter, Leafs star Mitch Marner, the fourth pick in the

2015 draft, put out: "I think everyone could see a little bit of frustration from him [Wright]. Just wanted to text him saying fourth is a nice pick. Nothing wrong going fourth."

Nice message, Mitch!

The Habs no doubt selected Slafkovsky, a six-foot-four, 225-pound winger, because they loved his skill and talent, but they also believed he had the mental resilience to play in the Montreal market. He had excelled at all levels, from the Olympics to the World Championships at a young age, under big-time pressure.

But he was also selected, in part, because he was a winger and the Habs ended up trading, which the public didn't know when the pick was made, for center Kirby Dach from Chicago earlier that day. They traded defenseman Alexander Romanov and a fourth-rounder to the Islanders for the thirteenth overall pick, then traded number thirteen with sixty-six to Chicago for the six-foot-four Dach, who was the third overall pick in 2019 but was a bit of a disappointment with the Blackhawks, with just nineteen goals in 152 games. The Habs rolled the dice that Dach would work out better for them at center and they could bring Slafkovsky along with the rest of their young talent, filling a need on the wing.

That's the fun part of being a GM on draft day, wheeling and dealing. I know how Kent Hughes felt, this one being his first draft. He got the job in mid-January after years of being a successful player agent. When I went into my first draft as GM, I had been an assistant coach, a head coach, an assistant GM. With Columbus, I had the entry draft and the expansion draft on back-to-back days. The tension and the stress were unbelievable, everything coming at you from every which way. And because we lost the coin toss for the draft order, we were picking fourth. Kent was picking first and the pressure would have been ten times greater being GM of the Canadiens with the draft in Montreal. He looked pretty calm and he made what many believe was a very bold move by not taking Wright.

Ottawa GM Pierre Dorion had an interesting day, also dealing with the Hawks. He acquired twenty-four-year-old forward Alex DeBrincat, a forty-one-goal scorer, for the seventh overall pick, number thirty-nine, and a third in 2024. Nice work by Dorion, although DeBrincat was going into the final year of his deal and required a very healthy $9 million qualifying offer or they'd lose him and get nothing.

No one could quite understand what was happening in Chicago. As they had dealt DeBrincat, the twenty-one-year-old Dach, and earlier in the season twenty-three-year-old winger Brandon Hagel, it was obvious a rebuild was happening. But it was puzzling to a degree that they were dealing young talent. Perhaps the Hawks were thinking ahead to the 2023 draft and the guy many believed would go number one, Connor Bedard (or perhaps Adam Fantilli, Leo Carlsson, Will Smith, or Matvei Michkov). As much as I hoped Columbus would finally win the lottery, it was the Blackhawks who jumped from three to one. Anaheim landed in the second spot and Columbus, damned again, fell from two to three after one of their worst seasons ever. It marked the tenth time they had a chance to win the first pick, but they've never won it. The Hawks, by the way, started that 2022 draft day without a first-round pick but ended the night with three. Rebuild in motion. And the first day after the 2023 lottery they sold $5.2 million in ticket packages in just twelve hours. Needless to say, Columbus was crushed.

"It was a pretty monumental day and huge land shift for our organization," said Chicago GM Kyle Davidson. "But it's almost the unofficial start of where we're headed and our ascension there."

There were a few other interesting story lines on the first night of the draft. The Vancouver Canucks, who selected center Elias Pettersson fifth overall in 2017, took defenseman Elias Pettersson in the third round. They are not related, but the younger Pettersson acknowledged that the older Pettersson is his favorite player.

There were other familiar names in the draft. Kent Hughes' son, Jack, was selected in the second round by the Los Angeles Kings. There were twenty-eight prospects related to former NHL players or executives taken, with the GMs and scouts no doubt betting on bloodlines.

There were teams that used their first pick to fix some mistakes and money problems, such as the Leafs, who moved their twenty-fifth overall pick to Chicago for the thirty-eighth overall pick but in the process were able to unload goaltender Petr Mrazek and the remaining two years of his deal at $3.8 million per. Some applauded the move, while others said the Leafs were without a true first-rounder again because they were once again fixing mistakes. In 2019, they used their first pick to acquire defenseman Jake Muzzin, a good addition. A year later, they traded their first to unload the final year of Patrick Marleau's contract. In 2021, they moved their first at the trade deadline to pick up forward Nick Foligno, which didn't work out because of injuries. In 2023, they traded their first as part of a package to acquire centers Ryan O'Reilly (who broke a finger shortly after arriving) and Noel Acciari. They also traded their first in 2025 to Chicago for a couple of pieces. They did get a 2023 first (which had belonged to Boston) back in a deal with Washington but also gave up twenty-two-year-old Rasmus Sandin, their first (twenty-ninth overall) in 2018. All of that impacts the prospect pool in the organization and time will tell how it all works out.

"I just felt our team earned it," said Kyle Dubas of the 2023 trades that involved some later-round picks as well. "I'd rather deal picks than our prospects pool." He referred to picks being a "mystery box" compared to prospects whom you know. Truth is, the Leafs had to make moves to try to win in the playoffs and perhaps save a front-office job or two. But it was Dubas who ended up leaving Toronto.

"With regard to the futures we don't want to deplete ourselves too much down the road," added Dubas, "but if we can add guys with term, which we did [in the Chicago deal], we can find ways to replace [the picks] as we move along, and we have a lot of confidence in our prospects."

Under a salary cap, teams need young players, with low entry-level salaries, to play and play well. The draft is really the only way to build a legitimate contender. Unlike the old days, teams simply can't spend whatever they can afford, so getting it right at the draft is more important than ever. Too many misses can be catastrophic to a franchise.

In many ways, that Montreal draft had a taste of everything magical about the draft, from a somewhat unexpected first overall pick, to trading top picks for roster fixes, to all the attendant uncertainties. Every GM and scouting staff member who left the Bell Centre after two days of drafting felt good about their picks and future, believing they hit home runs with every selection. But know this: There are no guarantees. The draft is a crap shoot. It's all about trusting eyeballs, experience, tips, analytics, hard work, and luck. There isn't one answer.

And it's worth noting that, going all the way back to that first draft in 1963, just eleven of the first overall picks went on to win the Stanley Cup with the team that drafted them! You never know what will happen down the road, even with your top picks.

The draft is the lifeblood for an NHL team and it can affect the future for years. It can be your salvation, or ruination. You can make trades to help your team, you can sign free agents, but the draft is still the most important element in building a winner.

Only time will tell how the 2022 draft class stacks up. Those top picks all had growing pains. Slafkovsky had many struggles in his first season and there were calls to send him to the Habs minor-league team in Laval before he suffered a knee injury in mid-January that ended his season. Wright only played eight games with the Kraken, averaging just over eight minutes of ice time. He was eventually sent to their American Hockey League (AHL) farm team for a two-week conditioning stint, during which he scored four goals. He returned to the Kraken for a game and scored his first NHL goal—against Montreal! He was then sent to play with Canada at the World Junior Championship. He captained the gold-medal-winning team, scoring four goals and seven points in seven games. After the tournament he was returned to Kingston, who traded him to Windsor for a potential run at a Memorial Cup a few days after he turned nineteen. But the top-seeded Spitfires were upset and swept by number eight Kitchener in the first round of the playoffs.

Nemec played with the Devils' farm team in Utica, while Cooley played for the University of Minnesota, as planned. He also played in the World Junior with seven goals and fourteen points in seven games, helping the Americans win bronze. David Jiricek, a Czech defenseman taken sixth by Columbus, played a handful of games in the NHL, but that was it for the first-rounders.

All of which proves that not everyone steps in right away and makes a big impact. Development is just as important as good selection. Unfortunately for the Canadian kids under the age of twenty, they have to go back to junior if they don't make it with the big club, while the Europeans can be sent to the AHL. It's one of the inequities of the collective bargaining agreement. You can be sure the Kraken would have preferred to send Wright to Coachella Valley of the AHL rather than Windsor of the OHL—and that's no disrespect to the Spitfires.

After the draft (and a few beers), the pressure goes back to the everyday operation of a team. There were five rookie GMs at the Montreal draft, overseeing their first selections: Hughes, Patrik Allvin (Vancouver), Davidson (Chicago), Mike Grier (San Jose), and Pat Verbeek (Anaheim). Trust me, they started feeling the pressure shortly thereafter. Being a GM in the NHL is the greatest job in the world, no question. In the 105-year history of the NHL, there have only been 207 of them, as of the start of the 2022 season. I was honored to be one of them.

Every aspect of the draft is significant. The 225th and final pick of the 2022 draft was nineteen-year-old goaltender Ivan Zhigalov, taken by the Avalanche. The kid was still sitting in the seats with his junior billets when his name was called. While Joe Sakic was talking with reporters, he made his way to the Avalanche table, the start of his career, both player and team full of hopes and dreams.

In the seven rounds, Colorado only had two picks; the other was defenseman Chris Romaine from Milton Academy in the sixth round, 193rd overall. The previous season, GM of the year

Joe Sakic had rolled the dice and traded away all his other picks to add pieces to his roster—and he won the Stanley Cup. But he still had a core group of draft picks on that championship roster, a key to winning the big prize.

"Draft, schmaft," as the great Cliff Fletcher once said when it came to trading picks and trying to win. That's what GMs have to decide with the precious currency that is a draft pick. Sometimes it works; sometimes it doesn't. But at some point, you have to draft well to be a winner.

CHAPTER ONE

THE HOCKEY LIFE

LET ME REINTRODUCE MYSELF. AFTER SIX DECADES IN HOCKEY, I'VE BEEN OUT OF THE spotlight for a few years but enjoying life nonetheless. There is life after hockey, but hockey will always be a part of my life. I have experienced the fantastic game as a player, assistant coach, head coach, assistant GM, GM, team president, and broadcaster. And as a proud parent.

My love of the game was born in Summerside, Prince Edward Island. I remember my mother, Fran, taking me skating when I was probably five years old. Sometimes my dad, Jim, would be there, too. I recall them joking that they would never have to worry about me being in hockey. A harsh scouting report.

But when I was growing up in PEI, hockey was a significant part of my life. My dad owned the Tartan Restaurant. We had a big backyard, and he always found time to maintain an outdoor rink. I remember when Dad would come home from the restaurant, which was also a pub, at 2:00 a.m. and I would go into their bedroom at 6:00 saying it was time for hockey practice. When I was fourteen, I walked into their room and announced it was time for practice. I guess he'd had enough, as he tossed me the car keys. From that point, I would drive a few of the guys to practice. The cops were my dad's friends and they'd tell him, "Jim, you can't be letting the boy drive to practice," and my dad would say, "But he's a good, safe driver."

Our backyard rink was a neighborhood meeting place. When I think back, George Matthews, our radio guy years later in Columbus, was always there. We became friends in the seventh grade. So was Jim Clark, whom I met in the second grade. He lived around the corner and later became a scout and trusted part of our management team as assistant GM with the Columbus Blue Jackets and later director of pro scouting with Ottawa. Our backyard was a special place to share the game of hockey with friends.

As a teenager, I stumbled my way into the lineup of the Charlottetown Islanders, part of the Maritime Junior A Hockey League. My teammates included Al MacAdam and Kevin Devine, two pretty good players. Unfortunately, even though Charlottetown was only about forty minutes away from Summerside, I got homesick after a couple of months.

So, I left the Islanders to join my hometown Summerside Junior Crystals. I remember my dad, who lived and died hockey every day, would come to my games with my mom. Dad always had a transistor radio with him and I thought that was neat. He would stand by the boards and listen to the games. Years later, Mom told me that wasn't a radio, it was a flask! He needed a shot or two to calm his nerves.

From my play with the Islanders and Crystals, I got noticed by the Montreal Junior Canadiens. Their GM, Phil Wimmer, and head coach, Roger Bedard, invited me the next year, 1971, to try out for their team as a seventeen-year-old, just sixteen months after Gilbert Perreault and the Junior Canadiens had won the Memorial Cup.

I remember flying from Charlottetown to Dorval Airport in Montreal, the first time I was on an airplane, thinking, Oh my God, what have I gotten myself into? But it was an amazing experience playing in Montreal and junior hockey hotbeds like Peterborough, Toronto, St. Catharines, and London. I was a center/winger and played with talents such as Ian Turnbull, Andre St. Laurent, and Mario Tremblay, who all went on to have terrific NHL careers.

Wimmer and Bedard were considered geniuses in junior hockey, but my first season the roster had changed a lot— Perreault, Rick Martin, Bobby Lalonde, Jocelyn Guevremont, and others had left for the NHL. I remember one game, Bedard was yelling at me between periods. They used to have a tray of sliced oranges on a table in the dressing room; next thing you know he's throwing oranges at me. I managed to get out of the way, but I got the message.

I wasn't playing much in my second year and was traded to Drummondville at Christmastime. It was very much a French-language-first community, and I didn't want to go there because I didn't speak French. I had a friend who played for the Brockville Braves, so I had him talk to his GM and we engineered a transaction to play there instead of Drummondville. I got a call saying that the $1,000 transaction fee check bounced, but it was eventually straightened out and I was free to join the Braves.

Brockville turned out to be a huge turning point in my life. I quit school in January and worked as a bricklayer's assistant, helped a carpenter, did some odd jobs. I was a bit of a disaster at the time. I was living with billets, and the day after the season ended they told me over dinner that this was my last meal with them. I remember it well: cream peas on toast! I remember packing my stuff and throwing it in the car and driving down Park Street in Brockville, with no place to sleep and five dollars in my pocket, thinking, What the hell am I going to do? I pulled into the driveway of one of the owners' homes, went to the door, and asked if I could stay overnight until I could find a place to live. I ended up staying there in part the next seven years.

I realized that I needed to finish my high-school education and over the summer I asked the principal if he would let me into school, grade twelve, on a trial basis. That's when I met Jill, my wife. Things really turned around for me then. I worked at a hockey school that summer, where I met a local goalie playing at St. Lawrence University by the name of Jacques Martin. Tony MacDonald, who became an essential part of the Carolina Hurricanes scouting staff, and future Ottawa Senators GM Randy Sexton also worked at the school. Every summer, even when I went off to university, I'd come back to stay with Ray and Polly Levia, the co-owners who rescued me. It was scary at the time, but they took me in. They became lifelong friends—they basically saved me. I had them at every home opening game in my career in Columbus. Sadly, Polly passed away a few years ago, but I still stay in touch with Ray.

With the Braves, I was good enough to play in a couple of Central Canadian Hockey League all-star games. My coach was Bryan Murray of the Pembroke Lumber Kings. He would later play a massive role in my hockey journey, becoming a friend and mentor. I was blown away with Bryan as a coach, how he communicated, and how he taught the game. I had an excellent all-star game. But, more so, I struck a chord with Bryan. He helped me progress.

But there were still a few more years for me to compete as a player after the Brockville experience. St. Louis Blues scout Frank Mario, who played fifty-three regular-season games with the Boston Bruins in the 1940s but mostly toiled with the AHL Hershey Bears and ended his professional career with the nearby Cornwall Colts, invited me to the Blues training camp in 1975. Frank initially told me I had been drafted by the Blues, which was exciting news, but as it turned out, Frank got a bit confused and I was only being invited to camp, but the Blues wanted to get that message delivered because a few teams wanted a look.

Back then, the Blues had farm teams in Salt Lake City, Columbus, and Johnstown. The Blues sent me to Johnstown. Three of my teammates there were Jack and Steve Carlson and Dave Hanson. You may know them as the Hanson brothers.

When I was running the Columbus Blue Jackets years later, Dave appeared on a local radio station. My son, Clark, and I were in the car listening to the interview. Clark couldn't believe I played with the famed Hanson brothers from the movie *Slap Shot*. Dave joked, "You know your GM here once played with us in Johnstown. He could have been in the movie with us, but he wasn't good-looking enough to make the cut." That was my movie *and* playing career: not good enough to make the cut. Clark was about nine when Hanson gave that radio interview. He looked at me and said, "You could have been in *Slap Shot*. Are you kidding me?"

The truth was when I arrived in Johnstown, I needed to find out if it was the best place to continue my hockey journey. I didn't know, but Bryan Murray had nominated me for a Hockey Canada university scholarship. So, I had a decision to make: chase my pro career or return home to pursue an education.

There was a veteran player at the Johnstown camp that fall named Reg Kent. He was thirty-plus and yet to get a sniff of an NHL game. After a few days there, a bunch of us assembled for dinner. I told Reg about my predicament, that St. Louis sent me down here and that I hoped it would work out, but that I also had this Canadian University scholarship offer.

I had offers from six schools, including one from the University of Prince Edward Island, less than an hour from my hometown. Reg told me, "Look, Detroit sent me here nine years ago, and I haven't heard a word from them since. Get the hell out of here and take the scholarship."

My next move was to discuss my situation with Johnny Mitchell, the Johnstown GM, who was a legend in the minors. He reaffirmed the advice from Kent—he said, "If you were my son, I would tell you to take the Canadian University scholarship." That's what he thought of my game.

I decided to attend classes at the University of Prince Edward Island. I played a few winters of varsity hockey there and worked toward a degree in education to become a teacher. I played at UPEI for two Island legends, Jack Hynes and Jack Kane, the latter the father of Canadian Golf Hall of Famer Lori Kane.

My first job teaching was at Holland College in Summerside. I coached the hockey team for a stint before taking over for the legendary Forbes Kennedy, who was an idol of mine, with the Summerside Junior Crystals at the end of the season. Forbie was a tough customer. He ended his career with the Toronto Maple Leafs and was involved in the game where Pat Quinn crushed Bobby Orr along the boards in the 1969 playoffs. Forbie fought a few times in that game, was called for a record thirty-eight penalty minutes, and punched linesman George Ashley to earn a four-game suspension.

My next teaching and coaching gig was at Three Oaks Senior High in Summerside. I later coached the Summerside Western Capitals in 1981 and won the league championship in my third season. I spent seven years in Summerside teaching high school, but I made a career decision of sorts. In my third year with the Capitals, still teaching, we lost a tough game. I was sitting in the staff room the next day and one of the teachers punched me in the shoulder. I was still pissed off we'd lost to Charlottetown the night before. I got up and put him up against the wall, cocked my arm, but didn't hit him. His name was Jim Hodge, a great guy, who goofed around at the wrong time. At the end of the day, I went to the principal and said, "I think I'm going to get my master's and try to get into hockey full-time." He said, "That's a good idea."

The plan was I wanted to pursue my master's in education psychology at the University of Western Ontario, in London. I also wanted to keep my hand in coaching. I wrote Don Boyd, the head coach of the London Knights, to see if he had an opening for an assistant coach.

Again, just like my time with Jacques Martin and Bryan Murray in Brockville, Don Boyd became a lifelong friend. I later hired him as my chief scout in Columbus.

After graduation in London, I was appointed head coach at the University of New Brunswick in Fredericton, thanks to a recommendation from Don. This was 1985. At the time, it was the highlight of my life. I felt I wanted to remain at UNB, coaching hockey and teaching for the rest of my life. I remember Jill and I went to dinner and I told her it was my dream job.

One of my big recruits at UNB was a player named Matt Stairs, who grew up in Fredericton and was a terrific hockey player. One day he came to me and said he was going to give baseball a shot. Good call, Matt. He went on to have a terrific major-league career, including a stint with the Blue Jays.

Besides teaching, one of the other jobs at UNB was to run a seven-week summer hockey school on campus. I called Jacques Martin to see if he was free to help out as one of the instructors. In spring 1986, Jacques coached the Guelph Platers, a team that included Gary Roberts, Steve Chiasson, and a couple of kids from out east, Jamie McKinley and Al MacIsaac, to the Memorial Cup championship. He also was an assistant coach on the Canadian under-eighteen team under head coach Dave Chambers. Still, Jacques agreed to come to Fredericton.

After the NHL draft in June, a newspaper report said Jacques was one of the finalists to become head coach of the St. Louis Blues. He called me shortly after, and I said, "You're calling to bail on me, aren't you?" That part was genuine, but there was another reason. Jacques asked me to meet him in St. Louis—he offered me a job as an assistant coach. I was making $40,000 a year at UNB and signed a two-year deal with the Blues at $35,000 and $40,000. I think I'm the only guy who ever had to take a pay cut to coach in the NHL, but it was worth it.

After exits in the first and second rounds in the first two years in St. Louis, the Blues replaced Jacques and me with Brian Sutter and Bob Berry. Thankfully, I wasn't out of work long. My old buddy from the Brockville days Bryan Murray called me the very next day asking if I would interview for an assistant coach position with the Washington Capitals. He hired me. It's so weird—I met a guy in 1974 and the next thing you know in 1988 I'm thirty-four years old and working for him. It was a dream job. He was a top coach in the NHL and Washington had a good team. Going from St. Louis to there was another big step for me.

One of my first "coaching life" lessons arrived one night when we were playing in Montreal. A few buddies from PEI flew up and we headed out to Crescent Street the night before the game. We're in a bar and it's about a quarter to two in the morning. I look around and through a cloud of cigarette smoke I see our captain, Rod Langway, shuffling on the dance floor. Well, he sees me, I nod to him, and I immediately head out. The next morning, at the skate, he comes up to me and says, "Coach, I won't say anything if you don't say anything." Deal!

In my second year in Washington, GM David Poile made the bold move of replacing Bryan as head coach with his younger brother Terry. The latter was running the Capitals AHL affiliate in Baltimore, the Skipjacks. I was assigned to replace Terry there. Things were going nicely in Baltimore until Poile promoted one of our top players, Nick Kypreos, and our number one goalie, Jim Hrivnak, after the first round of the playoffs. We lost to Rochester in the second round.

I got fired by Poile after that, my fourth year in the pros. I had $500 in the bank, Jill was pregnant with our daughter, MacKenzie, and we didn't have health insurance. We had to get out of the States and back to Canada. Talk about life in the NHL. Two weeks left in my contract and I'm fired. I'm lucky; I went twenty-two years in the NHL and never missed a paycheck, although a couple of times it was very close!

Bryan was hired as coach/GM of the Detroit Red Wings in mid-July 1990 and brought me in as an assistant coach a week later. I looked down the bench that first season, and there was Gerard Gallant, a kid I'd known since he was ten years old. I coached and taught him in Summerside and would later hire him as my head coach in Columbus. I remember one night in Detroit, Gerard was in the latter stages of his career, sort of hanging on. He's sitting on the bench, getting sour, and he pokes me in the gut with his stick. He says, "Tell that fucking idiot [Murray] to put me on the power play." I walked down the bench and said to Bryan that maybe we should give Gallant a shot on the power play, but I was careful to phrase the request differently. The Detroit years were so much fun and so frustrating.

In the fourth year, I was promoted to assistant GM of the Red Wings and also GM of their farm club in Adirondack. Again, I enjoyed being a manager. I'm incredibly proud of two moves that first year in management: buying Kris Draper for a buck and signing Tim Taylor. It's true, I got Draper for one dollar in a deal with Mike Smith, the Winnipeg GM. Taylor played for me in Baltimore.

When the legendary Scotty Bowman came on board as the Red Wings' head coach in 1993–94, we went to watch Adirondack play in Hamilton, Ontario, before Christmas. Scotty was impressed with Taylor and Draper, and they were called up shortly after. Both won Stanley Cup rings in 1997. Draper wound up winning three more afterward. Bryan Murray and I weren't around for those Stanley Cup wins in Detroit, though.

But Bryan and I hooked up for one final time with the Florida Panthers in 1994. Bryan was the Panthers' GM. I was brought in as player personnel director and as a pro scout. Bryan decided to let Roger Neilson go as head coach in summer 1995. Man, did I want that job. But Florida owner Wayne Huizenga wanted a big name, and there was no more prominent name available that summer than Larry Robinson. The former Montreal Canadiens Hall of Fame defenseman was an assistant coach with the New Jersey Devils, who won the first of three Stanley Cups in spring 1995.

Bryan and I met at the Bob's Big Boy restaurant in Birmingham, Michigan. I told him, "You'd be an idiot not to hire me as your head coach. I'm perfect for the job." We had been together for six years, and I had wanted a job like that my whole life. I'll never forget the look on his face. He told me to give him some time. He would have to persuade Huizenga and the team president, the legendary Bill Torrey, that I was right for the job. At the '95 draft, I met with Torrey and afterward I felt good about the interview and my chances. Bryan got his way. Two months later I got the job. I remember he called me as I was driving in PEI. I was back there helping out at a hockey school.

He gave me a three-year deal worth $275,000 a season. After the press conference to introduce myself as coach, I did a phone interview with TSN reporter Vic Rauter. He asked me if I was the fourth or fifth choice. All I could think was: Dickhead. So when the interview ended, I said, "Thanks, dick." He got something like five thousand faxes from PEI criticizing the question.

About the same time I was hired, the NBA Miami Heat hired Pat Riley as their coach. My first year, the legendary Don Shula was coaching the NFL Dolphins, then Jimmy Johnson took over, both Hall of Famers. The baseball Marlins had the great Jim Leyland as their manager. A few coaching stars there to say the least. I was the nobody of the group. I remember our marketing people asking, "How exactly did we get Doug?"

The Panthers announced me as their head coach on July 24. The Los Angeles Kings hired Robinson three days later. That season was ultimately the highlight of my career. Bryan put his balls on the line to give me that job. I will never forget him for that. Then, to have the kind of success we had that year, what a memorable ride. We finished fourth in the Eastern Conference regular season. The magical playoff drive began by dispatching the Boston Bruins in five games in the first round and the Philadelphia Flyers in six games in the second round.

Next on the docket were Mario Lemieux, Jaromir Jagr, and the Pittsburgh Penguins, who had won back-to-back Cups a few years earlier. They beat us in Game 5 in Pittsburgh to take a 3–2 series lead. No one gave us much hope of surviving. But Rob Niedermayer scored late in Game 6 to give us a 4–3 win, and Tom Fitzgerald put us ahead for good in the series finale midway through the third period in a 3–1 victory. John Vanbiesbrouck was sensational in goal for us, stopping fifty-nine of sixty-three shots in the final two games. I'll never forget walking off the ice in Pittsburgh. First Wayne Huizenga hugs me, and the next guy to hug me is Dan Marino, the legendary Miami Dolphins quarterback.

The playoffs are stressful for families, too. During the playoffs I had been staying in a hotel for seven weeks. We made the Harbor Beach Marriott our home base. My daughter, MacKenzie, was three or so at the time and I remember phoning home the night before that Game 7 in Pittsburgh. She said, "Dad, if you lose tomorrow what happens?" I said, "If we lose tomorrow the season's over." She said, "Dad, I hope you lose!"

We won. It was on to Denver for the Stanley Cup final (I remember Pat Riley phoning me looking for tickets!) to take on the mighty Colorado Avalanche, a stacked team that included Joe Sakic, Peter Forsberg, Adam Foote, and Patrick Roy. All the games were close except for Game 2, an 8–1 loss. It took a triple OT goal from Uwe Krupp in Game 4 to sweep us. After that Stanley Cup run, Huizenga and Bryan ripped up my contract and gave me a new deal, with a $50,000 signing bonus and two years at $455,000 and $550,000, plus 40,000 shares in Boca Resorts.

It was a huge deal for me. I was ecstatic. But I remember one day, my son, Clark, came home from school and said the kids had been teasing him. There had been an article in the newspaper about the salaries of Jimmy Johnson (Miami Dolphins), Pat Riley (Miami Heat), Jim Leland (Miami Marlins), and myself. Jimmy and Pat were earning $2 million a year, Jim $1.6 million, and they had me at $450,000. The kids were teasing him about how poorly paid his dad was!

After I was a Jack Adams Award finalist for coach of the year and an all-star game coach twice with Florida, we were slow out of the gate in my third season. Bryan made the difficult decision to replace me with himself as head coach.

I owe Bryan so much. Jacques gave me my start in the NHL, but Bryan made my career. He died in 2017 from cancer, and I miss him. You look at his career: Washington was a good team for a lot of years. Florida went to a final. Detroit eventually won a Stanley Cup with a group he helped build. So did the Anaheim Ducks a decade later, defeating a team Bryan coached, the Ottawa Senators. He was a remarkable hockey man and such a great person.

I received one more shot in the NHL with the Columbus Blue Jackets. How I became the expansion team's first president/GM is quite the story. Funny how things evolve, and I have my old friend and play-by-play man in large part to thank.

When Jeff Rimer was working in Washington with the Caps, he met an excellent and powerful fellow named John McCracken, a steel executive with Worthington Industries in Baltimore. Years later, when I was in Detroit, John visited and entertained a few clients at a Red Wings game. He phoned to ask me if it was possible to get them passes to hang out below the stands near the dressing rooms and press the proverbial flesh. That was no problem.

I'm glad I followed through because after I lost my coaching job with the Panthers, where Jeff had also been working, one of the first phone calls I received in 1998 was from John McCracken, promising me that he would put in a good word with his boss at Worthington, Mr. John H. McConnell. He just happened to be the proud owner of a recently awarded NHL expansion franchise in Columbus, Ohio. McCracken and Jeff had been talking and my name came up to become the team's first GM.

My first meeting with Mr. McConnell was twenty minutes from where we lived in Florida, at the prestigious Gulf Stream Golf Club. When I arrived, the valet asked me, "Coach, do you have a sports jacket?" I did not. He took me to a room to find one. The best fit was a little tight. But anyway, members of the club, some guests, and employees wanted to take pictures with me. Mr. McConnell loved it. He was impressed with my popularity as the former Panthers coach. I still had some cachet and I got hired. Outstanding. I told Mr. McConnell we would need to hire a president. He said, "Ah no, you just be the president." I guess he thought this was some traveling peewee team.

Suddenly, just like that I'm president and GM, and I had to put the hockey and business side together. I had to hire about two hundred people to fill out vice-president roles, ticket sales, marketing, and media relations. I went through the Panthers' media guide to figure out the many positions I had to fill. That was my training to be president. I brought in some friends from PEI, as I mentioned, Jimmy Clark, George Matthews, Jim Rankin, and later Gerard Gallant. And Jeff Rimer. I took a lot of shit from some of the media for bringing in the guys I knew well—the big joke on the island was that the Blue Jackets were the second-biggest employer behind Cavendish Farms!

I remember saying to George, who was doing play-by-play for the Western Capitals in Summerside, making twenty-five dollars a game, what would be your dream job? He said, "Doing play-by-play in the NHL." I said, "Well, your dream just came true." Jimmy Clark and I were in Vegas interviewing Bob Strumm for a scouting job, and Jim Rankin, a buddy since I was fourteen, flew out on points to join us. He was a liquor inspector in PEI and he told me he was struggling, going through bankruptcy. He asked me if I could hire him in Columbus. I said, "What are you going to do?" He said, "I could be your travel guy." I hired him and he did a great job. It meant a lot to me and a lot to folks in PEI that I hired friends, but they were also great at what they did. Our kids, Clark and MacKenzie, graduated from high school in Columbus. It was a fantastic experience. And all these years later, several people I hired are still with the organization.

I'll never forget for our first game in Columbus, Mr. McConnell sent his private jet to Summerside and flew up my mom and dad, my brother, John, and sister, Linda, a total of ten family and friends, for the home opener.

I had a funny experience a few years into my time in Columbus. I was walking through the Toronto airport when someone recognized me and yelled out, "Hey, MacLean, what are you doing now?" I said I was in Columbus. The guy said, "Don't worry, buddy, you'll fight your way back to the NHL!" When I got back to Columbus, I told my vice president of marketing, Marc Gregory, who was a great and talented guy, "We've still got some work ahead of us!"

When I was fired in Florida in 1997, I was sitting in the backyard when *Hockey Night in Canada* executive John Shannon phoned to ask me if I was interested in being an analyst. I worked one game in Montreal with the legendary Dick Irvin. I also wound up doing a few games for ESPN that spring. But I didn't think too much about a broadcasting career at the time because I still wanted to work in the NHL, and a few years later I was hired in Columbus. After I was let go by the Blue Jackets, I was busy helping Hollywood big shot producer Oren Koules and Jeff Sherrin pursue ownership of the Tampa Bay Lightning. Then another broadcasting opportunity arose a year or so after Columbus. I must credit Nick Kypreos and Bob McCown, both working for Sportsnet at the time, for getting my foot in the broadcasting door. And program director Nelson Millman.

In my last couple of years in Columbus, I started to think more and more about the possibility of broadcasting. But the best advice I received was not to take a broadcasting job just to get your next job in the NHL. I needed to be honest and not afraid to say what I thought. I had opportunities to remain in the game in those first few years at Sportsnet. Research in Motion (Black-Berry) co-CEO Jim Balsillie hired me as a consultant as he pursued buying the financially challenged Arizona Coyotes franchise. I later interviewed for the Coyotes GM job but lost out to Don Maloney. Same with the Minnesota Wild job when they decided to go with Chuck Fletcher. I thought I had the GM job with the Florida Panthers with Bill Torrey still in charge. But owner Alan Cohen chose to sell the team, and that job fell through.

I enjoyed my time at Sportsnet. I got to meet and work with many great people like Nick, Daren Millard, and Don Cherry. I was treated so well. Broadcasting was another part of an incredible ride as a hockey man.

Looking back, to see players like Kris Draper and Tim Taylor win the Stanley Cup; draft picks in Columbus like Rick Nash win a World Championship and two Olympic golds; Derick Brassard and Derek Dorsett go to a Stanley Cup final; and Gerard Gallant coach his way to a World Championship and a Stanley Cup final is exceptionally gratifying. There's not one guy I coached, managed, or drafted, or staff I hired, whom I would be afraid to run into and shoot the breeze with, because I like to think I treated them with respect. Many are lifelong friends. There are so many kids I drafted whom I still hear from.

As a kid growing up in PEI, the NHL was a long, long way away. All I ever dreamed about was one day playing in the NHL, but as I got older the dream changed. I wanted to be a coach. Dreams do come true, in large part because you work endless hours to make it happen, but also because you have families, friends, and people that step up and help along the way. I remember how supportive my mom and dad were; the time I was lost in Brockville but was rescued by my billets, Ray and Polly; how important my wife, Jill, and kids, Clark and MacKenzie, were along the way. And all the people I met in the game. The life I've had is pretty amazing, especially for a kid from PEI.

In the end, the draft is about having trust in the people you work with, that they will work hard at their jobs to put you and the team in the best position to succeed. And, of course, it's about taking a chance on a player, a person. It's a business, but it's also real life. The players aren't just pieces of a puzzle, they're people. Along the way, a lot of people took a chance on me at various levels of the game. I worked damn hard but was given opportunities, and for that I am very grateful. And I've been very fortunate to be in positions to give opportunities to others who deserved them.

CHAPTER TWO

THE HISTORY OF THE DRAFT

"HELLO, NUMBER ONE. THIS IS NUMBER TWO."

That is how Peter Mahovlich still greets his former Toronto St. Michael's College teammate Garry Monahan six decades later, when they catch up with a long-distance phone call.

The unique salutation goes back to what took place behind closed doors at the Queen Elizabeth Hotel in Montreal when the first NHL amateur draft, as it was called then, was conducted on Wednesday, June 5, 1963.

Monahan and Mahovlich, in that order, were the first two selected that day. But, like most of the hockey world back then, Monahan and Mahovlich had no idea what was taking place when GMs from the Boston Bruins, Chicago Blackhawks, Detroit Red Wings, Montreal Canadiens, New York Rangers, and Toronto Maple Leafs—the Original Six—assembled to take a chance on a group of sixteen-year-old Canadian players.

When Canadiens GM Sam Pollock rang the Monahan home in Scarborough, Ontario, Garry's father, Patrick, answered and immediately there was confusion.

"My dad thought Sam wanted to talk to my older brother Pat," Garry Monahan recalled. "Pat was a couple of years older, and he was the better player at the time. None of us understood the concept of a draft. This came out of the blue. There were no agents. For me, I got into hockey because I followed my brother around and played on his teams on the third or fourth line."

At the Mahovlich home in the midtown Toronto neighborhood of Leaside, a similar phone call occurred. When Peter Sr. answered, he thought it was the brother of a family friend, Doug Graham. But on the other end of the line was Don Graham, the longtime scout with the Detroit Red Wings.

"My brother [Frank] had heard from Maple Leafs scout Bob Davidson that they were interested in me," Peter Jr. recalled. "So, this was a total surprise. Next thing I knew, I was asked by the Red Wings scout Jimmy Skinner to play for the Hamilton Junior Red Wings the next year. We visited Hamilton, and my parents enrolled me at Cathedral High."

Pollock and then Canadiens eastern scout Scotty Bowman, who of course went on to become a legendary coach, pulled into the Monahan driveway a few weeks after the draft. They presented options for Garry to play for either the Montreal Junior Canadiens or the Peterborough Petes. The Canadiens sponsored both junior clubs. But Monahan's parents wanted their son, who wouldn't turn seventeen for four and a half months, to stay put at St. Michael's College School. So he didn't join the Petes until the following season.

It's no wonder neither Monahan nor Mahovlich knew about the first NHL draft. The four-round selection process occurred at the end of three days of league meetings. The next day there was a four-paragraph story in the *Montreal Star* about it. There was nothing in the rival *Montreal Gazette*. Instead, the 1963 draft was overshadowed by the big news of a trade that sent goaltender Jacques Plante and forwards Phil Goyette and Don Marshall from the Canadiens to the New York Rangers for goal-tender Gump Worsley and forwards Dave Balon, Len Ronson, and Léon Rochefort.

By the time Monahan attended his first training camp in Mon-treal in 1967, after three years in Peterborough, Worsley was the only player from that trade who remained with the Canadiens.

Monahan, a center, faced a tall order in cracking a power-ful Canadiens lineup with Jean Beliveau, Henri Richard, Ralph Backstrom, and Jacques Lemaire down the middle.

As a result, Monahan spent his first two seasons of pro bounc-ing back and forth between Montreal and their minor-league af-filiates in Houston and Cleveland, appearing in eleven games with the Habs one season, three the next. He then was traded al-most six years to the day after the 1963 draft to Detroit in a trade for his old St. Mike's teammate Pete Mahovlich.

"I tell people that Sam Pollock was the smartest man in hockey because he drafted me first overall, then he had the smarts to admit he made a mistake and then traded me," Monahan said with a chuckle.

Monahan played in 748 regular-season games and another 22 in the playoffs for Montreal, Detroit, the Los Angeles Kings, two stints with Toronto, and the Vancouver Canucks.

"Over the years, I've learned to have fun with my special

distinction of being drafted first in the first draft," he said. "When I'm doing an event for the Canucks, I like to present fans with a trivia question: Who was the first player selected in the first draft? I'm usually wearing a Canucks sweater with my name on the back, so I turn around to give them a hint."

Meanwhile, Mahovlich opened and closed his professional career with AHL Calder Cup championships with the 1966–67 Pittsburgh Hornets and the 1980–81 Adirondack Red Wings.

In between, he celebrated four Stanley Cups in Montreal and played in a combined 972 NHL regular-season and playoff games. He also played significant roles in Team Canada's victories in the 1972 Summit Series and 1976 Canada Cup.

Bowman, the scout responsible for the Canadiens taking Monahan all those years ago, was Mahovlich's coach in Montreal and one of the four co-coaches with Team Canada in 1976.

"I was visiting with Scotty Bowman not long ago," Mahovlich said. "And he says, 'It's a good thing I became a good coach because I wasn't a very good scout.' I know the careers of Garry and I took different directions. But I was fortunate to be on teams that won two Calder Cups and four Stanley Cups."

The first draft only went four rounds, with Detroit passing on its last two picks and Chicago electing not to take a player in the final round. As a result, only twenty-one players were selected, and only five made their way to the NHL. Besides Monahan and Mahovlich, only three others from the 1963 draft enjoyed NHL careers. The others, all selected by the Maple Leafs, were Walt McKechnie (sixth overall), Jim McKenny (seventeenth), and Gerry Meehan (twenty-first).

The amateur draft was the brainchild of NHL president Clarence Campbell. He wanted to phase out the sponsorship of amateur teams by the Original Six clubs. Instead, he wanted to create "a uniform opportunity for each team to acquire a star player." Campbell enlisted the services of Pollock, Detroit's Jimmy Skinner, Chicago's Tommy Ivan, and Stafford Smythe of the Maple Leafs to advise in forming rules for the draft. Pollock certainly paid attention.

There were a handful of flaws with the flow of young talent into the NHL back then. First and foremost, the Maple Leafs and Canadiens had a distinct advantage—and because of their proximity to the Canadian border, the Red Wings weren't far behind—in stockpiling good young players in their respective systems.

With the rare exception of a United States–born player, most of the talent back then came from Canada. The English Canadians lined up to play for Toronto, while their French counterparts desired a roster spot in Montreal. Between 1942 and 1963, the Maple Leafs and Canadiens each won the Stanley Cup eight times, with the Red Wings next at five wins. Bobby Hull and the Blackhawks were the only team outside the Big Three to break through with a league championship in 1961.

But even Detroit occasionally experienced the frustration of how unfair the player recruitment department was because of the mystique of the Canadiens and Maple Leafs in Canada. Consider how Dave Keon signed with the Maple Leafs. In 1954, a fourteen-year-old Keon was invited from his hometown of Noranda, Quebec, by Detroit to participate in a Red Wings–sponsored hockey school in Burlington, Ontario.

The Red Wings liked what they saw in Keon and offered him a spot on their sponsored junior B team in Burlington. But Keon's mother didn't like the idea of her son leaving home at such a young age. Besides, Keon's idol was Maple Leafs standout Tod Sloan, and the NHL all-star just happened to be Keon's cousin. So, Keon stayed home to play minor hockey in Noranda.

The Maple Leafs came calling a couple of years later and offered a scholarship for Keon to play at St. Michael's College. As a result, the Red Wings lost out on a future Hockey Hall of Famer.

Campbell also had concerns about possible legal threats because of the restrictive nature of the A, B, and C forms the teenage talent was signed to and the NHL's sponsorship of junior teams. Also, with expansion on the horizon, the league president wanted to level the talent-pool playing field.

Before the first NHL draft in 1963, an eighteen-year-old player, or a player younger with the consent of his parents, was signed to either an A, B, or C form. The A form committed the player to a tryout. The B form provided the team with an option to sign a player for a bonus. Finally, the C form committed a player's rights to the NHL team for life unless released, which rarely occurred because of the competitiveness between the six teams.

Before the draft, two of the more famous recruitment stories were Jean Beliveau and Bobby Orr. In Beliveau's case, the Canadiens first attempted to sign the big center in 1948, just ahead of his seventeenth birthday. Mickey Hennessy, one of the Canadiens GM Frank Selke's hired hands, approached the teenager as he walked home after his baseball game. Hennessey took Beliveau to a snack bar and offered him $100 and then upped the fee to $200 if the youngster would sign a C form with the Habs.

Beliveau balked. He asked Hennessy to talk to his father, Arthur. Mr. Beliveau did not want the Canadiens to control his son's future. Despite later visits to the Béliveau home from Canadiens captain Emile (Butch) Bouchard, young Jean instead agreed to attend the training camp of the Montreal Junior Canadiens, a team run by Sam Pollock.

Pollock released Beliveau that fall so he could play junior closer to home in Victoriaville in 1948–49, then the nearby Quebec Citadelles the following season before jumping to the senior Quebec Aces full-time in 1951.

The Beliveaus eventually agreed to sign a B form with Selke and the Canadiens. But except for a couple of brief stints with the Habs in 1950–51 and 1952–53, Beliveau remained with the Quebec Aces because he was paid a handsome $6,000 salary and an additional $3,000 with his job at Laval Dairy. It was only when the "amateur" Quebec Senior Hockey League turned fully professional that the Canadiens, who held his pro rights, were able to land the superstar.

Orr was discovered when he was thirteen. It was March 31, 1961, Good Friday, when Bruins head coach Milt Schmidt, scout Wren Blair, and a few other Boston executives rolled into the Wellington Street Arena in Gananoque, Ontario, to watch the hometown bantam team take on Orr and his Parry Sound team. Gananoque had taken the series opener in Parry Sound. Twelve days earlier, the Bruins had missed the playoffs for the second straight season. The Boston brass were there to scout a couple of local kids: captain Doug Higgins and defenseman Rick Eaton.

Schmidt, Blair, and the other members of the Bruins organization spread themselves to different sections of the arena among the 450 fans in attendance. When they gathered afterward, even though Gananoque won the game and the series, Schmidt and his associates were in unanimous agreement—they wanted the small defenseman from the visiting team, the kid named Orr.

There were two problems, however. First, the visiting party

from Boston noticed Montreal scout Scotty Bowman also was in attendance, and Orr's coach in Parry Sound was former Detroit defenseman Bucko McDonald. Although he finished his career with the Maple Leafs and Rangers, he worked as a scout for Detroit at the time. But Bucko and Bowman didn't stand a chance against the bulldog Blair. Bowman visited the Orr family at their Parry Sound home on Great North Road but was told by Arva and Doug Orr that Bobby's immediate future was to focus on his schooling.

Blair wasn't buying that. He moved into the local Brunswick Hotel and hounded the Orr family until they agreed to sign a C form on behalf of their son. Bobby actually was two years younger than Monahan and Mahovlich. But Bobby was ineligible for the first NHL draft in 1963 because he had already signed a C form, as most of the hotshot youngsters had. That's the main reason why only five of the twenty-one players chosen in the first draft made their way to the NHL.

Orr went on to play his first of four years with the Bruins-sponsored Oshawa Generals junior team in 1962. By the time he arrived in Boston, he didn't need much time to put the Bruins on equal footing with teams such as Beliveau's powerhouse Canadiens. In Number 4's fourth season in Boston, his team ended a twenty-nine-year Stanley Cup drought. The Bruins won again two years later.

By 1972, the NHL draft was almost a decade old. There already had been a few adjustments. Age and eligibility for the draft have changed several times since 1963. For the first draft, the players selected were limited to those who turned seventeen between August 1, 1963, and July 31, 1964. The A, B, and C forms and the sponsored junior teams had been eliminated in time for NHL expansion in 1967, which doubled the number of teams from six to twelve. The age eligibility was moved between eighteen and twenty. Any junior born after June 1, 1947, was a free agent.

The draft also saw the number of rounds fluctuate from four to two to three in the late 1960s only to increase to as many as twenty-five in 1974. It's now settled at seven rounds, since 2005.

Legendary defenseman Brad Park was one of those who didn't mind seeing the sponsored junior teams go by the wayside. After being drafted second overall in 1966 by the Rangers, he wound up being hamstrung on a couple of fronts by remaining with the Maple Leafs–owned Toronto Marlboros.

"The NHL decided to have a sixteen-year-old draft. You can't sign C forms anymore. You can draft, take these players, and put them on your junior team and groom them for the NHL," Park said. "That went on for a few years. My year was the last year they ever did it."

Park should have been chosen first by Boston in 1966, but the Bruins didn't want to pay the $3,000 fee to a competitor. Junior teams received $3,000 from NHL teams for each player selected in the NHL draft.

"I grew up in Toronto and was a big Leafs fan," Park said. "The Rangers had the second choice. Boston had the first choice. [Boston] scout Baldy Cotton told them I was the guy."

Instead, the Bruins chose defenseman Barry Gibbs from their sponsored junior team, the Estevan Bruins. After Park was taken second by the Rangers, the Blackhawks drafted Park's Marlboro teammate center Terry Caffery.

Imagine how many Stanley Cups the Bruins could have won with Park and Orr on the back end together. Ultimately, they briefly played together in 1975–76 when Boston acquired

Park from New York in a trade that sent Phil Esposito to Broadway.

After the Rangers drafted him, Park had a choice to either stay with the Marlboros or move to play for the Rangers-sponsored team in Kitchener. The Kitchener Rangers offered him twenty dollars a week, plus room and board. He was due for a raise to fifty-five dollars a week with the Marlboros, and he could live at home and not change schools. It was an easy decision to stay in Toronto and play a second season.

But the Marlboros didn't give Park a proper amount of ice time. Instead, they played Maple Leafs prospects ahead of him. On top of that, he missed part of the regular season with a bruised kidney and was knocked out of the playoffs with a knee injury.

"My coach with the Marlies was Gus Bodnar," said Park, whose teammates went on to win the 1967 Memorial Cup without him. "He was restricting my ice time because I wasn't owned by the Leafs, even though I was the best defenseman they had."

It also didn't help Park's cause when his father got into a verbal dustup in the stands with Dorothy (Dodo) Imlach, the mother of teammate Brent and the wife of Maple Leafs coach/ GM Punch Imlach.

"My father, when I was playing in junior, was very outspoken," Park recalled. "They were sitting behind the bench, and she was sitting in front of him. She would stand up, and he would tell her to 'sit down.'

"'Do you know who I am?' she would say. 'I don't care who you are' was his reply."

The following season, in 1967–68, the Rangers arrived in Toronto with only three healthy defensemen for a pre-season game against the Maple Leafs. The Marlboros had a Saturday night off, so the Rangers wanted Park in the lineup. It meant an extra one hundred dollars in his pocket.

"The [Rangers] scout tells me, 'They're going to call you up for the game,'" Park said. "I'm all excited. 'You're going to get a hundred bucks and get called up for the game.' They had to ask for Punch's permission, and Punch wouldn't allow it."

Park was angered at the moment and infuriated later that year when his Marlboros teammate Tom Martin was allowed to suit up for three regular-season games with the Maple Leafs.

After Park's draft year, the NHL raised the age of eligible players for its draft to twenty as the league expanded from six to twelve clubs. In addition, the six expansion teams selecting ahead of the Original Six were allowed to take overage players on previously NHL-sponsored junior teams in an attempt to even the playing field and expand the talent pool.

In 1970, the league had a new twist to the draft. The Buffalo Sabres and Vancouver Canucks were awarded expansion franchises. That year there was no doubt that Gilbert Perreault, a gifted, smooth-skating center with the Montreal Junior Canadiens, would be the number one pick. (I arrived the next season with the Junior Habs!) The league used a spinning wheel to determine who got the first pick. Who knew it would become the first of many NHL lotteries? Vancouver was given numbers two through six; Buffalo got eight through twelve. Number seven was left open for a respin. When the wheel was spun by NHL president Clarence Campbell, he at first determined it had stopped on number 1, but there wasn't a number 1 on the wheel. Sabres GM Punch Imlach was quick to notice the pointer was on number 11, so Perreault belonged to Buffalo. Apparently, eleven was Imlach's favorite number. Perreault went on to wear the number and he became a superstar and Hall of Famer. That was the first year, by the way, that Montreal didn't have dibs on the top Quebec juniors. Can you imagine if the Habs had gotten Perreault that year and Guy Lafleur the next?

Imlach had some legendary draft moments. In 1974, Imlach and the Sabres, with the 183rd overall pick, selected Taro Tsujimoto, the first-ever player selected from the Japanese Ice Hockey League. That year, the draft was conducted via conference call and by the time of the eleventh round, Imlach was fed up and wanted to go home. But before he did, he drafted Tsujimoto—who never existed! Imlach had asked his public relations director, the late Paul Wieland, who had a terrific sense of humor, to find some common Japanese names and they created Taro Tsujimoto of the Tokyo Katanas, another way of saying "Tokyo Sabres"!

Back then, of course, there wasn't a lot of international scouting and the league didn't have a register of all the potential draft picks. But with no easy way to verify the pick, the news of Taro lasted to training camp, with reporters wanting to know his whereabouts, before Imlach finally confessed. That would not happen today!

In 1979, the NHL lowered its age eligibility from twenty to nineteen as the NHL/World Hockey Association merger occurred. The NHL absorbed the Edmonton Oilers, Hartford Whalers, Quebec Nordiques, and Winnipeg Jets from the defunct WHA, and as a result the NHL altered its draft rules. The NHL Amateur Draft became the NHL Entry Draft because teenage professionals like Mark Messier and Glenn Anderson were allowed to be drafted. But not Wayne Gretzky.

There was considerable debate over whether Number 99 should have been tossed into the draft-eligible talent pool and should have been chosen first overall by the struggling Colorado Rockies. But he had a personal services contract with Oilers owner Peter Pocklington, and Gretzky was adamant about honoring the arrangement (and no doubt he wanted to avoid going to the lowly Rockies).

The draft was delayed by two months as the league mulled over the predicament. Eventually, the Oilers were allowed to keep Gretzky, but their first-round draft position was moved to the back of the pack. They chose defenseman Kevin Lowe with the twenty-first and final selection of the first round, plucked Messier in the third round (forty-eighth overall), and drafted Anderson in the fourth round (sixty-ninth). Three future Hall of Famers, and a fourth in Gretzky.

The following year the draft was open to the public for the first time. After bouncing around between the Queen Elizabeth and Mount Royal hotels as well as the NHL office in Montreal, the 1980 draft was held in the Montreal Forum.

Hockey fans poured into the storied building on Rue Ste-Catherine to experience firsthand the draft drama and where the future stars were headed.

In 1983, Brian Lawton became the first U.S.-born player to be selected first overall, by the Minnesota North Stars. It was a strong draft year, with Sylvain Turgeon going second overall to the Hartford Whalers, followed by Pat LaFontaine to the New York Islanders, Steve Yzerman to the Detroit Red Wings, and goalie Tom Barrasso to the Buffalo Sabres. Only Lawton didn't become a franchise player, but that's the draft!

The 1983 draft also was memorable because the St. Louis Blues refused to participate after the league denied the sale of the franchise to Canadian businessman Bill Hunter, who planned to move the Blues to Saskatoon.

Teams also began taking late-round gambles on European

players from communist countries. For example, the Canadiens selected goalie Vladislav Tretiak, a star in the historic 1972 Summit Series, in the seventh round and the Calgary Flames chose Sergei Makarov in the twelfth. The New Jersey Devils were the busiest in that department, taking Viacheslav "Slava" Fetisov (eighth round), Alexander Chernykh (tenth), and Alexei Kasatonov (twelfth).

The Montreal Forum also had the honor of hosting the first televised draft, in 1984. The CBC and French-language Radio-Canada had quite the story to tell. Mario Lemieux refused to leave his seat in the stands to shake the hand of Pittsburgh Penguins GM Eddie Johnston and other team officials after Lemieux was chosen first overall. Lemieux and his agent, Gus Badali, held contract talks with Pittsburgh before the draft, and Lemieux was not happy with the Penguins' offer.

"I don't feel the need to go down the stairs to the floor because I feel Pittsburgh doesn't really want me," Lemieux told CBC's Don Wittman on the broadcast. "That's why I'm staying here with my family and all my friends."

According to assorted reports, Johnston has said many teams tried to pry away the pick, including the Canadiens. Johnston said the Minnesota North Stars offered all twelve of their picks and the Quebec Nordiques offered Peter, Marian, and Anton Stastny and a first-round pick. The previous year Pittsburgh traded its first pick and missed out on the likes of Steve Yzerman, Pat LaFontaine, and Sylvain Turgeon. And with everyone agreeing Mario was going to be a generational player, Johnston said no deal.

"There was a lot of pressure because some people thought we should trade the pick and stock up," Johnston told *The Athletic*. "We hadn't been to the playoffs in a long time. The building was half-filled. A lot of people thought we didn't have much time left in Pittsburgh, that the team would move if things didn't turn around fast—and, basically, I could have had anything I wanted if I was willing to give up that pick. . . . I wasn't trading that pick. I told our owner he would have to fire me first."

A week after snubbing the Penguins, refusing to shake hands at the table and put on their sweater, Lemieux did sign with the Penguins, making $750,000 his first two seasons.

The Lemieux controversy was hardly the only big news that day: the host Canadiens made a big splash when they selected Petr Svoboda with the fifth overall pick. Few knew the talented eighteen-year-old defenseman had defected from then Czechoslovakia. He hid under the stands until Montreal GM Serge Savard called his name. Savard also landed a huge talent in the third round with the selection of goalie Patrick Roy, fifty-first overall.

For the first time in two decades, the draft moved from Montreal to the Metro Convention Centre in downtown Toronto in 1985. It just happened that the Maple Leafs held the first overall selection and chose Wendel Clark from the Saskatoon Blades, a versatile forward/defenseman who helped Canada win the World Junior Championship in Finland six months earlier. He became one of the most popular Leafs ever and was later used as a trade chip to acquire Mats Sundin.

Lemieux's case, while public, wasn't unique for top picks. Winger Craig Simpson, who played at Michigan State, reportedly told the Leafs not to take him first overall after he had a bad meeting with GM Gerry McNamara prior to the draft. I was an assistant coach with the London Knights at the time, working with Don Boyd, and we had big winger Jim Sandlak, who wound up going third to Vancouver. We were hoping he might slide up. Pittsburgh took Simpson with the second pick.

The draft returned to Montreal in 1986 but moved stateside for the first time the following year, to Detroit at Joe Louis Arena, where the Buffalo Sabres selected Pierre Turgeon first overall.

As the NHL draft entered the 1990s, there was increasing pressure in hockey to adopt a lottery system similar to the arrangement the NBA (where commissioner Gary Bettman had previously worked) had implemented in 1985 to avoid teams deliberately trying to lose games to finish last and obtain the first pick. The Houston Rockets were accused of blatant bumbling in 1982–83 to successfully land top collegiate player Ralph Sampson. A lottery, they figured, would disincentivize such behavior.

There had been considerable talk that the Penguins and Devils tanked to finish last and be able to draft Lemieux. For instance, as the story goes, late in the 1984 season Penguins GM Eddie Johnston sat out his best goalie in a game against New Jersey, which they lost.

The summer of 1993 played a massive role in tipping the scales for the NHL to guard against teams losing to gain the first overall selection. With two new teams starting their first seasons in 1992–93—the Ottawa Senators and the Tampa Bay Lightning—there was even more pressure to get it done. But it didn't happen yet. The Senators were awful in their inaugural campaign, winning just ten of their eighty-four games. They mustered only one victory in their final eighteen games. Still, despite all their ineptitude, they needed a 4–2 loss against the Bruins in the regular-season finale to remain tied with the San Jose Sharks at twenty-four points. But the Senators had one fewer win and secured the first overall selection.

The Senators had their eyes on Francophone standout Alexandre Daigle of the Victoriaville Tigres, a prolific offensive performer and charismatic personality off the ice. Ottawa ownership felt he would be the franchise's cornerstone for years to come.

"I'm glad I got drafted first, because no one remembers number two," Daigle told reporters on draft day at Le Colisée in Quebec City.

Daigle proved to be one of the biggest first overall flops in NHL draft history, while number two became a Hockey Hall of Famer. That was Peterborough Petes defenseman Chris Pronger. He went on to become a member of the Triple Gold Club: winning a World Championship, a Stanley Cup, and two Olympic gold medals, as well as a Norris Trophy and Hart Trophy. Daigle wasn't a horrible player; he just wasn't what you'd hope for from a first overall pick. He never became the superstar who was expected to take the Ottawa franchise to another level, and especially compared to Pronger.

"Hello, number one. This is number two." I'm pretty sure Pronger, unlike Mahovlich, never made that call, but he also wasn't shy over the years in reminding people of the infamous "no one remembers number two" comment. In fact, he has shared that, for that remark, Pronger's stick found the back of Daigle's legs whenever they played against each other.

Later that summer, after the draft, a firestorm engulfed the Senators when founding owner Bruce Firestone sold his shares and resigned from the club. *Ottawa Citizen* columnist Roy MacGregor was writing a book on the 1992–93 season. But then word leaked that a rival newspaper was about to report a story on something Firestone told MacGregor, play-by-play man Dean Brown, Ottawa radio reporters Gord Wilson and Al Rutherford, and local freelancer Moira Alfers at a post-draft party at a Quebec City nightclub.

Firestone revealed the club's slippery plan to make sure they finished last. The Senators founder allegedly contended that his team would pull their goalie if they had the lead or were tied in the season finale to ensure a season-ending loss. MacGregor also claimed Firestone said he guaranteed roster spots for the next season to four players if they made sure the Senators' slide continued in the late going.

"Any allegation that four players were promised preferential treatment to play less than their best is false," Firestone later said. "Having said that, I regret that the juxtaposition of certain remarks could lead some there to conclude otherwise."

The NHL commissioned an investigation in late August. Bettman and his legal team reviewed video of Senators games and interviewed Firestone and team officials, media members involved, players, head coach Rick Bowness, and others. The result was the commissioner found no improper conduct by the players or coaches but fined the Senators $100,000 because of the inappropriate remarks attributed to Firestone.

Seven months later, the NHL announced it had adopted a weighted lottery system to determine the order of selection for non-playoff teams. The league would implement the new lottery system in time for the 1995 draft.

From 1995 through 2012, the lottery system stipulated a non-playoff team club could not move up more than four positions in the draft order, meaning only the bottom five teams had a chance to win the first overall pick.

Over time the team finishing in last place has been given worse odds of getting the first selection, and beginning in 2022 a team could move up a maximum of ten spots, giving eleven of the sixteen non-playoff teams the possibility of gaining the top pick. But a team cannot win the lottery more than twice in a five-year span.

The weighted lottery system has failed to eliminate conspiracy draft theories, ranging from the alleged rigged Ping-Pong ball to allow the New York Rangers to claim the top pick in 2020 (Alexis Lafrenière) to the woeful Edmonton Oilers gaining the nod over the Buffalo Sabres for Connor McDavid in 2015.

But the dodgy draft lottery that got the most attention was to see which team would land the coveted Sidney Crosby in 2005. The league was coming off a canceled season because of a lockout. It was a whirlwind few days. The players ratified the new CBA on July 21 in Toronto, and the lottery was held the next day in New York at the Sheraton New York Hotel and Towers. The draft was held a week later at the Ottawa Westin.

The NHL head office decided the best way to determine the selection order was to include all thirty teams but weighted for clubs that made the fewest playoff appearances in the last three completed campaigns.

That meant the Sabres, my Columbus Blue Jackets, the Rangers, and the Penguins had the best chance with three Ping-Pong balls in the drum. Anaheim, Atlanta, Calgary, Carolina, Chicago, Edmonton, Los Angeles, Minnesota, Nashville, and Phoenix had two apiece. The remaining sixteen teams had one ball each.

The NHL had a problem in Pittsburgh. The once-mighty franchise that won back-to-back Stanley Cups in 1991 and 1992 was in the doldrums. The Penguins had missed the playoffs three years in a row and were financially challenged. The team needed a new building. The Mellon Arena, known as the Igloo, was one of the oldest in the league. There also were constant threats of the franchise being purchased and moved to Hamilton or Kitchener in Ontario, or Kansas City.

The lottery drama came down to Anaheim and Pittsburgh, with Ducks GM Brian Burke and Penguins president Ken Sawyer flanking each side of Bettman as he revealed the final pick. Pittsburgh won the day.

"Coming in with a four-point-five percent chance, and you end up there with a fifty percent chance, it's a good day," said Burke. "It would have been nice, but we're very happy to pick second." As fate would have it, many years later Burke and Crosby were united with the Penguins.

It worked out for both teams. The Ducks picked Bobby Ryan second, signed unrestricted free agent Scott Niedermayer, and traded for Chris Pronger the following summer to win the 2007 Stanley Cup. The Penguins won the first of three Stanley Cups with Crosby leading the way in 2009.

But to this day, the conspiracy theories live on and fans have created tanking slogans, such as "Not Winnin' for MacKinnon" and "Get Bad for Ekblad." And most recently, "Tank Hard for Bedard."

It has been quite the evolution for the NHL draft, from the pursuit of prospects as young as fourteen, the C forms, and the Quebec territorial rights to the generational picks from Lemieux all the way to McDavid and maybe Bedard. But what hasn't changed is that draft day is still a critical day for teams, the most important day. Like every other GM in the league, you hope you get a franchise player who will lead you to a Stanley Cup.

It's just not that easy.

CHAPTER THREE

THE VALUE OF DRAFT PICKS, PART ONE

IT WAS THE LATE, GREAT SAM POLLOCK WHO ONCE SAID, "PEOPLE BUILD TEAMS IN certain ways. I've always traded for futures—not pasts." Words every GM should be reminded of constantly.

I never met Pollock, who passed away in 2007 at the age of eighty-one, even though I played two seasons for the Montreal Junior Canadiens from 1971 to 1973, when he was doing some of his best work as the GM of the parent club. I sure wish I had met him. But I certainly heard a lot about him then and years later from Ron Caron, who was my GM during my two seasons as an assistant coach with the St. Louis Blues. Ron had been a scout with the Canadiens and he talked about Pollock with reverence what felt like every day.

To call Pollock a genius is almost selling him short. For fourteen years he was the GM of his hometown Canadiens, and during that time they won the Stanley Cup a record nine times. His name appears on the Stanley Cup a dozen times. He was the greatest GM in the history of the NHL, in my estimation.

Pollock realized the value of draft picks and how to use them to build one of the most successful franchises in all of professional sports. Born on Christmas Day in 1925, he was a gift to the hockey world. He had a successful management career with the Canadiens' junior teams and was eventually elevated to the big team as director of player personnel. In 1964 he succeeded the legendary Frank Selke as GM, and all of those Stanley Cup wins followed. Pollock understood long before many others the importance of the draft and what it meant to building and, in his case, maintaining a champion organization. He always seemed to be thinking a year or two or even longer ahead when it came to the draft, knowing the talent that was coming next. But he was also smart enough to prey on the desperate teams and GMs looking for a quick fix to turn around their fortunes. Of the many great stars who played for the Canadiens, most were their own draft picks. The rest were acquired in frequently lopsided trades.

Two of Pollock's shrewdest moves landed him two future superstars and Stanley Cup keystones, right winger Guy Lafleur and goaltender Ken Dryden, both the backbone of their 1970s championship teams.

Pollock was truly ahead of his time, really focusing on fleecing the 1967 expansion franchises. His most famous target was the owner of the California Golden Seals, the flamboyant Charlie O. Finley, who also owned the Oakland A's baseball team. In the early 1970s, the A's were one of the greatest baseball teams ever, winners of three straight World Championships and five straight pennants. They were colorful and game changers in their own right. Charlie was always front and center with both teams and perhaps it was because of his success on the baseball diamond that he was in a hurry to find it on the ice.

Pollock knew the 1971 draft was going to be special. Most predicted that the best player was going to be a phenom right winger named Guy Lafleur, who was from Thurso, Quebec, and was playing junior for the Quebec Remparts. Lafleur had great speed and a booming slap shot off the right wing. Then and now, drafting the homegrown talent was very important for the Canadiens. The other star-in-waiting in that draft was Marcel Dionne, a stocky center who left his hometown of Drummondville, Quebec, to play with the St. Catharines Black Hawks of the Ontario Hockey Association. They were two different players but great from an early age. In the 1960s, the Canadiens were allowed to draft the top two Quebec-born juniors. With the French-Canadian Gilbert Perreault taken first in the 1970 draft, imagine if the Habs were able to retain that territorial exemption. They'd have had both Lafleur and Dionne, and Perreault!

In his final junior season, as a twenty-year-old, Lafleur put up gaudy numbers: 130 goals and 209 points in 62 games. Dionne, born 48 days earlier, had 62 goals and 143 points in 46 games in a league that was deemed by many to be tougher to put up points in. They met that year in the Eastern Canada final, a lead-up to a Memorial Cup showdown with the Western Canada Hockey League (WCHL) champions. The series was ugly on and off the ice, with Dionne despised for leaving his home province to play in St. Catharines. The Black Hawks wound up forfeiting the series because of the nonsense on and off the ice, which included fans throwing eggs and other debris at the players in a rough fourth game in Quebec. Dionne's parents were assaulted in the stands and the team bus was attacked by an angry mob. There were death threats. After playing the fifth game in Toronto, a neutral site, the Hawks refused to return to Quebec City. Lafleur and the Remparts went on to beat the Edmonton Oil Kings in the Memorial Cup final.

All along, Pollock knew he wanted Lafleur but also knew he would never be able to get him without first making a trade to somehow move to the front of the line. Pollock also knew that Canadiens superstar Jean Béliveau was going to retire at the end of that 1971 season and he needed to find the next great one. And his former coach turned scout Claude Ruel was certain Lafleur would be great. The trick, however, was getting him. Pollock started to work on that early.

On May 22, 1970, Pollock worked his magic, a year ahead of the Lafleur draft. Seemingly figuring (and definitely hoping) the lowly Golden Seals would be the worst team during the 1970–71 season, Pollock made a deal with Finley and his GM, Frank Selke Jr., ironically the son of the former Habs GM. Pollock convinced Finley that he could help make the Seals more competitive sooner rather than later and all it would cost was that first-round draft pick. All owners, even in today's NHL, want to hear they can be competitive now, and it often prevents them from thinking clearly. Most GMs now protect the first-round picks they trade, meaning typically if the pick turns out to be in the top ten then the pick is pushed back a year. That protection is almost always built in now, but it certainly wasn't then. And Finley wanted to hear more about winning sooner than about drafting Lafleur. He would never have known.

Pollock traded forward Ernie Hicke and his first-round pick in 1970 to the Seals for defenseman Francois Lacombe, cash, and their number one pick in 1971. Ultimately, a steal. It should be noted, Hicke was a solid player. He went on to play two seasons with the Seals with his brother Bill before moving to the Atlanta Flames, playing 520 games overall and producing a very respectable 272 points. But he wasn't Lafleur. Heck, Sam even managed to get some cash thrown his way in the deal. Unrelated, Selke resigned as GM in November 1970, but those were crazy times in Oakland with Finley.

As shrewd as that deal was, Pollock still had to make another move just to be safe. During the 1970–71 season, the Los Angeles Kings started to stumble in the standings. They weren't yet close to the bottom, but there was a chance they might finish below the Seals and so would have the first overall pick.

As the story goes, Pollock realized he had to fortify the Kings to make sure they didn't finish last, so he sent them solid veteran center Ralph Backstrom, who was not happy in Montreal at the time, in exchange for Gord Labossiere, Ray Fortin, and a 1973 second-round pick, who turned out to be Peter Marrin, a good junior with the Toronto Marlboros.

Backstrom played parts of three good seasons with the Kings and a few more years after that in the WHA. None of the Canadiens' acquisitions ever played a game for Montreal, but more importantly, the deal ensured the Kings stood steady in the standings and the Habs got the prized first pick—in the same spring that they won the Stanley Cup and would soon add Scotty Bowman as their head coach.

In the book *Remembering Guy Lafleur*, written by the late Frank Orr, Pollock was quoted as saying "[I]n 1969–70, the Seals finished fourth in their division after a strong second-place finish the previous season. They definitely were a team on their way to good things and many thought they could win the West

Division. . . . There's no way I could have predicted that the Seals would be last in the NHL and we would have their draft pick, number one overall. Sometimes in hockey, it's better to be lucky than good."

As for the Backstrom trade, Pollock called the motivation "pure fiction and stronger words if you want them. Ralph will verify this. For personal reasons, Ralph wanted to move to a team on the West Coast and we talked about it. . . . The Kings were the only team to make an offer for him." In that 1970–71 season, the Kings finished fifth with sixty-three points, one more than Pittsburgh, and the Seals finished last with forty-five.

Lucky or good or both (I'm leaning to good), Pollock, of course, selected Lafleur with the Seals' pick, although to heighten the drama he did call a time-out before selecting him. The Flower would go on to win the Stanley Cup five times, the Art Ross Trophy three times, a Hart Memorial Trophy, and three Lester B. Pearson Trophies during his fourteen seasons with the Canadiens. He did have a slow start to his career, mostly just average his first three seasons to the point that Bowman wanted Pollock to trade him in his third season. But, I was told, Pollock told Bowman, "You can do whatever you want, bench him, sit him out, but he's going to be here a lot longer than you." Pollock had a personal unwritten rule that he wouldn't trade a player before he turned twenty-three. Six months later, in his fourth season and at age twenty-three, Lafleur became the superstar everyone, including Pollock, thought he would be and ultimately became a Hall of Famer. He finished with 518 goals and 1,246 points during his time with the Habs. After three years, he returned from retirement to play a season with the New York Rangers and parts of two with the Quebec Nordiques, completing his career circle.

Dionne, meanwhile, had a very good nineteen-year career. Drafted by Detroit, behind Lafleur, he played four seasons with the Wings, a dozen with the Kings centering the very successful Triple Crown line with Dave Taylor and Charlie Simmer, and three more years with the New York Rangers. He won a scoring title and Pearson Award, as well as twice winning the Lady Byng Trophy. His career numbers were 731 goals and 1,771 points in 1,348 games. But he never played on the caliber of teams that Lafleur did and never won the Stanley Cup. In fact, he played in just forty-nine playoff games. But he was still a Hall of Famer.

Interestingly, in the book *Triple Crown*, written by Ted Mahovlich—son of the Big M, Frank—Dionne insisted he didn't want to play for Montreal: "Detroit was the right place for me to go. I had too much emotion, they would have destroyed me in Montreal."

But it was easy to see why there was much debate as to who would be drafted first. Pollock never said it, but Dionne leaving Drummondville and the angst it caused in Quebec might have been a big factor in the decision. Whatever, Pollock got it right.

With the tenth overall pick Pollock moved in that trade in the 1970 draft, the Seals selected right winger Chris Oddleifson, who had a nine-year NHL career, mostly with Vancouver. Rumor had it that Pollock guaranteed Backstrom he would ensure that when he retired he would get the head coaching job at Denver University. Coincidentally, Backstrom went on to have a very successful college coaching career at Denver. That was the power Sam Pollock had in hockey.

Of course, Lafleur had a great team around him. A few months before Pollock had acquired the pick that ultimately became Lafleur, on January 23, 1970, he sent veteran winger Dick

Duff, who had won four Cups with the Habs, to the Kings for center Dennis Hextall and the Kings' 1971 second-round pick. That pick turned out to be future Hall of Fame defenseman Larry Robinson.

Two years before that, Pollock sent goaltender Gerry Desjardins to LA for the Kings' 1969 and 1972 first-round picks. Pollock ultimately traded the 1969 pick, but with the 1972 pick, fourth overall, he selected winger Steve Shutt from the Toronto Marlboros, who eventually played left wing on a great line with Lafleur and center Jacques Lemaire. Amazing foresight.

The acquisition of Dryden was an equally brilliant move by Pollock. Very few people realize that Dryden, sixteen at the time and playing junior B, was drafted by the Canadiens' archrival, the Boston Bruins, in the third round of the 1964 amateur draft, number fourteen overall. In the 1960s, the draft was totally private, held at the Queen Elizabeth Hotel in Montreal. No fans, no players, no agents, just team and league personnel. There were a maximum twenty-four players selected, over four rounds, who were turning seventeen years of age between August 1, 1964, and July 31, 1965, and not on any team's sponsorship lists. Dryden turned seventeen on August 8, 1964.

Players only found out which team had drafted them when they were contacted by the team. It was well known that Dryden would be attending Cornell University and at that time very few college players went to the NHL. Still, Pollock wanted Dryden, so seventeen days after the draft he traded two players Montreal had acquired in that same draft—Guy Allen (selected twelfth) and Paul Reid (eighteenth)—in exchange for Dryden and Alex Campbell, who had been selected second overall. The Bruins desperately wanted Allen, whom Montreal had selected ahead of Dryden.

NHL historian Dave Stubbs has reported that the Bruins actually had Montreal select Allen on their behalf, knowing the trade was coming. They saw him as being an impact player for years to come. Neither Allen nor Reid played a single game in the NHL.

Dryden, meantime, had an incredible career at Cornell before signing with the Canadiens. He went on to win the Stanley Cup six times and was the Conn Smythe winner, as the most valuable player in the 1971 playoffs. That season, the Canadiens called up Dryden for the final half-dozen games of the season, played very well, and then proceeded to lead the Habs to a Cup win, including a series victory over the Bruins. He also won the Calder Trophy, as rookie of the year, the following season, won the Vezina Trophy five times, and was inducted into the Hockey Hall of Fame in 1983. It was a lopsided trade to say the least. Incredibly, Dryden didn't actually find out he was drafted by the Bruins until 1974—ten years later—and by then he had broken their heart a few times.

To further emphasize Pollock's genius, especially with respect to the value of draft picks, he used picks acquired in trades to select future Montreal stars such as Robinson and Shutt, as mentioned, but also Bob Gainey and Guy Carbonneau. All four are in the Hockey Hall of Fame. With Gainey, Pollock flipped multiple picks with St. Louis, trading down from fifth to eighth, figuring Gainey would still be available. It's a risk, but you can trade down if you think the player you want will still be available later and you add another pick in return. With Carbonneau, Pollock had traded winger Jimmy Roberts to the Blues for a 1979 third-round pick, a terrific later-round selection.

Pollock almost hit an amazing home run in 1976. At the time, the draft age was twenty. Looking ahead, Pollock predicted the potential first pick of the 1980 draft would be a phenom from Brantford, Ontario, by the name of Wayne Gretzky. Yes, Sam was thinking four years ahead.

On September 13, 1976, Pollock sent high-scoring minor leaguer Ron Andruff and Sean Shanahan to the Colorado Rockies for the right to swap first-round picks in 1979 or '80. As it turned out, Gretzky never got drafted. When the WHA merged with the NHL in 1979, one of the terms of the agreement was the Edmonton Oilers got to keep Gretzky, who had a personal services contract with the owner. And what a draft that was in 1979. With the draft age lowered from twenty to nineteen (which Pollock couldn't have known would happen) and the underagers from the WHA also eligible, Rob Ramage, Mike Foligno, Mike Gartner, Rick Vaive, Craig Hartsburg, Mark Messier, and Kevin Lowe were among the many stars selected. More on that later.

As the 1979 draft evolved, the Rockies used the first pick to select Ramage, while the Habs didn't have a first-rounder—their sixteenth overall pick belonged to the Kings, who selected defenseman Jay Wells.

Pollock actually retired in 1978, but in 1980, owning the Rockies' first pick, the Habs hit pay dirt again, with the Rockies finishing last—meaning the pick Pollock had traded for in 1976 was now a first overall. Most GMs leave the cupboard bare, but not Sam. He left his successor Irving Grundman with that first pick in the 1980 draft, which was the first in which the public were invited to watch, held at the old Montreal Forum.

Grundman and Ron Caron, who was his assistant GM and a noted scout, selected Doug Wickenheiser, a big, rangy center with the Regina Pats. The brain trust believed Wick would be the next Jean Béliveau, in terms of centers, but also the next great superstar on the heels of Lafleur. Caron really believed it and Grundman trusted him, and Western scout Del Wilson, to make the decision.

That season Wick, who sadly passed away in 1999 far too young at the age of thirty-seven after a battle with cancer, was a star with the Pats. He had eighty-nine goals and eighty-one assists leading the Bryan Murray–coached Pats to the Memorial Cup. Wick was a heckuva player. Bob Strumm, who was the GM of the Pats and later worked for me in Columbus, felt Wick was a "can't-miss" superstar. Murray gave him a ton of confidence. But in Montreal, Wick was not handled well and the pressure on him was unreal.

There was tremendous local pressure on the Habs to select with that first pick slick center Denis Savard, who played for the Montreal Juniors and put up big numbers. When it comes to the draft, and even when hiring coaches and managers, the Habs have to be aware of the Francophone fan base. But Caron truly believed in Wick and most teams agreed he was the first pick. Winnipeg selected very good defenseman David Babych second, and the player all of Montreal and the province of Quebec wanted, Savard, went third to Chicago, which was the order most teams had it. Some had Babych first, but I've never heard of a team that had Savard first on their list. I'm convinced the heat of playing in Montreal, the pressure of being the number one pick, and the attendant public anger of Savard not being selected by Montreal rocked Wick.

Chicago had actually acquired that third overall pick in a shrewd move themselves. After the WHA merger, Quebec made a deal with Chicago to retain Réal Cloutier, a very talented player, sending their first-round pick to the Hawks. It worked out very well for Chicago.

Maybe the most devastating thing that happened to Wick was during his rookie season. The first time Savard and the Blackhawks came to Montreal, coach Claude Ruel made Wick a healthy scratch. Most hockey people say he never recovered from that embarrassment—further proof that the handling and development of your draft picks is as important as getting it right when you draft them.

Caron always believed in Wick, and when he became the GM in St. Louis he traded for him. That's when I first ran into Wick; I also had him in Baltimore of the AHL and again with Washington. Caron was a really sharp hockey mind, a lifer. Working with Ron in St. Louis was an adventure at times. He was one of my all-time greatest friends in hockey, but there were times . . .

As an assistant coach, making $35,000 a year, I had two suits. I had to mix and match a lot of shirts and ties to give the appearance I had more. As the eye in the sky in the press box during games, I had to sit next to Ron every game. To say he was fiery and intense doesn't come close to describing him. During a game, the Professor, as he was nicknamed, was wound very tight.

One night in Winnipeg, I was on the computer during the game. We were losing and he finally snapped and started yelling at me that "I'm going to throw that fucking computer out of the press box and I'm going to fire you tomorrow and hire Bob Gainey to be assistant coach." Between periods, I went down to the dressing room and I said to Jacques Martin, who was the head coach, and Bob Plager, who was the other assistant, that I had my fill with Ron, I couldn't take it anymore. Bobby, who was a great and funny guy, said to me, "Have a cigarette." He handed me the pack and I said, "I don't smoke." He said, "I didn't either until I had to sit next to Ron."

I finally quietly went to our public relations person and begged her to get me separated from Ron. Every city we went to, they'd put me at the end of the press box and Ron would be asking, "Why the hell do they keep moving you?"

At home games, Ron used to call down to the coaches' office between periods to rant. Eventually we stopped answering and he would throw a tantrum thinking his phone was broken and throw it against the wall.

There was one night, we were playing in Detroit and lost. Ron walked into the coach's room and said, "This is a goddamn joke. [Rob] Ramage, [Charlie] Bourgeois, [Ric] Nattress suck; why are you playing those guys?" I was fed up and I said, "Ron, you just named our whole right side of the defense. Who are we supposed to play?" Jacques didn't say anything. I walked out of the rink thinking I'm done now for sure. Jacques gets on the bus, walks by me, and shakes his head. The ride to the airport was about thirty minutes and I was a basket case. We get on the plane, I'm in my seat, and Ron walks by, punches me in the arm, and says, "You're okay!"

But as crazy as Ron could be, I loved the man. When I got hired in Columbus, before our first road trip I called Ron and invited him on the trip. It was my way to thank him for all he did for my career. Unfortunately, he was sick and couldn't come. But I really respected him as a person and a hockey man.

So, you can see Ron was an intense guy. It's easy to see he would have fought hard to convince his GM to make the Wickenheiser pick. But it was Pollock who set the draft table for the Habs before he retired. They just missed. It's worth noting that since Pollock retired the Habs have only won the Stanley Cup three times over that forty-five-year span.

Pollock tried to hit another home run in 1973, when the consensus first overall pick was Ottawa 67's defenseman Denis Potvin. The expansion New York Islanders owned the pick, but Pollock's "quick-fix" plan didn't sway GM Bill Torrey, who turned down a package of five players, all off the Habs roster. I worked for Bill in Florida, when we went to the Stanley Cup final in 1996, and he was a shrewd operator as well. To the day he died, in 2018, Torrey refused to divulge who those players were.

Bill pushed back on multiple offers from Pollock, and Denis became a key part of the Isles' four Stanley Cup–winning teams, which were in large part built through the draft. But Sam was on top of it. And he wasn't done dealing. He held the second overall pick, courtesy of a deal with Oakland, and traded it to the Atlanta Flames, who wanted to draft center Tom Lysiak. Sam offered up the second overall, another first, and a second that year. In return, Pollock got the fifth overall pick and the Flames' first-round picks in 1977 and 1978. Sam then traded the fifth pick to the St. Louis Blues, who wanted goaltender John Davidson. He was confident that with the eighth pick he could get the player he wanted and did: winger Bob Gainey.

"The Gainey draft developed out of a very large set of circumstances," Pollock said years later. "I always tended to look at the overall or big picture, such as how many players we had and how many players we were going to have to protect in a given year. Very seldom was my philosophy to win a championship first, especially at the expense of developing a good team, because if you worried about winning championships in one particular year, you could make some very bad mistakes. So, we got Gainey, a player who had the reputation of being a great defensive player and who had learned under the best—Roger Neilson in Peterborough."

Consider some of the other great trades Pollock made involving picks and future Habs superstars: Lafleur, Robinson, so many others, and that 1977 first-round pick got him winger Mark Napier. The hits just kept on coming. Hockey historian Todd Denault wrote that from 1969 to 1974, a six-year window, Pollock had seventeen first-round picks and eight second-round picks. In 1972 he had four of the first fourteen picks and two years later five of the first fifteen. Incredible. Any wonder they were so successful?

Over the years there have been some great GMs who were shrewd with their picks, the likes of a Ken Holland during his time in Detroit, Cliff Fletcher when he was in Calgary, Glen Sather with Edmonton, Bill Torrey with the Islanders—but there was never another Sam. And there never will be. Today, with thirty-two teams and a salary cap, draft picks have never been more important. Having good, young players on entry-level contracts is crucial. Teams aren't as loose with trading picks, especially top picks, as a result. And if they do trade a first pick, they will protect that pick in case they crap out and finish in the bottom of the standings.

Sam cautioned about worrying about winning one year at the expense of the future. He was, of course, right again. But because there are thirty-two teams and the salary cap, teams will make big deals and unload picks to win one Stanley Cup because it is so much harder to do. Sam was building to win nine Cups; teams today work toward winning one because it's so much more difficult to keep teams together for financial reasons. The expansion teams are given a much deeper talent pool to select from than back in the day and they aren't so desperate to make deals of the kind Pollock made.

Every GM tries to think years ahead when it comes to the draft, the way Sam did, but it's harder to get those first picks. And when a team is thinking ahead, say when a Connor McDavid became available or a Connor Bedard, it isn't typically a top team trying to rob a lower team, but a lower team aiming to make their pick number one. I'm not saying "tanking," but there are teams that will tear down leading up to a big draft.

Sam really was one of a kind, because of his smarts and foresight and because it was a different time. But his philosophy lives on and he was the one who drove it home for the rest of us.

Cliff Fletcher once told the *Hockey News* that another part of Sam's genius was "consistency and continuity. As far as consistency, how the day-to-day operation was run regardless of wins and losses. And continuity because he never believed in trading a young player (until, as I mentioned with Lafleur, he was twenty-three). When they traded a player, Montreal was pretty sure he wasn't going to be a contributing factor for them in the future. They were very conservative in the way they moved young players. Very conservative."

"Restocking the team was important to us," said Pollock. "We quickly realized that the draft was going to be the major area of importance."

Trading for futures, not the past. In today's game, however, maybe it's best put that contending teams are trading for the present because the future may be your replacement's problem.

CHAPTER FOUR
BUILDING A WINNER

ONE DAY, MANY YEARS AGO, WHEN I WAS AN ASSISTANT COACH WITH THE DETROIT RED
Wings, I found myself standing beside Steve Yzerman, the star
and captain, while he was shaving in the dressing room. "I'm a
pretty good player, eh, Doug?" he said.

"You're a great player, a star," I answered.

He shot back: "[Nick] Polano, [Brad] Park, [Harry] Neale,
[Jacques] Demers, [assistant coach Dan] Belisle, and you and
Bryan [Murray]—imagine how good I could have been if I had
just one good coach?"

I had nothing to say and that is rare for me. Stevie Y was
joking, he has a dry, sometimes cutting sense of humor, but he
also made a good point: Even a star player needs help to succeed.
Good coaching is needed, for sure, but stars also need to be surrounded by good players, and the best way to get good players is
through the draft.

Bob Strumm, a longtime junior hockey guru with the Regina Pats and Spokane Chiefs who helped build the first Canadian junior team that won gold back in 1982, had a theory. From his research in the early 1990s, he gleaned that a Stanley Cup champion typically had ten or more of its own draft picks on its roster. Basically, half the roster was drafted. That tells you how important good drafting is.

Recent history seems to prove him right. From 1995 to 2022, Stanley Cup–winning teams, especially those that have won multiple times, more often than not had stocked at least half their roster with homegrown draft picks. And the need to maintain that ratio is even more important in the salary cap era of the NHL.

Strumm was in the Red Wings front office in my first season with Detroit. Several seasons later, when I was being interviewed for the GM position with the Blue Jackets, Strumm kept reminding me of the importance of the draft. He had done the research. He had a book of notes and thoughts on how to start a franchise. Strumm later became my first pro scout with the Blue Jackets and then my director of pro scouting.

Yzerman and the Red Wings are a prime example of how good drafting helped to build a dynasty. When Bryan Murray was named the GM and coach of the Red Wings in July 1990, Yzerman was only twenty-five years old, but he already had played seven NHL seasons.

There were two good playoff runs in the late 1980s, with trips to the conference final against the Edmonton Oilers. But Wayne Gretzky and company had little difficulty dispatching Detroit in five games on both occasions. The Oilers would win their third and fourth Stanley Cups in those two springs, 1987 and 1988.

The Red Wings were a contender. But they stumbled under coach Jacques Demers after those two trips to the Campbell Conference final. In 1989, the Chicago Blackhawks, who finished well behind the Wings, knocked out Detroit in six games in the first round after Yzerman had a whopping 155 points in the regular season. The following year, the Wings missed the playoffs by six points, which prompted owner Mike Ilitch to make changes. Demers was replaced, and GM Jimmy Devellano was bumped upstairs to a new role as senior vice-president. Bryan Murray was brought in with a dual role, as coach and GM, and he hired me a week later as an assistant coach on a two-year contract.

Yzerman was a proud athlete. I remember one night I showed a video clip between periods during a game and I singled him out for a mistake on the penalty kill. "Number 19 was out of position on the play," I said.

The next thing I knew, he had followed me into the coaches' office. "Don't ever, ever call me out in front of the team again," Yzerman said.

I was shaking. My armpits were drenched. But then I said, "Well, do it right and I won't call you out."

Thankfully, he said he was joking and laughed off the incident. But that's how proud and intense he was.

Yzerman and the Red Wings are a fascinating case study in the difficulty of building a winner. The Red Wings, who had been dreadful for a decade, were fortunate Yzerman fell into their lap with the fourth overall selection in the 1983 NHL draft at the Montreal Forum. It was the first time since 1979 that they had kept their first pick. And it was Devellano's first draft with Detroit. He admitted an interest in three players. He liked the offense and size of Sylvain Turgeon, a left wing with Hull in the

Quebec league; a local kid named Pat LaFontaine, who was a slick center with Verdun in Quebec; and the heart and talent of Yzerman, who played with the Peterborough Petes.

But Devellano wasn't sure any of them would still be available at number four. Minnesota North Stars GM Lou Nanne ultimately chose a high-school forward named Brian Lawton first overall. The pick had belonged to Pittsburgh, but Nanne had acquired it earlier in the season. Devellano was ecstatic. He strongly felt the Red Wings would get a significant player to build around. The Whalers took Turgeon next and Devellano's old team, the New York Islanders, selected LaFontaine third. Yzerman fell to Detroit.

Lawton played parts of a dozen NHL seasons but was only average and at times seemed haunted by a brazen decision to wear number 98—just a little too close to number 99 in the eyes of many. But he wasn't close to 99 on the ice. While Turgeon had a decent career and LaFontaine enjoyed a Hall of Fame career shortened due to injuries, Yzerman was the best of the bunch.

But building the Red Wings around Yzerman into a championship team was an up-and-down, lengthy process. Stevie Y had played in 864 regular-season games and 113 more playoff games and was in his fourteenth NHL season before he finally lifted the Stanley Cup over his head at age thirty-two after his Red Wings swept the Philadelphia Flyers with a 2–1 victory on June 7, 1997.

By the time he accepted the prized trophy from commissioner Gary Bettman at Joe Louis Arena, to end a forty-six-year drought for the Original Six franchise, Yzerman had played for six head coaches (Polano, Park, Neale, Demers, Murray, and Bowman). Bowman, of course, is the all-time winningest coach in hockey, so maybe Stevie got the coaching upgrade he needed! He also had played under two GMs in Devellano and Murray. Devellano and Bowman shared management duties and Ken Holland was an assistant GM when the Red Wings finally won.

Interestingly, before Yzerman won his three Cups, three times he was nearly traded, once before Bowman had arrived and twice after. The first time was in 1991 when Bryan and I thought we had a deal with the Islanders for LaFontaine. One night Bryan told me the deal was going to be done and announced the next morning. It was LaFontaine and some other pieces for Yzerman. But the next day nothing happened, and it was never mentioned again. The second time was in 1992 when he was rumored to be part of a blockbuster offer to Quebec for Eric Lindros. The third time was in 1995 to Ottawa, supposedly for a package that included a young Alexei Yashin.

Once Yzerman was surrounded by the right players, many of them acquired through the draft, not only did Yzerman play great hockey and go on to win more Cups, but he also went on to become one of the greatest captains in the history of the game. And Bowman did push him hard to become a more complete player, good at both ends of the rink, with and without the puck. It's an example of how avoiding the temptation to trade, or allowing frustration to get the better of your thinking, can make a difference. Would the Wings have won had they traded him during those challenging years? Hard to say. But there have been a lot of instances when trading a top pick too soon can be disastrous.

With Detroit, Yzerman obviously was a big part of their success. But there were several other significant developments, beginning with a massive turning point at the 1989 draft at the Met Center in Bloomington, Minnesota. That was the year Mats Sundin went to Quebec first overall. The haul for Devellano and his director of scouting, Neil Smith, included reliable forward Mike Sillinger eleventh overall out of Regina, followed by defenseman Bob Boughner with the second-round pick out of Sault Ste. Marie—then Lidström at fifty-three, Sergei Fedorov at seventy-four, Dallas Drake in the sixth round, all the way to Vladimir Konstantinov in the eleventh. What a run of picks. Between them, Lidstrom, Fedorov, Drake, and Konstantinov have nine Stanley Cup championships.

"I don't think there was a better draft in the history of hockey than our draft, the Red Wings' draft, in '89," Devellano told NHL .com. "I'm also here to tell you there was some luck involved."

The Red Wings were leaders in developing with European talent. Devellano was intent on building his team through the draft and the philosophy was to find underrated Europeans, rather than just take chances on North Americans. Christer Rockstrom was the Red Wings chief European scout back then. Smith had hired him as a part-time scout and quickly confirmed he had a keen eye for talent. He was tipped off about Lidström from friends who played on the dependable defenseman's Swedish team, Västerås IK. Smith was the Wings' director of scouting, and he liked Fedorov over Pavel Bure. Smith also liked the toughness Konstantinov exhibited a couple of years earlier at the 1987 World Junior Championship, also known as the Piestany Punch-Up. At this time the Iron Curtain was coming down, so the Russians were much more available.

The bountiful 1989 draft was the last one for Smith and Rockstrom with the Red Wings. Neil became the New York Rangers GM a month later and took Rockström with him. The Blueshirts won a Stanley Cup under Smith in 1994.

But the Detroit drafts continued to produce bumper crops

without them. As Detroit's scouting director, Ken Holland took over from Smith, and Rockström recommended as his replacement in Europe fellow Swede Hakan Andersson, who became known as a superscout himself. Under his watch the Wings drafted Tomas Holmstrom in the tenth round in 1994. They later got Pavel Datsyuk in the sixth round in 1998, Henrik Zetterberg in the seventh round in 1999, and Johan Franzen in the third round in 2004.

Neil Smith was always big on Swedish talent; he was over there all the time. He married a Swedish lady. Hakan was Christer's assistant and hung out with him all the time. It was an easy transition. I arrived in Detroit after Neil left.

In 1990, the Red Wings drafted Keith Primeau and Vyacheslav Kozlov. The 1991 draft under Bryan Murray yielded Martin Lapointe, Jamie Pushor, Chris Osgood, and Mike Knuble, whom Detroit gave up on after only four pro seasons in the organization. But he went on to enjoy a one-thousand-plus-game career and managed to get himself into the post-season lineup for three games when Detroit claimed its back-to-back titles in 1998.

Darren McCarty was a significant addition from the 1992 draft. Two years later, the Red Wings selected future Stanley Cup winners in Mathieu Dandenault and Holmstrom. Year after year the Wings, with an excellent scouting staff, kept unearthing stars and supporting casts.

The roster later was fortified in 1998 with first-rounder Jiri Fischer and Datsyuk. Zetterberg was taken in the seventh round in 1999 and fellow Swede Niklas Kronwall in the first round in 2000. There also were Jiri Hudler, Valtteri Filppula, and Jonathan Ericsson in 2002, Franzen in 2004. All were Stanley Cup contributors, except for Ericsson. But Ericsson was an interesting case. In the same draft I took Rick Nash first overall, the Red Wings selected Ericsson, a defenseman, in the ninth round with the 291st and final pick. The very last pick. The Wings found talent in every round.

Ericsson did play in the 2009 Stanley Cup final for Detroit in his rookie NHL season. Despite various injuries late in his career, he still managed to suit up for a combined 756 regular season and playoff games. He also played for Sweden in the 2014 Olympics (silver) and two World Championships.

In our first season together with the Red Wings, Bryan Murray slipped off to Europe to take stock of European draft picks. He called me at 1:00 a.m. to tell me that after watching Lidström play for Västerås he thought Nick was so good that he would be the next Al MacInnis.

I replied, "Bryan, go have another beer, and we can talk tomorrow."

I felt he was either drunk or dreaming. MacInnis was a superstar, a perennial Norris Trophy contender. But Bryan was right. Lidström would play twenty seasons with the Red Wings with a combined 1,827 regular-season and playoff games, and win four Stanley Cups and seven Norris Trophies and be inducted into the Hockey Hall of Fame. Yzerman hired him to be his vice-president of hockey operations with the Red Wings in January 2022.

He was a star in his first practice and never looked back. I remember being on the ice as an assistant coach for that first practice thinking, How amazing is this guy? Not only did he never have a bad game; he never had a bad practice. He played with Brad McCrimmon that first season and the veteran was a suitable partner. But Nick probably was better for Brad at that point in his career. I remember Holland told me many times that the day Nick retired was the same day he would call it quits as GM.

My first day on the job in Detroit was a good one. Bryan picked me up at the Windsor airport and delivered unbelievable news. Sergei Fedorov had defected and was expected in Detroit within the week. Fedorov was with the Soviet national team at the Goodwill Games. The Soviets had played an exhibition game in Portland, Oregon, and were on their way to Kennewick, Washington, to begin the tournament when Fedorov slipped away from the Russian authorities. A few days later, we had Fedorov signed to a five-year contract. He scored thirty-one goals and seventy-nine points in seventy-seven games in his rookie season. In his fourth year, Sergei won the Hart Trophy, the Lester B. Pearson Trophy (renamed the Ted Lindsay Award in 2010), and the Selke Trophy for a brilliant fifty-six-goal, 120-point campaign, all at age twenty-four.

With Yzerman and Fedorov as a one-two punch, the Red Wings began a streak of twenty-five consecutive playoff appearances with Bryan as coach/GM and me as his assistant. We obviously weren't there for all of that amazing run, but we were there for the start of it. In addition, Lidström and Konstantinov arrived in Detroit a year after Fedorov's rookie season. But even with the captain and his three new European teammates in the fold, there still were growing pains.

In Fedorov's first season, the Red Wings were eliminated by the St. Louis Blues in the first round in seven games after Detroit was up 3–1 in the series. With Lidström and Konstantinov, the Red Wings finished first in the West in the regular season. Still, they needed to overcome a 3–1 series deficit to defeat Minnesota in seven games in the first round. The North Stars had finished the regular season with twenty-eight fewer points. The Blackhawks swept Detroit in the second round. Life got worse the following spring with another first-round flop when Nikolai Borschevsky scored for the Toronto Maple Leafs in overtime of Game 7. More changes were to come in Detroit after the 1993 playoffs.

There were whispers around the league that spring that owner Mike Ilitch wanted to bring in Mike Keenan as coach. Jim Lites, who was the president, and Devellano talked the Red Wings ownership out of that move and instead Devellano promised to deliver either Al Arbour or Scotty Bowman, both legends. Arbour did not want to leave Long Island. But Bowman was looking for a new challenge and a lucrative payday.

Bryan was stripped of his coaching duties. I was now his assistant GM and in charge of the Red Wings' AHL affiliate in Adirondack. Detroit performed beautifully in 1993–94 under Bowman, who arrived on the scene having coached the Montreal Canadiens to five Stanley Cups and added a sixth with Mario Lemieux and the 1992 Pittsburgh Penguins.

Again, the Red Wings finished tops in the West in Bowman's first year in Detroit. Fedorov scored fifty-six goals. They drew the San Jose Sharks in the first round, a team Detroit finished eighteen points ahead of after the eighty-four-game regular season. But in those days, it was a 2-3-2 playoff format, and the Sharks put themselves in a good position when they won the series opener 5-4 in Detroit thanks to Czech defenseman Vlastimil Kroupa's only playoff goal late in the third period.

The Sharks held a 3–2 series advantage when we returned to Detroit. The outlook appeared pretty darn good for the Red Wings when we hammered San Jose, 7–1, in Game 6 at Joe Louis Arena. But the deciding game did not go our way. Jamie

Baker's goal midway through the third period snapped a 2–2 tie and gave the number-eight-seed Sharks an upset first-round victory and placed the mighty Red Wings in disarray.

What made things worse for Detroit's ownership was that Keenan steered the New York Rangers to their first Stanley Cup championship in fifty-four years a few weeks later.

It was evident the Red Wings needed more reliable goaltending and playoff prowess. Bryan had traded goaltender Tim Cheveldae to the Winnipeg Jets for Bob Essensa that season and the latter did not work out. Osgood was still finding his way as a young goaltender in his rookie season. Yzerman still needed help to lead the Red Wings to the promised land. The Red Wings were a club in flux, a team searching for a goaltender and veteran leadership to help all those great draft picks.

A month after the Sharks' first-round upset, Bryan Murray and I were fired. Mike Ilitch, who died in February 2017, was a classy owner. It was a Friday afternoon when Bryan stuck his head into my office and said, "I've just been fired, and so have you." This was not a surprising development, considering another playoff flop. But I did not expect a thunderbolt when my phone rang at my Michigan home on the following Monday. It was Mr. Ilitch.

"You were fired on Friday," he said. "You have time on your deal?"

I informed him there was one more year remaining on my contract.

"Okay, if you don't have a job in a year, I'll hire you back," he said.

No wonder the Red Wings were such a success. But as generous and decent as Mr. Ilitch was, he also was challenging and intimidating and wanted to win.

He wasn't happy when Gerard Gallant, a Red Wings draft pick who scored thirty-eight, thirty-four, thirty-nine, and thirty-six goals in four successive seasons in the late 1980s and early 1990s, left as a free agent to sign with the Tampa Bay Lightning in summer 1993. I taught Gerard in high school in Summerside when he was sixteen. I first met him at the local rink when he was playing peewee hockey. I remember one day asking the kids, "What do you want to do when you finish high school?" and he said he wanted to be a mailman. I said, "You're going to Sherbrooke's major junior camp; if I was you, I would focus on hockey a little more!" Well, he obviously made it as player and later as a darn good coach in Florida, Las Vegas, and New York.

A few months earlier, in late January 1993, Bryan and I had a trade ready to go that had me sweating. The deal would send Jimmy Carson, Gary Shuchuk, and Marc Potvin to Los Angeles for Paul Coffey, Sylvain Couturier, and Jim Hiller. Bryan, myself, and Devellano went to the Fox Theatre on Woodward Avenue, where Mr. Ilitch had an office on the tenth floor, to get his permission to make the deal. The security guard told us, "If you guys come down from the tenth floor, I'll guarantee you'll be a changed person!" No one wanted to go up to meet Mr. Ilitch because we knew he wouldn't like what we had to say. It was the first time I was in his office, in my first year, and it was an intense meeting because Jimmy Carson was a Detroit kid, who played his minor hockey in the Compuware organization against Mr. Ilitch's Little Caesars team. Mr. Ilitch loved him. But Jimmy, who had been part of the Gretzky trade, was starting to slip. It was a pressure trade for us. Mr. Ilitch was pissed, but he gave us the approval. Before we left his office he said, "You fucking better be right."

The Kings made it to the Stanley Cup final that spring, but Coffey became an essential player for us and the team's future.

Funny story about Coffey, who is a great guy and was obviously a great player, another Hall of Famer, and was by far the best skater in the league. I remember I was the assistant GM during Bowman's first season and I got a call one day from Mrs. (Marian) Ilitch, who looked after the budgets. She said to me, "Can you tell me why Paul Coffey used twenty-two pairs of skates this season?" Most guys wore a couple, but Paul was so particular about his skates. The stiffer he could get the boot, the better. He would get a new pair and he and our equipment guy, Mark Brennan, would stitch them to make them stiffer. Then Paul would wear them, right out of the box. And he would wear a size smaller than he measured to keep them stiff and tight. But look at the results! I told Mrs. Ilitch how particular he was about his skates and if we had to buy twenty-two pairs it was worth it. If that cost the Wings a little money, I helped save them a lot of money in another transaction.

I must have impressed Mr. I, particularly with my acquisition of Kris Draper. He was quite the story. Kris came from a wonderful and thoughtful hockey family. His dad, Mike, had a successful junior, minor pro, and senior career, winning a pair of Allan Cups with the Orillia Terriers in the early 1970s. His uncle Dave won a Memorial Cup with the 1961 St. Michael's Majors. He became a junior coach and GM, a college coach, and one of the best NHL scouts in the history of the game, helping build the Quebec Nordiques/Colorado Avalanche into two-time Stanley Cup champions. Another uncle, Bruce, was Mike's twin. He was Dave's teammate when St. Mike's claimed its Memorial Cup in 1961, and played one game with the Toronto

Maple Leafs in 1962–63. But Bruce was stuck in the minors because there were only six teams back then. Sadly, he died too young, from cancer.

Mike often said that Kris had his uncle's skating legs. Kris never met Bruce, but as a pre-game ritual he thought about him and his grandfather Jack, who played minor pro for the Pittsburgh Yellow Jackets in the 1930s.

At seventeen, Kris joined the Canadian national team. The Winnipeg Jets drafted him in the third round (sixty-second overall) at the 1989 draft. He rejoined the Canadian national team for a second year but took a brief hiatus to join the Canadian junior team for the 1990 World Junior Championship in Finland, where he won gold.

Kris wore four sweaters in 1990–91. He played three games with the Jets, seven more with Winnipeg's AHL affiliate in Moncton, won a second World Junior gold with Canada in Saskatoon, where he shut down Pavel Bure in the gold-medal game, and finished the season with the Ottawa 67's under legendary coach/GM Brian Kilrea.

Draper then split the next two seasons between the Jets and Moncton, but more time in New Brunswick than Manitoba. He believed he should be an NHLer and grew frustrated with his situation.

Jim Clark was a part-time Eastern Canada scout for Detroit at the time. He liked Draper. I inquired about him with Jets GM Mike Smith. Smith liked Draper, but head coach John Paddock did not. Smith wanted to help the kid out and agreed to give Kris to us in a minor-league deal in summer 1993. The league intervened and said there had to be a transaction. We agreed on $1 U.S. as the return. And I did give Mike Smith a buck.

Kris didn't make the Red Wings out of training camp in 1993, Bowman's first year as coach, and wanted to take some time to contemplate his future, so he went home to Toronto. I urged our coach in Adirondack, Newell Brown: "You have to talk him into playing and that he has a future in this game."

Brown was persuasive. Draper did report to Adirondack. Bowman later watched Adirondack play around Christmastime against Hamilton, and Kris caught his eye. Draper was promoted in late January and never played another AHL game. He played in 1,157 regular-season NHL games and another 222 playoff games before he retired. He also was a member of each of the four Detroit Stanley Cup teams and went on to become the Wings' director of amateur scouting, and a damn good one.

Jim Clark, now director of pro scouting with the Ottawa Senators, deserves plenty of credit for the Draper development in Detroit. Draper's story proves again that players can be drafted by one team and it doesn't work out, but a different situation can make a world of difference.

Draper, Maltby, Lidstrom, McCarty, and Holmstrom were the only five members to play on all four Red Wings Stanley Cup–winning teams between 1997 and 2008. Draper played a massive role on the four championship teams on the grind line with Maltby and Joey Kocur, who later was replaced by McCarty.

Still, after the addition of Draper, the Red Wings needed to add more elements to their roster to get over the hump. After our departure and the loss to the Sharks, Bowman, Devellano, and Holland took over the Red Wings' personnel decisions. Veteran Mike Vernon, who won a Cup with Calgary, was brought in to solve the goaltending woes, acquired from the Flames at the 1994 draft.

The next season was shortened, due to a lockout. Play didn't begin until January 1995. But the Red Wings made a giant leap forward in the shortened season. Famed Russian veteran defenseman Viacheslav Fetisov was added at the trade deadline, and Detroit finished the forty-eight-game regular season on top, winning the Presidents' Trophy.

The Red Wings continued their world-beating ways in the first three rounds of the playoffs, dispatching the Dallas Stars in five games, gaining a measure of revenge with a sweep of the Sharks in the second round, and taking care of business in the West final with a five-game ousting of Chicago. Detroit entered the 1995 final against the New Jersey Devils as the heavy favorite. The Devils finished fifth in the East and won only twenty-two of their forty-eight regular-season games. But it took the Devils only eight days and four games to claim their first Stanley Cup title, sweeping the Red Wings in a shocker.

The Red Wings were beaten again the following year. After another Presidents' Trophy regular season, they lost in the West final in six games to Patrick Roy and the Colorado Avalanche, which was not a major upset but certainly a disappointment.

Meanwhile, Bryan had been hired to run the Florida Panthers in August 1994, and he brought me along with him as his director of player development. He hired me to replace Roger Neilson as head coach to begin the 1995–96 season. It would have been something had the Murray/MacLean leadership duo faced off against the Red Wings in the 1996 Stanley Cup final. But the opponent instead was the Avalanche, and we were swept by the former Quebec Nordiques.

The Red Wings were still a few moves away from achieving their Stanley Cup championship chops. Bowman acquired Igor

Larionov in fall 1995 and he, Yzerman, and Fetisov worked well together, forming a strong leadership group. They liked each other and had plenty of input with Bowman in terms of ice time, line combinations, and the like. This was a big step forward for the Red Wings, but the big moves to put the team over the top were three trades in the 1996–97 season. First, in October the Red Wings acquired Brendan Shanahan and Brian Glynn from Hartford for Coffey, Keith Primeau, and Detroit's 1997 first-round selection. Then Greg Johnson was moved to the Pittsburgh Penguins in exchange for Tomas Sandström. The final transaction landed Larry Murphy from the Maple Leafs for future considerations.

Not only did they give up a first-round pick, but Primeau was Detroit's first-round selection (third overall) in the 1990 NHL draft, a month before Bryan and I arrived on the scene. It shows just how close they thought they were to winning it all that they were willing to give up such assets to bolster their team. We see a lot of that these days, with contenders moving their first picks to acquire assets to win now.

The 1990 draft was a big one. Quebec took Owen Nolan first, Vancouver chose Petr Nedved next, followed by Detroit with Primeau, Philadelphia taking Mike Ricci, and Pittsburgh selecting Jaromir Jagr fifth. Imagine the Red Wings in the 1990s and beyond with Jagr instead of Primeau. But Primeau was no slouch. He made the Red Wings out of training camp that fall. One of my duties as assistant coach was to work on his skating after practice, particularly his crossovers. Once again, Yzerman skated over to me with a question.

"Do you and Bryan think this guy is going to play in the NHL?" the captain said.

I told Stevie Y that I thought Primeau would be a star.

"He'll never play in the NHL," said Yzerman, who had watched the kid stumble through the early part of the season as an eighteen-year-old.

The Red Wings assistant GM at the time was Nick Polano. He was instrumental in Fedorov's defection that summer and the late Petr Klima finding a way out of former Czechoslovakia in 1985. He and then Red Wings president Jim Lites also hatched the masquerade of getting Konstantinov out of the Soviet Union in 1991. A Soviet contact was given money, which was used to bribe doctors to say the defenseman had a rare cancer and needed to go to the United States to be treated properly.

I mention Polano because he and Jimmy D didn't like each other. Polano wanted the Red Wings to select Jagr over Primeau in 1990, but Devellano had his mind made up. Primeau had size, and he was coming off a season with fifty-seven goals in sixty-five games in junior with the Niagara Falls Thunder. He enjoyed a lengthy career, playing in a combined 1,037 NHL regular-season and playoff games. But again, imagine how good those Detroit teams would have been with Jágr.

Polano never missed an opportunity to rub it in on Devellano. He often slipped Jagr's statistics underneath Devellano's office door. But Devellano and Co. did just fine in stocking the shelves with homegrown talent. They smartly signed significant free agents (especially later for the 2002 championship team), made first-rate trades, and fixed the goaltending problem.

The Red Wings won again in 1998 despite the heartbreaking limousine accident that left Konstantinov crippled. But there was no dramatic roster overhaul. Veteran forward Brent Gilchrist was added through free agency. They lost Vernon in a trade for two second-round picks with San Jose because they knew he would be scooped by Nashville in the 1998 expansion draft. Then Detroit bolstered their blue line with the addition of Jamie Macoun and Dmitri Mironov. The Red Wings acquired Macoun from the Maple Leafs for a fourth-round pick, and Mironov came aboard from Anaheim in exchange for Pushor and a fourth-round choice.

The Detroit players were determined and motivated to Win One for Vladdy, and the heart of the roster was pumping with draft picks. There still were homegrown players in Yzerman, Lidstrom, Lapointe, Kozlov, McCarty, Holmstrom, Fedorov, Kocur, and Osgood. But now more young players from the past drafts like Anders Eriksson (1993 first round, twenty-second overall), Mathieu Dandenault, and Mike Knuble also stepped up in the playoffs. This meant the Red Wings had twelve draftees on the 1998 championship roster, one more than the year before.

Two other youngsters from the second title-winning team were defenseman Aaron Ward and backup goalie Kevin Hodson. They weren't Detroit draft picks, but Bryan Murray and I acquired Ward in the 1992 off-season from Winnipeg for Paul Ysebaert. Ward didn't see any action in the 1998 post-season, but he did play in fifty-two regular-season games.

Hodson was an undrafted Memorial Cup–winning goalie with the 1992–93 Sault Ste. Marie Greyhounds. Chicago signed him out of junior, and after a year split between the Soo and their AHL affiliate in Indianapolis we signed him for Adirondack just before the Memorial Cup. I was really impressed by him. He was the top goaltender in that tournament. After three full seasons in the minors where he was a star for us, and a fourth pro season of limited action as the Red Wings' third goalie with only six regular-season appearances, Hodson became the backup in the

1997–98 season. He saw brief action in Game 5 of the second round against St. Louis. It puts a smile on your face when an underdog acquisition like Kevin works out. I was proud of that signing, as well as Tim Taylor, whom I signed when I was GM in Adirondack. I had coached him in Baltimore; he was a second-round pick with the Caps. He became a valuable piece for the Wings, along with Draper.

The Red Wings remained strong the next three seasons, losing twice to Colorado in the conference semifinal and once to Los Angeles in the quarterfinals. In the 2002 Stanley Cup run, the Red Wings had a new cause. It was Win for Luc, Steve, Dom, and Fredrik and one more for Brett and Chris.

Luc Robitaille, Steve Duchesne, Dominik Hašek, and Fredrik Olausson were popular and distinguished veteran players nearing the eighteenth holes of their careers. But they were without a Stanley Cup. Brett Hull had won with the Dallas Stars in 1998–99 but wanted to add another title. Chris Chelios was sixteen years removed from his first Stanley Cup with the Montreal Canadiens in 1985–86.

With that championship, the Red Wings captured a third Stanley Cup in six years. It was an aging gang this time around, but again a considerable part of the mix were Detroit draft picks in Yzerman, Fedorov, Lidstrom, McCarty, Fisher, Dandenault, and Holmstrom, plus newcomer Pavel Datsyuk.

That makes it only eight draft picks. But before old Strummer suffers a medical episode, we should point out that not only were backup goalie Manny Legace and Jason Williams homegrown players, but also draft pick defenseman Maxim Kuznetsov played in thirty-nine regular-season games. Unfortunately, however, he didn't see any post-season action.

Williams was signed by the Red Wings as a free agent after four years of junior with the Peterborough Petes in September 2000. He was developed by Detroit and saw action in nine of the Red Wings' twenty-three playoff games in 2002. Legace was a late-round draft pick of the Hartford Whalers in 1993 after his brilliant World Junior performance for the gold-medal-winning Canadian team. He bounced between the Whalers/Carolina Hurricanes organization and the Los Angeles Kings before the Red Wings signed him as a free agent in July 1999, briefly lost him on waivers, and then reclaimed him two weeks later. Legace became Osgood's backup in 2001–02.

Many hockey experts predicted the Red Wings would suffer in a salary cap world because they freely spent in the free-agent market. But after the Carolina Hurricanes and Anaheim Ducks celebrated championships in the first two years after the lockout-canceled 2004–05 season and the league instituted a salary cap, the Red Wings were again top of the heap.

In 2007–08, Detroit's roster was still heavy with draft picks: Datsyuk, Zetterberg, Hudler, Holmstrom, Franzen, Filppula, Osgood, McCarty, Kronwall, Darren Helm, and Drake, traded as part of the Bob Essensa deal in March 1994. But Drake returned to Detroit as a free agent in July 2007. By this time Yzerman had retired and now captain Lidström passed the Stanley Cup first to Drake in the on-ice celebrations, who retired at age thirty-nine five weeks later.

Added to the list of eleven draft picks were Tomas Kopecky and Derek Meech. They played seventy-seven and thirty-two regular-season games, respectively, but didn't see any playoff action. Next, Brett Lebda and Matt Ellis signed as undrafted free agents out of the University of Notre Dame and the junior St. Michael's

Majors, respectively. Lebda played nineteen games in the Red Wings' Stanley Cup run, but Ellis was a black ace. They may not have been drafted, but chief amateur scout Joe McDonnell and his Red Wings staff unearthed the two contributors.

After the Red Wings won their fourth Stanley Cup in eleven seasons (one year wiped out because of the 2004–05 canceled lockout season), the NHL saw four teams win multiple championships in the next thirteen years in the Pittsburgh Penguins (2009, 2016, 2017), Chicago Blackhawks (2010, 2013, 2015), Los Angeles Kings (2012, 2014), and Tampa Bay Lightning (2020, 2021).

Strumm's theory holds up for these minidynasties, too. The 2009 Penguins had ten draft picks, and eleven picks for the 2016 and 2017 championship seasons.

Because the 2004–05 season was scrapped, there was quite the debate at the GM meetings about how the draft would be conducted in June. A generational player—Crosby—was at stake. There was plenty of campaigning on how your particular team could land him and teams wanted the same lottery setup as in previous years. The NHL wanted all teams to have a chance due to the mothballing of the season.

The Penguins finished last in the 2003–04 season, and the NHL wanted Crosby in a Pittsburgh hockey market that had hit the skids. The lottery was held in New York in late June, and the NHL got their wish. Sid the Kid was Pittsburgh bound. As a GM who ended up with the sixth pick of the 2005 draft, I was sick to my stomach.

The Penguins were a lousy club for four years. Their failures landed them luck in the draft lottery with number one picks like Marc-Andre Fleury in 2003, Malkin (second overall) in 2004, Crosby in 2005, and Jordan Staal (second overall) in 2006. Those four draft selections, plus the drafting of Kris Letang in the third round in 2005 (sixty-second overall), set up the Penguins for many years. Penguins legend and owner Mario Lemieux also made an astute move in replacing Ray Shero as GM with Jim Rutherford before the 2016–17 season. Rutherford made sharp deals to bring in quality veterans like Patric Hornqvist, Phil Kessel, and Ron Hainsey.

Other beneficial moves made, especially in the U.S. College free-agent market, were the signings of Conor Sheary and Carter Rowney. In addition, defenseman Brian Dumoulin was brought aboard in a trade with Brandon Sutter for Jordan Staal in 2012. But the core of these Penguins teams was established by the success of the four mentioned drafts, especially the hotly contested 2005 draft.

As for the Chicago Blackhawks, their first Stanley Cup of the modern era, in 2010, was earned with ten draft picks, such as Patrick Kane and Jonathan Toews. The 2013 winning team contained many of the same picks, adding one more to bring the total to eleven. And the same number for 2015: eleven draft picks on the roster.

The Blackhawks' success at the draft table has been a topic of conversation in the league for many years. Yes, they were a terrible team for a long time, but their staff still made some extraordinary picks in the early rounds and deeper in the draft.

I recall traveling to a game in Alberta with then Blackhawks GM Dale Tallon in the 2006–07 season when I ran Columbus. It was late in the season, and we kept one eye on the players we were scouting and one eye on how our respective teams were performing. The season ended, and the Blackhawks won the draft lottery. They selected Patrick Kane with the first pick. I was fired after the season, more than two months before the draft. As stated earlier, you have to be bad sometimes to be good. The Blue Jackets never won the draft lottery. Most years I was there, the lottery was unlucky and we moved down.

But the Blackhawks' made the most of their draft picks. One exciting selection for them was defenseman Duncan Keith. He was taken in the 2002 draft in the second round (fifty-fourth overall) out of Michigan State. He was undersized, played in forty-one games, and scored three goals and fifteen points.

The Blackhawks longtime Western scout Bill Lesuk, who played more than 750 career NHL and WHA games with the Boston Bruins, Philadelphia Flyers, Los Angeles Kings, Washington Capitals, and Winnipeg Jets, deserves credit for Chicago's interest in and subsequent drafting of Keith. Lesuk, a left winger, who played three regular-season games in late December for the 1969–70 Stanley Cup champion Boston Bruins and another three games late in their playoff run. The Blackhawks management didn't have much interest in Keith, who was ranked ninety-fourth among North American skaters by Central Scouting. The Hawks thought Lesuk was off his rocker. But Lesuk didn't back down and got his way.

Keith went on to win the Norris Trophy twice, the Conn Smythe in the Blackhawks' last championship, and play in more than 1,350 career regular-season and playoff games in the NHL. It's a good thing the Blackhawks listened to Lesuk, even though others later took credit for taking Keith.

Brent Seabrook was an intriguing selection. We had the fourth pick in the 2003 draft and discussed Seabrook. However, our Western scout, Sam McMaster, saw him play all season and predicted he would never play in the NHL. Instead, we chose Nikolai Zherdev. It's incredible how scouts see players differently.

Seabrook was selected fourteenth overall. He won three Stanley Cups, Olympic gold for Canada in 2010, and performed in 1,237 combined NHL regular-season and playoff games.

Although Dustin Byfuglien was only around for the first title, he was a steal in the eighth round (245th overall) in 2003. It was undoubtedly the unrestricted free-agent signing of Marian Hossa on July 1, 2009, that helped push the Blackhawks over the top. Hossa, a Hall of Fame two-way forward, had been to the Stanley Cup final with Pittsburgh in 2008 and lost, then lost again with Detroit in 2009. In Chicago, he won three titles in his last eight NHL seasons.

As for the Los Angeles Kings, it should come as no surprise that when they won two Cups, in 2012 and 2014, both times they had twelve homegrown draft picks on the team.

When the Kings won their first Stanley Cup in franchise history, they accomplished this feat as an eight seed in the Western Conference. On December 20, 2011, Kings GM Dean Lombardi made a coaching change, hiring NHL veteran coach and executive Darryl Sutter. Sutter replaced Terry Murray—yes, Bryan's brother—who, in my opinion, had done a solid job taking a young group of draft picks and molding them into a solid core. Sutter was six years removed from his last coaching gig in the NHL with the Flames and a first-round exit in 2006. Lombardi and Sutter had a history together in San Jose. Lombardi felt Sutter was precisely what the Kings needed to take the next step. And again, Lombardi was right on the money.

As with previous Stanley Cup champions, the Kings' draft picks were massive contributors. Jonathan Quick, a third-round pick in 2005, was a star in both championships, capturing the Conn Smythe Trophy in 2012 as the playoff MVP. Drew Doughty, the first-round (second overall) choice in 2008, swiftly blossomed into a young stud defenseman and emerged as a leader. He would do whatever was necessary to win.

Anze Kopitar was a first-round pick (eleventh overall) in the 2005 draft and emerged as not only a scoring leader but also an excellent two-hundred-foot forward. Dustin Brown was a first-round (thirteenth overall) selection in 2003. When the Kings became contenders, he transformed himself into a veteran, physical leader, and captain.

All these significant draft picks were pushed to the top when Lombardi acquired proven winners like Jeff Carter, Justin Williams, Colin Fraser, and Mike Richards, and an excellent leader in Willie Mitchell.

The Tampa Bay Lightning have become a powerhouse, winning back-to-back Cups in 2020 and 2021, with ten draft picks on the team for each championship. And it all comes back to Steve Yzerman. He was the GM who built the Lightning into a contender through the draft, free agency, trades, and player development.

Yzerman inherited Steven Stamkos, the first overall selection in 2008, and Victor Hedman, the second overall pick in 2009. But then Yzerman added two more cornerstone players in Nikita Kucherov (second round, fifty-eighth overall, 2011) and Andrei Vasilevskiy (first round, nineteenth overall, 2012). Yzerman also landed Mikhail Sergachev, Erik Cernak, and Ryan McDonagh through significant trades. In addition, Kevin Shattenkirk was an unrestricted free agent signing by Yzerman's successor, Julien BriseBois.

The Lightning scouting staff was also good at plucking young undrafted free agents. They signed Tyler Johnson after his over-age season with the Spokane Chiefs and Yanni Gourde. After his Quebec Major Junior Hockey League (QMJHL) MVP season with the Victoriaville Tigres, Gourde bounced around in the minors with Worcester, San Francisco, and Kalamazoo for two seasons. Finally, the Lightning got him, and after two and a half more seasons in the minors, he became a full-time NHLer and two-time champion.

The Lightning had a knack for development. Johnson played two seasons in the AHL before being promoted full-time to the Lightning in 2013. Alex Killorn was similar. Anthony Cirelli spent most of his first year as a pro in Syracuse before finishing the 2017–18 season in Tampa Bay. Ross Colton skated a similar path in 2020–21. He ended the season with the Lightning and scored the Stanley Cup–clinching goal in the 1–0 finale against the Montreal Canadiens. Think about how good Brayden Point and Cirelli became, and they were third-round picks in successive years.

Tampa's run of back-to-back Cups ended, of course, in 2022 when they lost in six games in the final to the very impressive Colorado Avalanche, who proved again how important the draft, and patience, are toward building a winner. Five seasons after finishing dead last and by twenty-one points, the Avs under the leadership of former star center Joe Sakic—who had twice led them to Cup wins on the ice, including 1996 against me and the Panthers—were the Cup winners again.

And much of the heavy lifting was done through the draft. The Avs selected winger Gabriel Landeskog second overall in 2011. He went on to become captain. With the first overall pick in 2013 Sakic took Nathan MacKinnon, another star. Quite often by the time the Memorial Cup is played in late May or early June, the scouting is typically over. Mario Lemieux, for example, after a great regular season, didn't have a great Memorial Cup with

Laval, but it obviously didn't impact his draft status. MacKinnon, on the other hand, had one of the greatest tournaments of all time and validated the Avalanche's decision to take him ahead of defenseman Seth Jones, who had been the consensus number one.

Sakic said afterward that "Nathan's lived under the microscope for some time and he's always lived up to that occasion. He's the most explosive player in this draft. He wants to be a difference maker, he is a difference maker."

In 2015, Sakic selected talented winger Mikko Rantanen tenth overall. Now, Landeskog and MacKinnon were no-brainer picks and Rantanen was a great find, but perhaps the best selection was in 2017. Despite finishing last overall by a wide margin, the Avs dropped to fourth in the lottery, while New Jersey moved up four spots to number one, Philadelphia moved up from thirteenth to number two, and Dallas moved from the eighth spot to number three. See why I hated the lottery?

The Devils took talented center Nico Hischier from Halifax first, the Flyers took Brandon center Nolan Patrick second, and Dallas took Finnish defenseman Miro Heiskanen third. With the fourth pick, the Avs took defenseman Cale Makar, who was playing for the Brooks Bandits in the Alberta Junior Hockey League. While a lot of scouts liked Makar, there were some who worried that he was playing at a lower competition level than some of the other top prospects and his ranking might be skewed. Well, after a couple of seasons at UMass-Amherst he arrived in Colorado and in his third season at age twenty-three won the Norris Trophy, Conn Smythe Trophy (the youngest to win the Conn since Bobby Orr in 1970), and Stanley Cup—a brilliant talent. In my opinion, he has a chance to become a Lidström, one of the all-time greats, to win all those trophies multiple times.

Sakic added another nice piece in 2019 in defenseman Bowen Byram with the fourth pick. He also added forward Alex Newhook that same draft, sixteenth overall. In total, the Avs had six homegrown draft picks on that championship team but used picks to acquire talent to push them over the top, such as goalie Darcy Kuemper and top-pairing defenseman Devon Toews.

Kudos to Sakic, who was in his ninth season as GM when they finally won, but there was a lot of losing and pain and high picks before they got there. They made good on the picks, stuck to their plan, and their owner remained patient—another key.

And kudos to Yzerman for his part in building the back-to-back champions in Tampa. At the time, you don't think about whether a player you're coaching will be a future NHL GM or coach, but I've always had the utmost admiration for Stevie Y's hockey mind. Even if he didn't think I was a good coach way back when. The bottom line is championship teams are built through great drafts, most often with at least ten homegrown talents on the roster, as Bob Strumm once told me. Up to 2022, Stanley Cup winners were all built through the draft to a certain extent. Stevie Y is doing a good job back in Detroit, building around young, drafted talent.

The Boston Bruins, who dominated through the 2022–23 season before being upset in the first round of the playoffs, had a dozen of their draft picks on their outstanding roster, including stars such as Patrice Bergeron, David Krejci, Brad Marchand, and Charlie McAvoy. Like so many of the contenders these days, when it came to the 2023 trade deadline the Bruins traded some draft capital for missing pieces, but that's the way it is in the NHL: Contenders who have stockpiled draft talent trade picks to win now. As of this writing, the Bruins don't have a first pick again until 2025 nor a second until 2026, and they haven't had a first and second pick in the same year since 2017. But they've been in the Stanley Cup hunt.

Drafting and developing has always been critical and having those ten draft picks on your roster continues to be the benchmark. It's more important now than ever if you want to win the Stanley Cup.

I should mention that the two Stanley Cup finalists in 2023, the Vegas Golden Knights and Florida Panthers, are an anomaly. Both had five picks playing for them during the season. Vegas, which benefited from a strong expansion draft and shrewd moves, have traded away three first-round selections and a couple of first picks in their amazing six-year history. They have been a "win now" team from the day they entered the league, the owner boldly saying they would win the Stanley Cup within six years, and so they did. Vegas only had one draft pick on their roster when they won the Cup. But both teams have also traded for several highly regarded former first-round picks, the likes of Jack Eichel in Vegas, and Matthew Tkachuk, Sam Bennett, and Sam Reinhart with Florida. I don't believe this will be a formula teams follow moving forward.

Arizona Coyotes GM Bill Armstrong is a long way from winning a Stanley Cup in the desert, but his plan is to win through the draft, the way St. Louis did when he was assistant GM with the Blues. "It's easy to look at the standings and say, 'the Coyotes, they suck,'" Armstrong told *The Athletic*. "We really deliberated hard about where we were going. We could have just re-loaded and gone at it and made the playoffs once every four years—if lucky, get by a first round, but most times get beat out. We had the conversation, 'We want to be great here. And the only way to do that is through the draft.'"

CHAPTER FIVE

THE VALUE OF DRAFT PICKS, PART TWO

THE SIMPLE TRUTH IN THE NHL IS YOU CAN'T JUST SPEND TO WIN AND YOU CAN'T spend to fix your mistakes, either. Those days are long gone and they're not coming back. That's a dangerous game to play regardless, even if you can afford it. And some teams simply don't have the money to do it even if they wanted. But because of the salary cap, having more younger, inexpensive players has become even more vital than ever. And if the players get good in a hurry, even better, although that creates financial challenges sooner than later, too. But that's something you have to live with and it's still a good problem to have.

As we've seen, teams that consistently do well at the draft table are more likely to become contending teams, and Stanley Cup champions typically have at least ten or so players who are homegrown draft picks. Teams that draft well and don't do well over time are often low-budget teams that can't afford to pay the kids when they develop into stars.

Draft picks are a valuable currency. Contending teams trade future or current picks for players they hope will improve their team, who they think can be the missing piece or pieces for a championship team. In 2023, for instance, a total of fifteen players, in a dozen deals, were moved at the trade deadline with a first-rounder going the other way. Teams also move up in the draft in order to acquire a player they believe won't still be available when their turn to pick comes around. Whatever the scenario, drafting the right player can undoubtedly set up a franchise for future success. That's also easier said than done. Buffalo, for instance, has missed the playoffs for a record twelve straight seasons, dating back to 2011. In the eight drafts leading up to 2022, they had selected first or second overall four times. It doesn't always work, although there are finally signs of life in the Sabres with an improving young team.

When you look back at the history of the draft, it is at best a crapshoot. But one thing is for certain: Mistakes made with the first picks, especially in the top five overall picks, can be devastating to a franchise. It can set them back for years. GMs' careers and legacies are often determined by these selections. It must be remembered, of course, that GMs are selecting players who are eighteen years old and don't always develop as hoped, or at the speed teams had predicted and need.

As a coach, I didn't mind if my GM traded away a first pick. But I knew it was scary for him. As a GM, I never traded a first pick for a player; I only did it to move up or down in the draft. And that wasn't because I was smarter than everyone else. I was the GM of an expansion team and I was never tempted to make such a bold move because we were never in a position where that one crucial piece could put us over the top. These days, more and more teams are trading firsts for that missing piece. It's still a big, risky strategy.

It's hard to put a precise value on a pick in terms of a trade, but if you are going to trade a first pick—the selection at a future draft or the top pick you already drafted—then you have to get an impact player in return. It's a dangerous game, but many GMs have rolled the dice, for various reasons, and there's something to be learned from their successes or failures.

On June 6, 1986, frustrated Vancouver Canucks GM Jack Gordon decided to trade his former number one draft pick, Cam Neely, on his twenty-first birthday no less. Neely had been drafted three years earlier, ninth overall, but head coach Tom Watt wasn't impressed with Neely's defensive play. Watt was also the assistant GM, so he had considerable input into personnel decisions. And the Canucks had a glut of right wingers with Stan Smyl and Tony Tanti, with Neely playing behind them.

So, Gordon traded Neely and his 1987 first pick, which turned out to be third overall (defenseman Glen Wesley, who became an all-star) to the Boston Bruins and GM Harry Sinden in exchange for twenty-five-year-old center Barry Pederson, who was a very solid player and went on to play three-plus seasons with the Canucks before playing with Pittsburgh, Hartford, and finally ending his career back in Boston. But because of injuries, Pederson was never the same player that he was with the Bruins, where he had earned 116 points a few seasons earlier.

Neely would go on to play ten seasons with the Bruins, earning 694 points in 726 games before his career was cut short by a serious leg injury. He was inducted into the Hockey Hall of Fame in 2005 and is now president of the team.

Wesley would play seven seasons for the Bruins and go on to play 1,457 NHL games, earning 537 points. When the Bruins eventually traded Wesley to Hartford, they acquired three first-round picks in return. In a way, that initial trade ended up being Neely and four first-round picks for Pederson. To say the least, those types of deals hurt for a long, long time. That's the risk of trading a twenty-one-year-old top pick. Remember, the legend Sam Pollock had the unwritten rule of waiting until a top prospect was twenty-three before moving him out. Given that players are starting in the NHL at a younger age these days, that number would be adjusted, but the point remains the same: Patience is a virtue!

Floyd Smith, GM of the Toronto Maple Leafs, was frustrated with his team during the 1989–90 season. In an attempt to shake up the team, he traded their first pick in the 1991 draft to the New Jersey Devils in exchange for twenty-seven-year-old defenseman Tom Kurvers. The Leafs did manage to recover and make the playoffs that spring, but the next season they opened 1–9–1 and struggled throughout with the spectre hanging over their heads of having possibly traded away the first overall pick in the 1991 draft: the couldn't miss, guaranteed first overall pick Eric Lindros, a local boy who was expected to be the next great player in the NHL. And so he was, though his journey was interesting, to say the least.

The Leafs didn't finish dead last, but they were close. And it was an agonizing season for Smith and his management team. The Leafs actually made a deal with the Quebec Nordiques to help ensure the Leafs didn't finish last and the Nordiques did—it would have been too embarrassing to finish last after trading away the first overall pick. The Nords weren't terribly interested in improving because Lindros would be the reward (or so they thought) for finishing last. The Leafs sent winger Scott Pearson, a sixth overall pick three years earlier, and two second-round picks to the Nordiques in exchange for Aaron Broten, Lucien DeBlois, and Michel Petit. Quebec finished last with forty-six points, the Leafs second last with fifty-six. But the San Jose Sharks were entering the league and were given the second overall pick (first in all other rounds). So, the pick the Leafs had traded away wound up as the third overall in 1991. With that pick, the Devils selected defenseman Scott Niedermayer from the WHL's Kamloops Blazers.

Niedermayer went on to play eighteen seasons, was a four-time Stanley cup champion, and was selected as one of the one hundred greatest NHL players. He was inducted in the Hockey Hall of Fame in 2013.

Kurvers, who sadly passed away in 2021, was a good player and played seventy games that first season with the Leafs and had a very respectable fifty-two points. He played just nineteen games in that fateful following season and was dealt to the Vancouver Canucks.

It's worth noting the Sharks, with the second pick, took Spokane Chiefs right winger Pat Falloon, who played 575 games, scoring 143 goals, and earning 322 points, proving again how unpredictable top picks can be.

But how much better would the Leafs have been in the years to come if they had held on to their pick? The pressure to win and an impatient, unpredictable owner (Harold Ballard) was the impetus behind the deal, but it was a deal that ultimately stung.

Very few GMs haven't done the same and gambled to make their team better at some time in their careers. When I was a

GM, every time I was asked for my first pick, I always thought about those types of trades. I would look at the history of teams that were not good trading their picks and where it put them as franchises years down the road. As the GM of an expansion team, every time I got a call it was for a first- or second-round pick. Like I said, I never traded a first pick for a player. I only traded it to move up or down in the draft and to add more picks. (I must have learned from Pollock's fleecings.) Before our first draft with Columbus, I traded a second-round pick to Colorado to get goaltender Marc Denis. He was coming into his own with the Avs, but they couldn't protect him in the expansion draft, so I made the deal to make sure Minnesota couldn't take him ahead of us.

When I was discussing this book with former GM Brian Burke, who at the time was the president of hockey operations with the Pittsburgh Penguins, he said, "Well, obviously you'll discuss the greatest trade in draft day history."

Of course, Burkie.

If it wasn't the greatest in history, Burke's big deal was right up there. The story of the Sedin twins is, in fact, one of the greatest draft day deals in the modern era. The 1999 draft was considered one of the worst in many years. The consensus number one pick was center Patrik Stefan, from the Czech Republic, who had played two seasons in the International Hockey League (IHL). Daniel and Henrik Sedin were considered by most scouts to be the next two top picks.

I remember scouting the twins at the World Junior tournament in 1999 in Winnipeg and wondering, along with all the other hockey people, how the twins would react to being broken up and going to separate teams. Their agent, Mike Barnett, was telling everyone who would listen that they wanted to be drafted by the same team. But no team had multiple picks at the top of the draft, so we all thought it would never happen. But Burke thought differently.

The Canucks were a dreadful team, in a rebuild, and had the third overall pick, behind Tampa with the first pick and the expansion Atlanta Thrashers at number two. The Canucks knew they had a good chance of getting one of the Sedins. But they wanted both.

At one point during the season, Burke had actually soured on the Sedins after a poor showing at the World Junior tournament in Winnipeg and was open to trading his pick. But his scouts, notably former Canuck Thomas Gradin, convinced him to keep an open mind after the World Championships in Norway in the spring. With his mind made up, Burke set out to get them both, but it would not be easy. In fact, it required three deft trades.

First, Burke worked out a deal to acquire Chicago's fourth overall pick by trading defenseman Bryan McCabe (recently acquired in the Trevor Linden deal) and a first pick in the 2000 draft. Burke then traded that fourth overall pick, along with two third-round picks, to Tampa to acquire the first overall pick. But his work still wasn't done. He was able to trade the number-one pick to Atlanta, as long as they promised to use it on Patrik Štefan. That gave Burke the second and third picks, and a clear path to the twins.

Burke was running a huge risk, but Atlanta made good on their promise, and Burke was able to draft the Sedins, back to back, second and third overall.

This tremendous draft day work set the stage for a major turnaround of the Canucks' future, as the Sedin twins went on to become the greatest players in team history. They were inducted into the Hockey Hall of Fame together in 2022.

Burke's magic continued at his next stop, as GM in Anaheim. With forward Rob Niedermayer already in the fold, he then was able, with Rob's assistance, to convince his brother, Scott, a great defenseman, to sign as a free agent. Yes, the same Scott Niedermayer the Leafs missed out on by trading their top pick.

Coupled with the trade to acquire big defenseman Chris Pronger from the Edmonton Oilers, it gave the Ducks an amazing blue line and helped lead them to a Stanley Cup. Years later, then Oilers GM Kevin Lowe (the Oilers' first-ever pick in 1979) said Burke was intent on making the Pronger deal happen and every time they talked when the ask went up Burke said, "Yes, let's get this done." And so they did.

On July 3, 2006, Anaheim sent winger Joffrey Lupul, defenseman Ladislav Smid, a 2007 first-round pick (number thirty), a 2008 second-round pick (number fifty-three), and a 2008 conditional (if the Ducks reached the 2006–07 Stanley Cup final, which they did) first-round pick (number twenty-two). Those picks turned out to be Nick Ross, Travis Hamonic, and Jordan Eberle. The Oilers got five pieces; the Ducks got a Cup.

Burke then moved to Toronto as GM, but his magic didn't entirely make it across the border. Impatient after his first season with the Leafs, and not looking to have a long rebuild, he acquired high-scoring winger Phil Kessel from Boston, who was a restricted free agent.

Burke sent three picks—the Leafs' first and second in 2010 and first in 2011—for the twenty-two-year-old winger, then signed him to a five-year, $27.5 million deal. While Kessel scored a lot for the Leafs, the team still struggled and Burke's worst nightmare was realized—with the second overall pick, Boston selected a great talent, center Tyler Seguin. The following year, the Leafs not much better, the Stanley Cup champion Bruins owned the ninth overall pick courtesy of the Leafs, which they used to select defenseman Dougie Hamilton. Neither player is with the Bruins now, but they got a lot of production from both. And they were very good players who would have helped the Leafs.

Burke was an excellent GM, a Cup winner, and he wasn't wrong in his assessment of Kessel, who was a very good player. It's just sometimes we are all guilty of overestimating how good our teams are and assessing the right time to give up futures for a missing piece.

When I was coaching in Florida, we tried to rush things along as well. After coaching the Panthers to the 1996 Stanley Cup final, where we were swept by Colorado, I still truly believed we had a team that could contend for a number of years. We had a unique group of players who really believed in each other. As the next season began, ownership and upper management decided to mess with our chemistry. How much pressure was applied to GM Bryan Murray? Hard to say, but we started making moves. We had gotten close and in the franchise's fourth season they wanted to go all the way. I later heard from Bill Torrey, our president, that the owner, Wayne Huizenga, expected us to win the Cup. His logic was, you made it to the final the year before, this year you win.

Two of our fan favorites, center Stu Barnes and defenseman Jason Woolley, who were both instrumental in our previous season success, were traded to Pittsburgh for twenty-two-year-old center Chris Wells, the Penguins' first pick, twenty-fourth overall in 1994. When the trade was announced even my nine-year-old son, Clark, asked, "Dad, are you guys crazy?" Good question,

Son. I didn't disagree. Wells played parts of four seasons—141 games with seven goals and twenty-five points. The trade was the start of the decline of the Panthers.

Early in the 1997 season, we were struggling, but we were still close to a playoff spot despite numerous key injuries. Rob Niedermayer, our number one center, was injured and out for six weeks. Murray felt the team needed a jolt and size down the middle, so he traded the Panthers' 1998 first pick to San Jose for Viktor Kozlov, a six-foot-four, 232-pound center the Sharks had taken sixth overall in the 1993 draft.

A week after the trade, I was fired by the Panthers, so I didn't get the opportunity to work with Kozlov. He had plenty of talent but in my opinion never reached his potential. That season he had twenty-three points in forty-six games. He would play seven seasons for the Panthers, scoring more than twenty goals only once—essentially a secondary player.

Meanwhile, the Tampa Bay Lightning, on March 24, 1998, traded defensemen Bryan Marchment and David Shaw to San Jose for Andrei Nazarov and a first-round pick (Florida's pick from the Kozlov deal). The Panthers finished a disastrous 1998 season second last overall. But that wasn't the worst of it. The Panthers' nightmare continued when they wound up winning the draft lottery but didn't own the pick! Instead, that pick belonged to Tampa—from Florida, via San Jose.

You could say the Panthers' nightmare got even worse because with that first pick overall in the 1998 entry draft the Lightning selected center Vincent Lecavalier from Rimouski of the Quebec Junior league.

The owner of the Lightning at the time, Art Williams, declared that Lecavalier would be "the Michael Jordan of hockey."

He wasn't quite that good, but he was very good and he did lead the Lightning to the 2004 Stanley Cup championship. He played 1,212 NHL games, scoring 949 points, and won the Rocket Richard Trophy as top goal scorer in 2007. His number 4 was retired by Tampa.

The message and lesson, once again, is that trading future number one picks is an amazing gamble. That deal set the Panthers up to be a bottom-feeder for many years to come, especially with other things that happened around the franchise. Bryan Murray was a very successful GM and he expected the trade to make the Panthers a contender, but that is the risk when the player you acquire doesn't have the impact you needed and that number one pick you've traded away turns out to be someone truly special.

As a GM you are often faced with the situation at the draft table of your scouting staff wanting a certain player, so you do everything possible to acquire him. It's great when it works, but it can also backfire.

It happened at the 2007 draft. Columbus GM Scott Howson, who took over after me, was encouraged by his staff to move up to acquire Russian winger Maksim Mayorov in the fourth round. Columbus traded three fifth-round picks to Dallas to make this move. Dallas, with one of those picks from Columbus, selected Jamie Benn 129th overall from the Victoria Grizzlies of the British Columbia Hockey League (BCHL). As of this writing, Benn has played more than one thousand games and earned more than eight hundred points with the Stars; he is team captain and a franchise player. Meanwhile, Mayorov, selected ninety-fourth overall, played twenty-two games in parts of four seasons with the Blue Jackets, finishing his NHL career with two goals and one assist.

In 2011, Columbus made a significant draft day move that shook up the draft. This time Howson traded their former seventh overall pick, Jakub Voracek, the eighth overall pick, and a third-round pick (Nick Cousins) in the 2011 draft to Philadelphia for center Jeff Carter. Howson figured this would give the Blue Jackets a number one center to play with Rick Nash.

Philadelphia used the eighth pick to draft center Sean Couturier, who became a really good player. The trade turned out to be an even worse disaster for the Blue Jackets as Carter refused to report and finally, when he did, demanded to be traded. His agent, Rick Curran, had told the Jackets not to make the trade, but they did it anyway and it was a big part of why Howson was eventually fired. Carter played thirty-nine games for the Blue Jackets before being moved to the Los Angeles Kings, in February 2012, for defenseman Jack Johnson and a conditional first-round pick. Carter twice won the Stanley Cup with LA and scored the game-winning goal in the first championship.

Lou Lamoriello has won the Stanley Cup three times due to amazing drafting and scouting, as well as astute trades. At the 2013 draft, Lou knew his New Jersey Devils needed a proven goaltender and decided to make his move. Lou moved the ninth overall pick to Vancouver to acquire Cory Schneider. With that pick, the Canucks selected center Bo Horvat, who had an outstanding junior career with the London Knights. At the time, Lou was quoted as saying, "You never know if an eighteen-year-old is going to work out."

Most hockey people thought the deal was a good one for the Devils. Schneider gave the Devils solid, even spectacular, goaltending at times. They got four solid seasons out of him, but due to injuries and inconsistency his game slid dramatically.

Meanwhile, Horvat gave the Canucks several good seasons and was named team captain before being acquired by Lamoriello and the Islanders in 2023. How do you criticize Lamoriello for the Schneider trade after the success he has had in the NHL building franchises? He got the goaltending upgrade he needed but long term lost the deal. And later his job in New Jersey.

Peter Chiarelli, then GM of the Edmonton Oilers, felt he needed to improve his team's blue line and believed trading for young defenseman Griffin Reinhart, who was drafted fourth overall in 2012, was a good gamble. He certainly came from a good pedigree, with his father, Paul, a former NHL star and brothers, Max and Sam, both drafted to the NHL.

In the deal, the New York Islanders received the sixteenth and thirty-third picks in the 2015 draft. Prior to that deal, the Isles didn't have a pick in the first two rounds. Isles GM Garth Snow then sent that thirty-third and his seventy-second pick to Tampa Bay for the twenty-eighth overall pick. With the sixteenth, the Isles selected speedy center Mathew Barzal from Seattle juniors and with the twenty-eighth pick winger Anthony Beauvillier from Shawinigan. Barzal is a star with the Islanders and has taken the place of John Tavares as their centerpiece up front. Beauvillier has become a solid NHL forward. Reinhart, meanwhile, played twenty-nine games for the Oilers during the 2015–16 season, recording one assist. Prior to the trade, Reinhart played eight games with the Islanders, earning one assist.

Trades like that happen on a regular basis at the draft as GMs gamble, trusting their scouts' advice that they are getting a player who will help their organization for years to come. Obviously, the critical question that has to be answered is who, potentially, are we giving up a chance to draft and are we prepared to do that? Needless to say, the Oilers thought it was a good gamble. It wasn't. That deal was the start of Peter's trouble and eventually losing his job.

Sometimes deals work out well for both teams. Take the big trade between St. Louis and Buffalo on July 1, 2018. The Sabres sent a disgruntled Ryan O'Reilly to the Blues in exchange for big center Tage Thompson, taken twenty-sixth overall in 2016, Vladimir Sobotka, Patrik Berglund, a 2019 top ten protected first pick and a 2021 second.

The deal worked out great for Blues GM Doug Armstrong, who added some other key pieces. But with O'Reilly that next season, the Blues won their first Cup. He won the Conn Smythe and Selke Trophies and was later named captain. Not bad. As for the Sabres, at first blush the deal didn't look good for them. Berglund decided to return home, Sobotka eventually was traded, and Thompson was up and down between the minors. But four years later, Thompson started to emerge as a star, while the Blues traded O'Reilly to Toronto in the final year of his contract, although he did fetch them a first-round pick, a couple of minor leaguers, and a second and third pick. It's a classic case of the Blues getting what they wanted, a team leader and a Cup win. And in time the trade benefited the Sabres, with Thompson emerging. And it could get even better if that first pick (thirty-first overall) used to take defenseman Ryan Johnson and the second pick, traded to Vegas for defenseman Colin Miller, work out. Thompson looks like a stud and the Sabres could be the long-term winners, though both teams ultimately won. Again, it's a case of identifying the value of your picks.

When deals don't work out and your team struggles, they haunt you forever. The media always brings them up. When Peter Chiarelli's job was in trouble, those failed deals were always mentioned. They drive you absolutely crazy and they eventually cost you your job. You are constantly reminded of the value of a draft pick, especially a top pick.

The temptation is sometimes tough for GMs. At the 2022 draft in Montreal, the Ottawa Senators acquired winger Alex DeBrincat from Chicago for three picks, including the seventh overall selection, a second, and a third. It was part of a three-way deal with the Canadiens that got the Habs center Kirby Dach, the Islanders landed defenseman Alexander Romanov, and Chicago received another first-round pick, thirteenth overall.

Only time will tell how that deal works out for all involved. Rest assured, there will be a happy GM, maybe two, *maybe* three, but I'm sure there will eventually be an unemployed GM. And it remains, if you don't have enough of your picks on your roster, in the neighborhood of ten, you're not likely to win.

CHAPTER SIX

THE LINDROS RULE

ONE OF THE MOST FASCINATING, CONTROVERSIAL, AND IMPACTFUL DRAFT SELEC-
tions ever was also a no-brainer. But it played out in a way no one
could have imagined.

The year was 1991 and the consensus first overall pick
was Eric Lindros: a behemoth of a player, six feet four, 230
pounds, a supersized, superskilled center. He was born in London, Ontario, but grew up and played his minor hockey in
Toronto. From an early age he was labeled The Next One, as
in the next one after The Great One, none other than Wayne
Gretzky, or the Magnificent One, Mario Lemieux. Yes, Lindros was that good, but a completely different player than
Gretzky or Lemieux. Lindros ultimately became a dominant
figure, the best player in the game. But all of that came later.
What happened during his draft is one of the greatest stories.
And craziest.

For context, Lindros and his parents, Bonnie and Carl, were very particular about where Eric played. For instance, when he was fifteen years old he was drafted first overall by the Sault Ste. Marie Greyhounds in the OHL, the same junior team Gretzky had played for, despite telling the club he had no intention of playing in the Northern Ontario city. Lindros' parents didn't want him to play in the Soo, worried that the travel and the remote location might adversely impact his education. So, he refused to report, instead playing for Detroit Compuware in the North American Junior Hockey League. Eventually owner Angelo Bumbacco and part-owner Phil Esposito traded him to the Oshawa Generals for three players, some draft picks, and $80,000—essentially because of a rule created for him, which allowed first-round picks to be traded. It wouldn't be the last time a new rule was made because of Eric Lindros.

Lindros did not disappoint. The legendary Bobby Clarke, who would eventually become his GM in Philadelphia, called Lindros the "best sixteen-year-old player I've ever seen. He could play in the NHL right now." Lindros was a beast with Oshawa, where Bobby Orr had played. He led the Generals to the Memorial Cup and a win. The next season he was named the CHL's Player of the Year. And he put up amazing numbers. He was the real deal.

Which is why, when it came to the 1991 NHL draft, the first overall pick was obvious. Lindros first, then all the rest, although the third overall pick in that draft, Scott Niedermayer, was a heckuva player, too.

That year, Quebec once again owned the first overall pick. They had taken Mats Sundin first overall in 1989 and Owen Nolan first overall the next year, but the Lindros family were not interested in playing for *les Nordiques* or, more specifically, owner Marcel Aubut. Despite the public relations spin making Eric and his family out as the villains, Lindros' reluctance to play in Quebec was not about the province, or the culture, or the language (Eric wound up marrying a Quebecois lady and owned property there)—it was about Aubut. There were plenty of whispers at the time that Aubut had told his hockey staff to stop winning games to ensure they got the first pick. That did not sit well with the Lindros family. A few years ago, Lindros publicly said Aubut was the reason, "absolutely."

Despite all of that, when his name was called at the 1991 draft, Lindros made his way to the Nordiques table and shook hands with the hockey staff and accepted the Nordiques sweater but would not put it on. He had no intention of ever wearing that sweater as long as Aubut was around.

"We kept hearing Eric didn't want to come to Quebec," Pierre Page, GM of the Nordiques at the time, told me. "We heard the stories, but it didn't influence us because he was that good. It was an easy decision to draft him. Those players, like Bobby Orr or Wayne Gretzky, come around every forty years. We used to say he was a six-foot-five Gretzky. But he was really a six-foot-five Gordie Howe. An incredible talent."

Lindros was so good that a few months after he was drafted, at the age of eighteen, he was invited to training camp with Team Canada for the 1991 Canada Cup tournament. He definitely made an impression, especially on coach Mike Keenan, who cut Steve Yzerman to give Lindros a roster spot. He played well, too, with three goals and five points in eight games, and he made a statement of what kind of player he was with a bone-crushing check on Swedish defenseman Ulf Samuelsson. Further proof he was the real deal. He went on in that 1991–92 season to play with Oshawa for a handful of games, as well as the national and Olympic teams.

"We thought there might be a chance for him to come [to the Nordiques]," said Page. "But the last time we met with him, we brought in Guy Lafleur, who really thought he was going to make a big impact on him. Well, Guy came out of the meeting and was so insulted. He said, 'There's no way he's coming to Quebec.' Guy was so shocked. At the meetings, it was Bonnie who ran the show. That meeting was the kicker."

After drafting Lindros, the Nordiques had two years to sign him or he would go back into the draft. Those were and still are the rules. It was a year after drafting him, after the Lafleur meeting, that they realized it was hopeless.

"I was more stubborn, thinking we could convince him," said Page. "But after one year Marcel said the guy is not coming. We couldn't screw this up."

They even offered him a ten-year, $50 million contract.

"Absolutely we made that offer," said Page, "and he ended up making less money. That was good money, but there was zero interest, none at all. The thing is, I kept telling people he's entitled to say no. He never broke a rule."

The Nordiques were not going to win a standoff, so they had to trade Lindros' rights and get assets in return. It is, after all, a business. And prior to that 1992 draft was the right time for a couple of reasons. First, if they waited until toward the end of the two-year period, they would have lost leverage, as everyone would have known Lindros was about to be eligible for the draft again; that would have made the Nordiques desperate. Second, the Nordiques wanted to acquire draft picks in time for the 1992 draft. Even though Lindros wasn't interested in Quebec, he had tremendous trade value—it was still a wise move to draft him. The key was to assemble the right deal.

According to Page, the Nordiques hired Sherry Bassin, who had traded Lindros from the Soo. They asked him how he dealt with Lindros and his parents and how he evaluated him. The Nordiques had read a lot and settled on the "Herschel Walker" model and results.

If you're not familiar, the Walker trade, in October 1989, was the largest player trade in the history of the NFL. Several teams made offers, but it involved trading Walker, a star running back, from the Dallas Cowboys to the Minnesota Vikings. A third team, the San Diego Chargers, was also involved and the deal ultimately involved eighteen players and draft picks. The Cowboys were a horrible team looking to rebuild, while the Vikings thought Walker was their missing piece. As it evolved, the Vikings at first thought they were the big winners, but they never made it to the Super Bowl, while the Cowboys used their picks to rebuild and went on to win three Super Bowls in the 1990s. The deal, obviously, was massive and eventually became one of the most lopsided in sports history.

Well, the Lindros deal wasn't lopsided, but it was massive. And in the case of Lindros, the Nordiques, who became the Colorado Avalanche in 1995, went on to win two Stanley Cups after their move. But before that, there were plenty of teams interested in Lindros. The Nordiques were even involved in serious trade talks with their provincial rivals, the Montreal Canadiens.

"Serge Savard [the Habs GM] had a Lindros for Patrick Roy and a bunch of players deal on the table," said Page. "Serge and Patrick did not get along. We didn't do it because there were other good offers."

Savard in fact offered captain Guy Carbonneau, prospects Jim Campbell and Craig Darby, defensemen Eric Desjardins and Sylvain Lefebvre, winger Mike McPhee, and Roy.

You know the old saying, sometimes the best deals are the ones you don't make? The following season, in 1993, the Canadiens won a record ten overtime playoff games and won the Stanley Cup with Patrick Roy winning the Conn Smythe Trophy. Had they made that deal for Lindros, would they have won the Cup? We'll never know, but without Roy . . . Years later, the Avalanche did get Roy and gritty winger Mike Keane in exchange for goalie Jocelyn Thibault (selected with Philadelphia's first pick in 1993, one of the three first-round picks in the Lindros deal) and wingers Andrei Kovalenko and Martin Rucinsky. And Colorado beat my Florida Panthers in 1996 to win the Stanley Cup. But even then, without the other pieces they got in the Lindros deal, they don't win the Cup.

As the draft approached in June 1992, the interest in Lindros surged and at one point the Nordiques had fourteen teams very interested in making a deal. As a GM, if you're doing your job well, you have to make the call to find out the price. Lindros was a generational player, a difference maker to a team, a type of talent who isn't often available at that age via trade. Teams interested got hot, then cold, but all of a sudden, a week before the draft, it got crazy. The Nordiques rented the fifth floor of the Hyatt Hotel in Montreal, brought in a five-star chef (Aubut enjoyed a fine meal), and security guards. The management team slept in three shifts to make sure they were always fresh for trade talks.

"We met all night," said Page. "I remember meeting Cliff [Leafs GM Fletcher] at three thirty in the morning. He made an incredible offer, but it wasn't as good as the other ones."

The Leafs' final offer was star center Doug Gilmour, fan favorite Wendel Clark, defensemen Dave Ellett and Ken Baumgartner, forward Darby Hendrickson, goaltender Felix Potvin, draft picks, and $15 million. In return, the Leafs would get Lindros, the Nordiques' first pick that year (fourth overall), goaltenders John Tanner and Stephane Fiset, and Kovalenko.

"Cliff had offered so much, all of a sudden he started to sweat and he said, 'Pierre, there is no way I can do this. I'm nervous. This is too much.' I said, 'Don't worry, you're my former boss [in Calgary], you treated us so well, if you don't want to make the trade that's fine.' He really wanted to bring Lindros to Toronto," said Page.

Toronto was one of three teams Lindros preferred, according to Page. Lindros wanted to go to Chicago to play for Keenan, who put him on the 1991 Canada Cup team. That was Lindros' first choice. Toronto was second and the New York Rangers were third. Interestingly, he didn't want to go to the Los Angeles Kings, which, given his star and marketing power, seemed like a logical fit, although Gretzky was still with the Kings and affording two big stars might have been difficult.

Calgary also made a strong offer, including players such as Joe Nieuwendyk, Gary Suter, and Mike Vernon.

"They put out an offer, but they changed their mind right away," said Page. "The next day the deal was off."

There was also St. Louis in the mix, with my old boss Ron Caron offering up Brendan Shanahan and Brian Sutter among others. But while Toronto and Chicago and Calgary had terrific offers, throughout it was the Philadelphia Flyers that had the best one.

"Towards the end a lot of teams cooled off, including Philly," said Page. "We kept meeting, all the scouts, Pierre Gauthier and Gilles Leger, all the coaches, Marcel Aubut—everyone was involved and we kept writing on the board what we wanted from each team and Philly was always the most appealing of them all, but Philly didn't seem interested. We kept trying to meet with everyone again that week [leading up to the 1992 draft] and then Philly didn't budge. New Jersey cooled off, Detroit was out, Toronto we met the night before with Cliff until three thirty in the morning and that's when he said, 'I can't give up all those players; there's no way.' That was gone."

Detroit had offered an interesting package that included Steve Yzerman. Remember, he didn't win a Cup until 1997, so there was a different feeling about Yzerman at the time. I was an assistant coach with the Wings, working for Bryan Murray. And there was pressure to win. Our first offer included Steve Chiasson, my old pal Gerard Gallant, Martin Lapointe, Yves Racine, Mike Sillinger, Yzerman, and $15 million. The second offer was Lapointe, Racine, Sillinger, Yzerman, and the money. Quebec wanted Sergei Fedorov instead of Yzerman, but Bryan wouldn't budge. They kept asking for Fedorov, Gallant, Lapointe, Keith Primeau, Racine, Vincent Riendeau—but no way. In return we were asking for Lindros, Craig Wolanin, Herb Raglan, Steve Maltais, and one other player.

That night before the draft things got very interesting. According to Page, at 1:30 a.m. (the early morning of draft day) Aubut went to the suite of Flyers president Jay Snider and presented an offer.

"I've read the reports and to clarify Marcel Aubut didn't make two deals," said Page. "We had all those deals and then all of a sudden we had none. Marcel kind of panicked the night before at one thirty. He went with the list that we wanted from Philly, he wrote it on a piece of paper, and he threw it at Jay [Flyers president Jay Snider] and said, 'Come on, Jay, make the frickin' deal.' Jay said, 'I have to check with my hockey people, I can't do this at one o'clock in the morning without my hockey people.' He left the piece of paper there and on the piece of paper the names were Duchesne, Forsberg, Hextall, Hoffman, Ricci, the first pick in 1992, '93, and '94, and fifteen million dollars."

Quebec had originally asked for Rod Brind'Amour to be in the deal, but the Flyers wouldn't include him.

Later in the morning, around ten thirty, Page was negotiating with Keenan, but those talks hit a wall because Blackhawks owner Bill Wirtz didn't want to include the money in the deal. There's a reason why his nickname was "Dollar" Bill.

"So, the next morning I'm meeting with Keenan at ten thirty and it looks like we have a deal, there's a bunch of players, seven picks, but Mike had to go talk with Wirtz about the money and he wasn't interested at all," said Page. "While I'm talking with Mike, the phone rings and Marcel—I'm sitting across from Mike and Marcel is next to me—the phone rings and Marcel picks it up. He never tells me who was calling. And I don't really hear too much of what he's saying because I'm so focused, talking to Mike. Well, basically, that phone call was Jay Snider saying they accepted the deal. So, all of a sudden, we don't have a deal with Mike Keenan anyway, but at ten thirty Jay says, 'We accept the deal.' But Marcel says we don't want the deal, we're making a deal with Chicago. Why did he say no? Good question, because we all wanted that deal. We can just say 'yes' to Philly and 'no' to Mike and Chicago and it's all done. Instead, we have zero deals. Marcel refused the deal with Philly that we wanted because he thought we were making the deal with Chicago, which was not as good. But the Philly deal was by far the best one."

Knowing there wasn't a deal with Chicago and not knowing the Flyers had accepted, Page was going to speak with the Rangers, who had expressed earlier interest.

"To me, he [Aubut] didn't make the deal with Philly, or Chicago, and he didn't make the deal with New York, so he didn't make two deals. After the Chicago deal died, I met with [Rangers GM] Neil Smith and at eleven fifty that morning the deal is done with New York. I'm walking out of the Hyatt to the Forum and Jay and other people from Philly are walking in really, really pissed off. I don't know anything because Marcel apparently said no, we don't want that deal because we have a deal with Chicago. But we didn't. All of a sudden, I go to the draft and Neil blasted me. He says, 'Well, you're a nice guy, you make a frickin' deal. . . .' I had no idea what he was talking about."

The Flyers were angry the Lindros deal "didn't happen" at the time because owner Ed Snider, who wasn't at the draft because he was undergoing surgery, had told Jay and the staff to make the deal. Snider didn't want to miss out on the generational player, especially with plans in the offing to build a new arena.

Things were muddy. Aubut felt he didn't make a deal with the Flyers, who thought they had made one, and Page felt that he had made a deal with the Rangers. So, there were two deals, sort of. But the NHL sent the whole mess to an independent arbitrator from Toronto, prominent labor lawyer Larry Bertuzzi, who immediately asked for the league's bylaws and, specifically, the rules for what constituted a trade.

"I asked one simple question, give me all the written materials about what constitutes a trade . . . and any background information I need to know," said Bertuzzi. "I was handed a single sheet of paper, with two lines on it, saying if there was a dispute over a trade it would be settled by the league president or an independent arbitrator."

There was no formal language for what constituted a trade or how to file one.

"I received evidence from other clubs about how trades were made, what constitutes a trade," he said. "What I learned was, it was a relatively informal procedure, usually engaged in by the general managers, who effectively operated, I think, by the rule that said: 'Burn me once, shame on you; burn me twice, shame on me,' and so they knew they had to deal with each other and as a result dealt with each other informally and fairly. So the absence of rules was replaced by the presence of an awful lot of good faith amongst the general managers."

In the end, Bertuzzi ruled that the Flyers deal was binding because Aubut had left the piece of paper with the trade offer and it included Lindros' phone number. Bertuzzi referenced that as being a "critical" piece. Aubut had said he wouldn't give up the number until a deal was done, and Flyers GM Russ Farwell did call Lindros.

"All of a sudden we have to go to arbitration and lose the case and one hundred thousand dollars, which was the best thing possible," said Page. "New York was a good deal, Chicago was a good deal, Toronto was a good deal, but Philly was a much better deal. It's a crazy story for sure, but Marcel wanted the Philly deal, then he turns it down and I didn't even know."

There was a lot riding on this, for every club involved. The Rangers were reported to have upped the ante to $20 million, although Page thinks it was $15 million.

"We agreed to fifteen million dollars," said Page, "unless Marcel made a deal for more. When I left at eleven fifty, it was fifteen million dollars, Tony Amonte, Alexei Kovalev, John Vanbiesbrouck, Doug Weight, and three firsts."

But the Philly offer was better: Peter Forsberg, Mike Ricci, Ron Hextall, Steve Duchesne, Kerry Huffman, the Flyers' 1993 first-round pick, and $15 million for Lindros. The original deal included the Flyers' 1992 first pick, which because of the circumstances they kept and selected Ryan Sittler. Bertuzzi ultimately got the Flyers to send Chris Simon and a 1994 pick to compensate.

In 1996, before the Avalanche won the Stanley Cup, sweeping my Florida Panthers, we had to play Lindros and the Flyers in the second round and he was the only guy we talked about in our meetings. He was on that "Legion of Doom" line with John LeClair and Mikael Renberg. They were frickin' scary. Lindros used to crush people and he was an animal in that series. I had to play Rob Niedermayer and Brian Skrudland against him shift to shift. How we ever won that series was beyond me because he was that good, but we beat them in six games.

I remember we had a nineteen-year-old defenseman named Ed Jovanovski, who was the first overall pick in 1994. He was a big kid, six feet three, 220 pounds. During that series Jovo buckled Lindros with a hit. Our bench came alive. That was the kid's coming-out party. It was a big moment in that series, which had lots of story lines. The Flyers coach was Terry Murray, the brother of our GM, Bryan. Remember, Terry replaced Bryan when he got fired as the head coach in Washington. So, there was some tension. And prior to landing the Detroit job, Bryan thought he had the GM job with the Flyers. So many overlaps.

Thinking back, I was as impacted by the trade as almost anyone. Our Panthers team had to play him in that second round—and he was hard on our team, physical, scoring, inflicting injuries. Then in the final we play Colorado, which had been fortified by the Lindros trade.

As for the Avalanche winning the Cup, a big part of their success was Forsberg, who became one of the best power forwards in the game. But he wasn't a sure thing heading into the Lindros draft, selected sixth overall.

"We saw him play when he was eighteen and he was five foot eleven, one hundred sixty-five pounds," said Page. "He was not fast, not slow, but he was skilled and gritty. Anyone who says he was going to be a superstar is lying. He was good, but he was not above average fast. He was just nasty, gritty, and skilled. Then, a year and a half later, he's six foot one, two inches taller and twenty-five pounds bigger, and faster, which is unusual. We hit the jackpot. We knew he was good. Inge Hammarstrom, who was a Flyers scout, has said he wouldn't have done the deal one-for-one for Lindros. To be honest, at that time, Lindros was way, way better. Peter got better and better, became a two-way player. He was the best player in the NHL at one time, according to Glen Sather.

"It's the old saying in hockey, Cliff Fletcher used to say it all the time—it doesn't matter if you give up four, five, six, seven players, if you get the best players, you do it. Lindros was a six-foot-five Gordie Howe. Forsberg could have won four Stanley Cups. He was a gritty Jacques Lemaire, who won eight. Philly just didn't find the pieces to go around him to help Lindros win Stanley Cups. He just had to win four or five Cups and he would have been one of the best players in the history of hockey. John Elway did the same thing as Lindros, but he helped the Denver Broncos win two Super Bowls in 1998 and 1999."

Cliff was right, if you get the best player or players (essentially Forsberg and Roy for Thibault), you win the trade, but there is still a balancing act to make sure you don't gut your roster in the pursuit. The Flyers did miss the playoffs the first two years they had Lindros—it took time to build up the roster around him. After two playoff losses, in year five they were in the Stanley Cup final, but they were swept by Detroit. Even so, Lindros did not disappoint on the ice.

But that balancing act wasn't the only problem. Injuries, specifically concussions, were a major factor in Lindros' career. He played thirteen seasons—eight with Philly, three with the Rangers, one each with Toronto and Dallas—but never a full season, averaging fifty-eight games per. He even missed a full season because of concussion issues. But for a time, he was the best player in the game, winning that 1991 Canada Cup, winning the Hart and Pearson trophies in 1995, an Olympic gold medal in 2002, and a silver in 1992. He lived up to his billing and he was inducted into the Hockey Hall of Fame in 2016.

Forsberg, of course, became a superstar. He remained in Sweden for three seasons before joining the Nordiques in 1994–95. But, as Pierre said, Forsberg grew in size and skill during that time. Injuries impacted his career as well, but he was in the same class as Lindros and he got the two Stanley Cup wins and was inducted into the Hall of Fame in 2014, two years before Lindros. It was a trade that worked out well for both teams, but a little bit better for one.

"Lindros wanted nothing to do with Aubut," said Page. "But he also had no interest in nineteen other clubs. We got lucky with the Philly deal, which basically is a case of we won in court. Marcel didn't make the deal. I didn't make the deal. The arbitrator made the deal. Basically, Bertuzzi kept trying to figure out how to solve it. Legally, a piece of paper is a legal binding contract if you don't take it back, especially when Jay Snider called and accepted the deal at ten thirty before I made the deal with the Rangers."

This is where the second "Lindros rule" comes into play. It was after *l'Affaire Lindros* that the NHL, under the new leadership of Gary Bettman, the next season put the "trade call" in place. Meaning, teams have to call the league's central registry office and they review contract terms, salary cap implications, whether picks involved actually exist, all of that sort of stuff. When the league has all the information, there is a trade call with the teams to go over the details. But a trade is not a trade until the league says so.

For that reason alone, the Lindros trade could never go down again the way it did. The league has cleaned up that process. And it will likely never happen again because that type of player is typically not available in today's NHL. He was available at age twenty, a superstar in waiting. I mean, if Connor McDavid or Nathan MacKinnon were made available at age twenty by Edmonton or Colorado, if they had refused to sign with their team, there would have been a lot of teams kicking the trade tires, the same as with Lindros, but I can't imagine the offer on McDavid or MacKinnon would be as big, and that's not a slight on either star player. It's just with the salary cap and how rosters have to be constructed today financially, and how important high draft picks are today because of that, it's hard to fathom a comparable deal.

Maybe the closest recent comparison was the second overall pick in the McDavid draft, Jack Eichel. He was traded by the Buffalo Sabres, who drafted him, when he was about to turn twenty-five, in his seventh season. But that trade was nothing close, in part because of the changing landscape of the game but also the fact Eichel was coming off a major injury.

There is a difference between a generational player and a good player. The only possible comparable is if McDavid or MacKinnon was on the market—what would the price be? It would be astronomical, but still not close to what was paid for Lindros. Same goes for Crosby or Ovechkin. Lindros was a six-foot-five Gordie Howe, and all the hoopla. What if Connor Bedard was put on the market? What team could afford to give all those picks, players, and money? I just don't see it in today's NHL. That's not to say the deal wouldn't be significant.

When his season was over, Montreal Canadiens executive vice president of hockey operations Jeff Gorton was asked if he would try to make a "Lindros-like trade" if he didn't win the lottery (which he didn't) to acquire the first overall pick to select Bedard.

"I'm not sure how to answer that," he said. "The Lindros trade, they gave up quite a lot there, it ended up going in one team's favor when it looked like it was the other team. . . . All I can tell you is if I just put myself as a fan, [Bedard] looks pretty good. There's no denying that."

"The Lindros draft and trade will go down in history," said Page. "But it was all worth it because the team won the Stanley Cup twice and could have won it twice more the way Forsberg and Roy were playing. At the end of the day that's what it's all about."

CHAPTER SEVEN
SCOUTS AND THE DRAFT LIST

GENERAL MANAGERS RELY HEAVILY ON THEIR SCOUTING TEAM. IT'S CRUCIAL TO SEE top prospects yourself, in various junior games or competitions, but at the end of the day you have to rely on what your pros are telling you. The players you draft are your foundation. And if you can find a gem deeper in the draft, even better.

Take the Tampa Bay Lightning, back-to-back champions in 2020 and 2021. Former GM Steve Yzerman saw center Brayden Point play as a sixteen-year-old, two years before he was draft eligible. Yzerman actually went to Moose Jaw to scout Morgan Rielly, in a 2012 playoff game, with Tampa Bay's director of amateur scouting, Al Murray, who was based a forty-five-minute drive away in Regina.

Murray told Yzerman he liked Point, even though there was concern about his skating and he was just five feet nine, 160 pounds. Yzerman wound up liking Point, too. The organization kept an eye on him. He played for Canada's under-eighteen team at the 2013 Ivan Hlinka tournament, helping his country to gold and winning MVP honors. The following spring, he played for Canada at the World U18 Championship after leading Moose Jaw in scoring with thirty-six goals and ninety-one points in seventy-two games.

Tampa Bay went into the 2014 draft in Philadelphia hoping to fortify its blue line. So, with their first three picks, the Lightning chose defensemen Tony DeAngelo (nineteenth), Dominik Mašín (thirty-fifth), and Johnathan MacLeod (fifty-seventh). Then Yzerman and his staff turned their attention to Point.

He entered the draft thirty-first on the NHL Central Scouting Service list of North American skaters. He was invited to play in the Canadian Hockey League (CHL)/NHL Top Prospects Game in Calgary five months earlier, but only as a replacement for an injured Sam Bennett.

Yzerman talked to many teams about swapping picks so he could take Point in the third round. Finally, twenty-two spots after MacLeod's name was called, the Minnesota Wild agreed to a trade. The Wild also liked Point and Louis Belpedio, a defenseman with the U.S. under-eighteen program. So, Minnesota shook hands on a swap of third-round picks, settled for Belpedio at number eighty, and got an additional seventh-round selection (204th overall) from Tampa Bay that the Wild used to draft Jack Sadek.

The Lightning, which moved up one spot to get Point, deserves credit for taking a chance on him and for his development. He did play—and win gold—for Canada at the 2015 World Junior. However, his development started shortly after the 2014 draft when he began to work with Tampa Bay development coach

Stacy Roest, who had been an undrafted player and was briefly a teammate with Yzerman in Detroit in the late 1990s.

Roest hooked up Point with skating guru Barbara Underhill. She was a former World Champion pairs skater with Paul Martini and transformed into a highly sought-after skating coach in the 2000s. Point developed into a premier talent.

The Lightning was rewarded by sticking to its plan, its draft list, typically a one-hundred-player ordered list of prospects. In Point's second NHL season, Tampa Bay advanced to the East final and then won the back-to-back Stanley Cups, with Point scoring twenty-four goals in the two successful post-season runs.

Yzerman clearly had somebody he trusted in Al Murray, as well as his Western Canada scout, Brad Whelen, who had seen Point the most. In fact, it has been reported by Joe Smith in *The Athletic* that just before Yzerman selected Point he asked Whelen for one last rundown. He was quoted as saying, "He's not very big, not all that strong, I'd say he's more quick than fast. But I do know one thing. When it all matters at the end, he'll be the one there."

Yzerman made the pick and the rest is history. What a great third-round pick—and he was the only Lightning pick from that draft to play for the team.

Whelen added in that article that Yzerman's successor, Julien BriseBois, has told the scouts "skating is something you can improve. If you're not a smart hockey player, you can't just pick it up." It's hard to argue with their success at the draft table and on the ice. Al Murray, who has added assistant GM to his résumé, has earned high praise for his ability to find gems outside the first round, such as Point, but also Nikita Kucherov (who won the Hart Trophy, Ted Lindsay Award, and Art Ross Trophy in 2019) in the second round, Anthony Cirelli (third round), and Mathieu Joseph (fourth).

Other notable mid to late picks for the Lightning include Alex Killorn (third round), Ross Colton (fourth round), and Ondrej Palat (seventh round). There's a reason they won back-to-back Cups and went to the final the year after. And it's why BriseBois has felt confident moving first-round picks for help at the trade deadline. He sent a couple of firsts and two players to Chicago in March 2022 to add Brandon Hagel, knowing he has internal growth. But Hagel was also on an affordable contract ($1.5 million per year for two more seasons) and the first-round picks would be late, so almost like seconds. BriseBois used the same logic to add the likes of Blake Coleman, Barclay Goodrow, and Nick Paul, affordable players with term.

In 2023, prior to the deadline, BriseBois traded five draft picks (a first in 2025, a second in 2024, and a third, fourth, and fifth in 2023) and Cal Foote to pick up big winger Tanner Jeannot. A lot of GMs were surprised at the price. At the time, it left Tampa with only a sixth and seventh in the 2023 draft.

"At the end of the day, I know there's a perceived value of those picks, but we have a really good idea of what the actual value of those pics is," said BriseBois about the Jeannot trade. "Individually you can go, 'What's the first-round pick worth? What's the second-round pick?' And so forth and so on. When we look at what that's worth to us, based on the odds of those picks turning into good NHL players down the road, I'd rather have the good player right now for this season and next and help this group win right now. Because I know what the odds are of those picks turning into players. I also know what the odds are of those picks turning into players that can help us win while we have this group of players right now in their prime, ready to go for another long run. The odds of that are zero. None of those picks were going to help. None of the players we were going to draft with those picks are going to help us win this year, or next, or probably the year after that. So, when you put it into context and you frame it that way, it ends up being a pretty easy decision actually."

One of the most important jobs a GM has is hiring a director of amateur scouting to lead this very important department. He has to be the absolute right person, because he will hire a staff to scour the world looking for talent that will be the key to your success or failure. Typically, this person is a former scout who has grown into the position by developing a reputation of being an excellent scout and has great leadership skills. He will watch in the vicinity of two hundred games a year. Most earn in the range of $175,000 to $300,000, but they are invaluable and should be key decision makers in the organization, not only for amateur scouting. They will have input into trades, especially when prospects are involved, coming or going. The scouting staff typically has the best book on those players. I would talk to my director of amateur scouting on a daily basis about all aspects of the organization.

For me, in Columbus, it was Don Boyd. I first met Boyd almost four decades ago. I had just finished a coaching stint in my hometown, steering the Summerside Western Capitals to their first Prince Edward Island Junior. A championship in twelve years. I decided to pursue my master's degree in educational psychology at the University of Western Ontario. But I also wanted to continue to coach. So, I contacted Boyd, who then was the head coach of the London Knights, to see if he had room for a part-time assistant coach. He hired me, and a friendship was born.

After a season together, I moved back east to coach the University of New Brunswick, while Boyd later became a scout with the Quebec Nordiques, helping build a roster that would win a Stanley Cup in Colorado in 1996. But by then, Boyd found himself back in junior for one final gig as the GM/coach of the OHL Sarnia Sting. He would later work for the Ottawa Senators and St. Louis Blues before I snagged him for the Blue Jackets.

Scouts come in all shapes and sizes. Some are former players, and some can barely skate. Boyd was a former goalie from Dryden, Ontario. The highest level he played was a few seasons at Bowling Green University.

Jimmy Devellano, for instance, never played the game. But he certainly had a passion for hockey at a young age and he knew talent. He was a rink rat, living in downtown Toronto. He worked as a government claims adjuster during the day and coached some minor hockey in the evening. He also kept a close eye on the exploits of the Toronto Maple Leafs and the Junior Toronto Marlboros, and with every chance that presented itself he would introduce himself to others immersed in the game.

When the NHL expanded in 1967, he pestered St. Louis Blues GM Lynn Patrick for a job. Patrick finally gave in and hired Jimmy D as a part-time scout. There was more expansion five years later. Bill Torrey had been hired to run the New York Islanders. I later worked under Bill with the Florida Panthers. He told me how he hired Devellano. Torrey had set up a meeting in his hotel room. When Jimmy D knocked on the door, he was dressed in his favorite suit. Bill said, "He looked like a clown, with all the different colors in the jacket."

But Jimmy D had a keenness and persistence. He was hired and helped the Islanders go on their dynastic run of four consecutive Stanley Cups, and they darn near got a fifth. Devellano was around for the first three before being hired to run the Red Wings. Now he's a seven-time NHL champion and in the Hockey Hall of Fame as a builder. Devellano worked his way up in the Islanders management hierarchy under Torrey. Devellano first became director of amateur scouting and later assistant GM.

One of the many tasks as the director of amateur scouting is to build a staff in North America and Europe. In Columbus, Boyd's first move was to hire Paul Castron as the assistant director of amateur scouting. Another was hiring Kjell Larsson as our European scouting director. He had an impressive coaching résumé at the international level in France and Switzerland and pro teams at home in Sweden. He had a really solid background, but we didn't get off to the best start.

The first time I met him was on a scouting trip in fall 1999. He picked me up at my hotel in Stockholm and we went to a junior game about an hour outside the city. We arrived in the town, but Kjell drove around for thirty-five minutes trying to locate the arena. He finally stopped to grab a coffee and to ask for directions. We found the arena in time for the second period. After the game, when I got back to my hotel room, I phoned Boyd to needle him.

"I'm not sure about your new European guy," I said. "He couldn't find a rink an hour from his home. How will he be able to find any players for us if he can't find a rink?"

I still laugh with Kjell about that first impression. He wound up working fourteen years for Columbus (long after I departed) and another six for one of Sweden's top teams, Stockholm AIK, before he retired in 2021, because he had a keen eye for talent.

Boyd also brought in Artyom Telepin as our Russian scout. He was another dandy. Having an excellent Russian scout is critical because not only is he your scout, but when you're in Russia he's your driver and bodyguard. I would not go anywhere in his homeland without him.

Others on our staff told me Telepin's apartment wasn't in great shape. So, I decided to treat him and his wife to a couple of nights' stay at the Moscow Marriott during the 2001 World Junior tournament so we could celebrate New Year's together. Finally, after five days, they returned home. Boyd said to me, "His wife wouldn't move out. She loved the Marriott."

Artyom, who now works for the Montreal Canadiens, would show up for three weeks of training camp in Columbus with only his shaving kit. Then, after about three or four days, I would ask a staff member to take him shopping for some clothes. But, of course, that was his plan all along, and I got sucked in. Another time he asked me for a raise. He was making $30,000 as a part-time scout. I offered him $40,000, and he accepted. Artyom met with the Blue Jackets financial guy to set up the payments. The CFO called me: "Doug, he wanted it all at once and in one-hundred dollar bills." Turns out he wanted the money all at once because he was planning to buy a house in Russia. It always was a treat dealing with the Russians.

We also added a scout in Czechoslovakia, as it was known at the time. His name was Milan Tichý, and he was drafted by Chicago in 1989 and had a five-year pro career, though he only played twenty-three NHL games. He worked twenty years for Columbus and he's still in the league, hired in 2022 by Edmonton as their head amateur scout. He was a tremendous person and a really good scout.

Draft-eligible players are eighteen years old and born before September 15, a negotiated cutoff date. The logic is kids born in November or December could be almost a year younger than a kid born at the start of the year. Those born before September 15 are eligible to be drafted for three years. Players with late birthdays are only eligible for two drafts.

Scouts usually don't begin zeroing in on players until they are in their draft year. But there is a trend in scouting these days in which some organizations employ scouts to watch underage players. These scouts only watch players who would be available for a draft in two years. However, most teams have their scouts file reports on underage players only if they appear to be outstanding future talents. They're not too focused on the underagers because seventeen-year-old kids can change a lot in a year, especially physically.

Another trend that has been evolving over the past two decades has been the use of video to enhance scouting. The Buffalo Sabres made the most noise in the use of video under GM Darcy Regier and former owner Tom Golisano. Regier already used video, especially in the pro scouting department in the early 2000s. Then Golisano bought the Sabres, and he severely cut the hockey operations department budget, forcing Regier and his staff to rely more on video to keep an eye on prospects as well as trade targets in other NHL organizations.

At the time, the Sabres were using video strictly to save money. Today, they have built up their scouting department. But no two teams have the same size scouting department, or front office.

In the last two drafts under Golisano's rule, 2010 and 2011, the results were troubling. The Sabres made fifteen picks mostly using video. Only four played in the NHL, with only two—forward

Joel Armia and defenseman Mark Pysyk—suiting up for more than twelve NHL games. Pysyk was taken twenty-third overall in 2010, while Armia was selected sixteenth overall in 2011.

Most feel video is a good backup tool. But a scout still sees much more in person. For example, you can watch how the player prepares in the warm-up and reacts on the bench to a teammate who messed up. Or how he plays away from the puck—all sorts of things. But you also may have face time with the team's GM, coach, or the player himself. That being said, video played a more prominent role during the height of the COVID-19 pandemic, but teams have returned to in-person scouting again.

A former GM running the Maple Leafs a decade ago likes to brag to his peers about how he commanded his video scouting department to edit every single shift of Morgan Rielly's 2011–12 season, his draft year. Brian Burke omits the part of the story where Rielly's season with the Moose Jaw Warriors was limited to eighteen regular-season games, five more in the playoffs, because of a severe knee injury. Regardless of the small body of work that season, Toronto still drafted Rielly fifth overall and he has been much better than the four players taken ahead of him in the 2012 draft: Nail Yakupov (Edmonton), Ryan Murray (Columbus), Alex Galchenyuk (Montreal), and Griffin Reinhart (New York Islanders).

A GM receives all the blame and most of the credit for draft picks. He is, after all, responsible for all hockey-related decisions. But depending on the GM, most don't spend a lot of time in the cold rinks of junior and college hockey or Europe. Moreover, the role of the GM has changed. Over the years, GMs have been devoting more time to be with their clubs on game days, at home and on the road.

Unless you're Rick Dudley, who had stints as a GM in Ottawa, Tampa Bay, Florida, and Atlanta, most GMs limit their scouting trips to the World Junior tournament, the CHL/NHL Top Prospects Game, the under-eighteen Ivan Hlinka tournament in the summer, and the occasional U.S. College or European excursion to check up on a top prospect on your team's radar. Dudley was a different animal. He is a scout at heart. He wore the treads off his tires, preferring to drive over flying. He once added up the number of games he saw in a season at close to three hundred.

How much time a GM spends scouting depends on his philosophy and situation. For example, Blue Jackets GM Jarmo Kekäläinen has a scouting background. He would spend a lot of his time on the road scouting. A GM like Detroit's Steve Yzerman would spend a similar amount of his time on the road scouting, but because of the extensive rebuild he has in front of him.

Most GMs will hit the road in the late season to get a look at players the scouting staff believes will be in their draft wheelhouse. But even with the increased technology and some GMs spending more time than others looking at prospects, trust me, the director of amateur scouting makes decisions with his staff on which prospects are drafted. Rarely does a GM overrule what the scouting staff recommends.

When we stole Steve Mason in the 2006 draft in the third round (sixty-ninth overall), it was a situation in which Boyd believed Mason had incredible potential. The challenge, however, was Mason was the London Knights' backup netminder in 2005–06 to overager Adam Dennis. The previous season, Dennis helped the Knights win the Memorial Cup against Sidney Crosby and the Rimouski Oceanic.

The trick for Boyd and his staff was to feel comfortable enough with Mason, despite his lack of playing time. He was limited to twelve regular-season appearances with London and four more in the playoffs in his draft year. But Boyd had a plan. He urged our goalie coach/scout Rick Wamsley to watch Mason in as many of his games as possible. They also didn't miss an opportunity to watch Mason in practice and his junior B outings with the Petrolia Jets. He made nine starts in the regular season and five more in the playoffs for Petrolia. Mason went from a third-round pick to a World Junior champion with Canada in 2008.

He was traded by the Knights to the Kitchener Rangers when he starred for the Canadian junior team. He had Kitchener on course to win the Memorial Cup, but he missed the prestigious junior championship after undergoing arthroscopic knee surgery in mid-April. Without Mason, the Rangers lost to Tyler Johnson and the Spokane Chiefs in the Memorial Cup final.

Mason didn't take long in the NHL to prove Boyd and Wamsley right. He played in sixty-one games, winning thirty-three, to win the 2009 Calder Trophy as rookie of the year. He was a valuable selection for our organization. With Mason in goal, the Blue Jackets made the playoffs for the first time in club history. The 2006 draft proved to be productive. We chose center Derick Brassard from Drummondville sixth overall in the first round. In the seventh and final round, Medicine Hat forward Derek Dorsett was drafted 189th overall.

I was proud to see both players traded to the New York Rangers in April 2013 after I had left the organization. They became valuable playoff performers and went to the 2014 Stanley Cup final with the Rangers. Brassard went to two more East finals with the Ottawa Senators in 2017 and the New York Islanders in 2020. He has played in more than one hundred Stanley Cup playoff games.

Unlike Dudley, most sane scouts see between 170 to 220 games a year spread over ten or eleven months. A typical scouting staff would include five Canadian scouts, four U.S.-based scouts, and three more overseas, based in Russia (prior to recent world events), the Czech Republic, and Finland or Sweden. In turn, these scouts are assigned to defined areas.

In Canada, scouts will cover the QMJHL, the OHL, the WHL, as well as junior A Tier II and high-school loops, and to a lesser degree Canadian universities and colleges.

The U.S.-based bird dogs will cover the United States Hockey League (USHL), North American Hockey League (NAHL), the U.S. College scene, and prep schools.

The European scouts cover their particular areas, but they will also do a lot of crisscrossing, especially with all the tournaments like a Channel One Cup in Moscow at Christmastime or a Kalahari Cup in Helsinki in November.

Some teams also employ part-time scouts to help with the workload, with the hope these scouts develop into full-timers.

An amateur scout would earn a salary between $50,000 and $90,000, far less than their director. But some directors earn more because they also have an assistant GM title. But a regular scout is the lifeline of your organization. They're in it for the love of the game; the challenge of predicting a prospect like Mason will make a difference.

The low scouting salaries are part of the proverbial hockey culture. The NHL front office in New York prides itself on keeping its non-player-related costs to a minimum. In other words, if an NHL team sets a budget of $100–$120 million, salaries would make up $82.5 million. Toss in AHL salaries and bonuses and that takes you to perhaps $88 million.

The scout's role is not only to grade a prospect but also to project where the young player will fit on the roster or depth chart, like a franchise player, a top-four defenseman, a top-six forward, a role player, an NHL regular, or an impact player. Most teams use a rating scale of 1 to 7. A franchise player would have a perfect score of 7, like a Connor McDavid, Sidney Crosby, or Auston Matthews. Toronto forward Mitch Marner would have been a 6, which is what we had Gilbert Brule rated at. A 6 is projected to be an impact player, while an NHL regular with extra qualities, such as penalty killing or checking, would be a 5 or 5½ (think Edmonton center Ryan Nugent-Hopkins). Oilers forward Zach Hyman would be a 5. The late Bob Probert would have been a 5 or 6 because he was a tough guy who could score thirty goals.

A player like Sean Kuraly was a 4 in Boston, but in Columbus he's a 5 because of a different role as someone who could move up and down in the lineup in a pinch. A tough guy like Jody Shelley or Colton Orr would be a 3, a role player. A 2 is a minor leaguer, who could be called up to fill in for an injured regular. You don't want a 1.

There are a variety of scales used by teams in scouting talent. For example, we employed a 1 through 7 scale in Columbus with several grading areas such as skating, puck skills, offense, defense, hockey sense, compete level, physicality, size, and strength.

Organizations put different emphasis on these categories. For example, some teams stress size and strength, and skating ability. Other clubs pay more attention to hockey IQ and skill, such as Tampa with Point. But each team has a specific system for how it grades prospects and projects their development based on their individual skill sets.

Over the years, a lot of teams have become less fixated on size than skill and compete level. Players such as Point, Marner, Johnny Gaudreau, and many others have shown smaller players can thrive in the altered NHL. I don't disagree, but a lot still believe a big player with skill, all other things being equal, is a better pick, especially for playoff time.

Where does character fit into the grand scheme of grading? This again is a significant part of a regional scout's job. Some are more sociable and better at finding out things about a player's character and behavior (good or bad) than others. Sometimes you're tipped off by a contact. For example, London Knights head coach Dale Hunter and his brother/GM, Mark Hunter, turned our attention to defenseman Marc Methot. He was a big part of the Knights team that defeated Crosby and Rimouski in the 2005 Memorial Cup final. Methot wasn't a high-profile guy, but they told us to keep an eye on him; he was a leader in the dressing room and had an upside to become a solid NHL defenseman.

He was still there when we selected him in the sixth round (168th overall) in the 2005 draft. He wound up playing a combined 662 regular-season and playoff games for the Blue Jackets, Senators, and Dallas Stars. Sometimes you couldn't help but take a second or third look at prospects in franchises like London or the Portland Winter Hawks, teams that had excellent reputations in developing players.

A regional scout is on the front lines and needs to know a prospect's personality and off-ice habits as much as what the scout sees from the player on the ice. So, the scout almost needs to be a little bit like Lieutenant Columbo, obtaining information and a characterization of the prospect from people around him, like coaches, teammates, and billets. One scout, who worked with Central Scouting for a while, said they always used to interview the player's mother because "the moms were always honest. If there was a sense they could be a pain in the butt, the player would often be a pain as well."

But one thing you have to remember in this part of the process is you're dealing with seventeen- and eighteen-year-old kids. Sometimes you have to rely on your gut and project how a prospect will mature, or not. There are stories where teams scratched a prospect off their lists because of too many red flags in terms of character flaws. The question a GM and his scouting staff need to ask is: "At what round are we able to look past these character issues and take this player, knowing the potential risks?" That's why getting to know the kid on and off the ice is so important.

One very sad story involves a kid named George Pelawa, a big winger who had a great senior season playing high-school hockey in Bemidji, Minnesota. In fact, he was named the top high-school player in 1986. Pelawa was interviewed by many teams, including the New York Rangers. During their interview, they asked him what his interests were. He said, "Hockey, booze, and broads." They asked him what his favorite team was. He said, "Calgary." Incredible. Well, the Rangers, who had the ninth pick, took defenseman Brian Leetch, who became a star. Pelawa fell to sixteen, but he was drafted by his favorite team.

The reason he loved Calgary was because Joel Otto, a big center with the Flames, was his favorite player. Pelawa watched him play for Bemidji State. The draft that year was in Montreal, and when the Flames called out his name Pelawa was so excited he didn't bother using the stairs to get down to the draft floor but instead was jumping over the rows of seats until he got his leg stuck in one of the chairs and needed help to get out. Sadly, at the age of eighteen, three months after his dream came true, Pelawa was killed in a car crash. Sure, there were some red flags there with his attitude, but we'll never know how he might have matured had fate not been so cruel.

Then there's the case of goalie Glen Hanlon and the Vancouver Canucks. There is no denying Hanlon became a good and dependable teammate in his thirteen-year NHL career with the Canucks, Blues, Rangers, and Red Wings. After his playing days concluded, he also went on to a successful coaching career in the NHL, AHL, Russia, Europe, and junior.

The Canucks had significant interest in Hanlon after he led the Brandon Wheat Kings to the top of the 1977 WHL standings and a trip to the WHL final against the eventual Memorial Cup champion New Westminster Bruins. He also won the Del Wilson Memorial Trophy as the league's Goaltender of the Year. Vancouver GM Jake Milford (from Charlottetown, Prince Edward Island) brought Hanlon in for an interview and noticed he was suffering a bit with a limp. Milford, knowing the reason for the limp, asked the goalie what was wrong. Hanlon replied he fell off a ladder while painting. Well, Hanlon fell off a ladder all right. But he wasn't painting. He was sneaking into his girlfriend's apartment. Despite the fib, Hanlon was a character guy and Milford wanted to see how he would respond.

Regardless, the Canucks drafted Hanlon in the third round (fortieth overall). He made 137 regular-season appearances with Vancouver before being included in a trade to St. Louis in exchange for Jim Nill, Tony Currie, and Rick Heinz, missing out on the Canucks' run to the Stanley Cup final in spring 1982.

Goaltending is the most challenging position to scout. They have different skill sets, including size, athleticism, compete level, hockey IQ, skating, puck handling, and mechanics. In terms of size these days, the cutoff is usually six feet two. Mason had size. He was six feet four. But a guy like five-foot-eight John Vanbies-brouck, who was a big part of why the Florida Panthers made it to the 1996 Stanley Cup final when I was head coach, would not get much of a look these days.

Some scouts focus more on athleticism and size over savvy and the technical aspects of the position. It's also advantageous to have scouts keenly aware of how some teams are more challenging to play for in goal because of the system and strength of the team in front of them. A weaker team can make it harder to evaluate a goalie.

Quite often, because their development takes longer, sometimes four to six years, goalies are drafted in later rounds, unless you're a phenom like Marc-Andre Fleury or Carey Price. And there have been first-round goalie misses such as Rick DiPietro, who went first overall to the Islanders in 2000. There have been others who went in the first round, such as Spencer Knight thirteenth overall to Florida in 2019, the highest a goalie had been taken since Jack Campbell went eleventh in 2010. From 2000 to 2006 twenty goaltenders went in the first round, but only a dozen or so since.

Having said all that, Tampa's twice-Cup-winning goalie, Andrei Vasilevskiy, was a first-rounder. Same with Fleury and the Penguins for their Cups. Everyone knows you typically don't win without a great goalie, so a lot of teams have expanded their goalie coaching departments and are including more former goalies on their scouting staffs.

A scout's calendar begins in the summer with under-eighteen tryouts for Hockey Canada and USA Hockey in preparation for the Hlinka tournament, which pits the best seventeen-year-olds in the world against each other, usually in August. September has showcase games for the USHL in Pittsburgh, BCHL, and Alberta Junior Hockey League.

Whether full-time or part-time, regional scouts will begin the season in the fall with a list of fifty or so players they have targeted to follow in their area. By the end of the season, the list will be reduced to twenty or so. For example, in a U.S. region, a scout will trim his list of college players, national developmental teams, USHL, NAHL, prep, and high school down to a reasonable list. Recently, the Jets had twenty-two players on their one-hundred-player list from all the U.S. regions. Usually, this is how many Canadians would be on a team's list. November is a big month for European scouts because of all the international tournaments. February is similar for the Euros.

December, or more often January, is when most teams summon their scouting staffs together for meetings and compile their first list of prospects. These meetings, which can cost upward of $150,000, take place in southern locales because it's warm and a nice break from the cold of winter and the rinks.

It is the first occasion of the season when a team can bring together its scouting staff. Prior to the mid-term meetings, there have been Zoom calls and lots of conversations about players, which ones to keep a close eye on. As the meetings draw closer, scouts in the various regions have started to assemble lists for their region. At the mid-term, each scout would put ten to fifteen names on the board, and from the input the top one hundred names would be shaped.

It was always interesting to listen to the discussion on every player as the list came together. There is plenty of crossover in today's scouting environment, so many of the scouts have kept a close eye on some of the same players because of tournaments in North America and Europe. Key scouts in Europe would know players in North America, and some Canadian or U.S.-based scouts would have a good read on the best prospects in Europe. As a result, there would be some great debates among the scouts. It could also be a time for some older GMs, who have been through the process many times, to catch up on their shut-eye. Just ask Glen Sather.

One year, when Slats was with the Rangers, they were having their final scouting meeting and he was asleep at the end of the table. Now, that's not a shot at Slats, who had a Hall of Fame career. Like I said, a lot of GMs, especially an experienced one like him, wouldn't get too deeply involved in the list process, but they liked to be able to spend some time with the scouting staff and for any GM the two or three days were a great break from the pressures of the season, the rigors of the job. It could be refreshing to get away from the team and those pressures for a few days.

In December, the World Junior takes center stage on the scouting scene. Almost every NHL GM attends this tournament at some point. But, for most GMs, this is the first opportunity to see most of the top-end under-twenty talent. Even though 90 percent of the World Junior participants are already drafted, GMs are there to watch their prospects as well as the undrafted players.

You could write a book just on the mischief GMs and scouts get into during the World Junior. In 1994, when the tournament was in Ostrava, Czech Republic (a four-and-a-half-hour train ride east of Prague), I was working for the Red Wings. Of course, this was about the time we started to stockpile Russian talent in Detroit with Sergei Fedorov, Vladimir Konstantinov, and Slava Kozlov.

Sitting around a bar one night in Ostrava were three Russians. When they heard I was with the Red Wings, they told me to be careful because "we want to kill you." They hated Detroit with a passion because of all the talent we had poached, the likes of Fedorov, Kozlov, and Konstantinov.

I learned my lesson. So, when we drafted Nikolai Zherdev fourth overall in 2003 I sent my scout Jim Clark out to the next World Junior in Finland.

During another European excursion with Bryan Murray in Stockholm, we arrived late back at the International Hotel. After going to bed, I woke up at 5:00 a.m. to go to the bathroom. Anyone who has been to Europe knows how small the hotel rooms are. So, I go through the door I think is for the bathroom, but I find myself out in the hallway—naked. I'm panicking. I decided to go down the stairwell and look for a maid to give me another key. But there was no maid in sight.

I went back up to my floor, the ninth, and knocked on the room across the hall. A Swedish guy answers the door to find a Canadian without any clothes on. "No key, no key," I said to him. He was nice enough to get dressed and go down to the front desk to get me a key. That's life on the road.

After the World Junior, the next major event on a scout's season-long agenda is the CHL/NHL Top Prospects Game, which showcases the top-forty draft prospects from the WHL, OHL, and QMJHL. This game can sometimes be a nightmare for scouts because a GM can interfere with the scouts' process if he falls in love with a player after only seeing him once, unlike the scouts who have seen the player multiple times. In January 2005, the prospects game was in Vancouver and was supposed to pit Sidney Crosby, the best from the East, against Gilbert Brule, the best in the West. Crosby, however, bailed on the showcase. He cited a nagging injury and fatigue from the World Junior in Grand Forks, North Dakota, contested two weeks earlier. As a result, Brule, a center with the Vancouver Giants, dominated in his home rink before a capacity crowd of 16,331 at Pacific Coliseum, scoring three times in his team's 8–4 win. Crosby still went first overall. We snatched Brule sixth.

There are more U.S. prospects games in February, like the USA Hockey All-American game. These games don't garner the same attention as the CHL/NHL Top Prospects Games, but the importance continues to rise. For example, more than two hundred scouts and GMs attended a recent USA Hockey All-American game in Plymouth, Michigan.

March is also a critical time because major junior and U.S. College hockey playoffs are in full flight. In many cases, the playoffs in these leagues are the last chance to make a final assessment of a particular player. The U18 IIHF World Championship is contested in April. Unfortunately, not all the best players are available for this tournament, but it's still important to see players compete.

The list comes together at a team's scouting meetings in late April or early May. There will be some minor adjustments made before the draft in June because there are a few events to consider. In mid-to-late May, there is the four-team Memorial Cup championship and the NHL Combine in Buffalo, in which one hundred players are invited based on their NHL Central Scouting Service ranking and requests from NHL teams. Most teams will conduct close to sixty interviews at the combine, but not all scouts watch the fitness testing. Instead, some teams prefer their fitness staff to take in the physical testing proceedings.

There is also the IIHF World Championship, an event where a few top prospects may be suiting up for their country, but it's also a chance for scouts to keep an eye on draft picks as well as free agents. One of the classic stories from a World Championship happened in 1997 in Helsinki. John Ferguson Sr. was the San Jose Sharks' chief scout back then. He was high on Finland's Olli Jokinen. Downstairs in the Hesperia Hotel was a famous nightclub. Fergie was having a nightcap—well, early-morning cap—with some other scouts, and he sees Jokinen on the dance floor. So, Fergie goes up and asks Jokinen, "Shouldn't you be in bed?"

Olli told Fergie to "fuck off, old man." Fergie was so pissed the Sharks selected Patrick Marleau second overall a few weeks later. Jokinen went third to the Los Angeles Kings. I would say Jokinen did the Sharks a big favor. Marleau went on to play 1,779 regular-season games, breaking the all-time record previously held by none other than Gordie Howe. Jokinen had a good career, but he never reached the potential that Fergie had expected of him.

With scouting sometimes you just never know what will help make the final decision! On the flip side, the Montreal Canadiens fell in love with Juraj Slafkovsky at the 2022 Winter Olympics and then the World Championships, where he was terrific, and wound up taking him first overall in 2022.

I remember being told when I was in Columbus that the Florida scouts were debating the goalies in the 1999 draft. They were going to select a goaltender, but while the scouts were putting together the list the debate got heated. One scout was a big fan of a kid named Ryan Miller, who played for the Soo Indians of the NAHL. Tim Murray, who was a terrific scout, shouted out: "He has a better chance to be a scarecrow than an NHL goalie." Miller was six feet two, maybe 170 pounds. Well, Florida drafted a goalie, Alex Auld, in the second round, while Miller was taken by Buffalo in the fifth round. Auld had a decent NHL career, but Miller was a star for many years. It's funny, but when Murray was a rookie GM in Buffalo, in 2014, all those years later, he traded Miller to the St. Louis Blues in a blockbuster at the trade deadline. His first impression was a lasting impression. Miller, by the way, had his number 30 retired by the Sabres and was inducted into their hall of fame in January 2023.

But in terms of assembling the list, it starts in earnest mid-season and gets revised and fine-tuned as the season goes along. Throughout the year the scouts are filing reports on players, rating them for the different categories, and it all goes into the team's database. As you move through the scouting meetings, you build lists by regions and leagues and countries. And eventually you assemble your overall list, and that involves input from all the scouts, many of them fighting for players they've watched over the course of the season. Typically, a GM won't have too much input because he hasn't seen a lot of the players in action. At the end of the day, the chief scout will break any deadlocks in ranking debates.

In the process, you take the top guys from each league and put four or five names from each on the board. Once you put them in order, you add more names. It's a continual five-name list on the board. The scouting department has it down to a science. They'd have twenty-five names down the side, pull out the top five, then keep going. It was a two- or three-day process.

We would compare our list to what Central Scouting, the league's independent scouting department paid for by the NHL and headed up by Dan Marr, produces, although they don't combine North America and Europe into one master list. We would use it more for identification purposes, to make sure we hadn't missed someone, or if there is a wildly different ranking. We would look at some of the scouting services as well, including a guy like TSN's Bob McKenzie, who works really hard on his draft rankings. Bob talks to ten top scouts, gets their rankings, and assembles his list. Why not have a look?

Even after all that, you still need good fortune to come out ahead on draft day. Teams generally don't stray too far from their list and sometimes that's a good thing, sometimes not. Think about the Winnipeg Jets. In the 2015 draft, they really liked winger Lawson Crouse and tried to trade up in the first round. Florida owned the eleventh pick but wouldn't deal and took Crouse, a very good player. The Jets held on to their pick, number seventeen, and selected winger Kyle Connor, who scored forty-seven goals in 2021–22. In the 2013 draft, the Jets tried to trade up to get defenseman Samuel Morin, who wound up being selected by Philadelphia at number eleven. The Jets got defenseman Josh Morrissey at thirteen. Morin is now a forward and struggled his first few years. Connor and Morrissey became the Jets' two best players. Obviously, they had Crouse and Morin rated higher on the list, but everything turned out well. Like I have said, it's not a perfect science!

Regardless, if you're stumbling around before the draft, still trying to figure out who your pick is, you're in the wrong business. And when you're spending $2 to $3 million a year to prepare that list, you better make it the number one priority.

CHAPTER EIGHT

RICK NASH, FIRST OVERALL

SOME MEDIA PEOPLE HAVE SAID IT WAS THE BEST WORK I EVER DID AS THE PRESI-dent and GM of the Columbus Blue Jackets. They are right, but talk about peaking early.

Back in fall 2000, in our first season, there was a lot of conversation between myself and our director of amateur scouting, Don Boyd, about the need to find a face of the franchise, a player who would take our team from hapless expansion team to potentially a contender, much sooner rather than later. Every GM has that thought and conversation at some point—the need to find the next great one through the draft.

As ours was an expansion team, the need was even more acute, especially with the expansion draft rules back then so much different from today. Vegas and Seattle, the most recent additions, were afforded a much deeper list of available talent off NHL rosters and, as a result, the chance to be good right out of the gate. For us, we did our best in the expansion draft, then we were left trying to make trades to upgrade, but our lifeblood was going to be the entry draft.

I vividly remember that I learned very quickly in Columbus just how important it was to find that face of the franchise. I remember one day that first year, my son, Clark, who was in grade five, came home from school and he said, "Dad, hockey's not going to work here. They hate hockey. All they want to talk about is Ohio State football."

People had no idea the pressure on us to be good, to be noticed, because of the Ohio State Buckeyes. The people in Columbus and Ohio love them and it's still an issue for hockey in Columbus. They are so big. We needed to find that player, to find the success, to get into that mix.

The next great one Boyd and I talked about early wasn't eligible for the draft until 2002, another season away. I'm not saying we had the foresight of a Sam Pollock when it came to getting aligned for the draft, but Rick Nash was on our radar big-time long before he was draft eligible. And I mean big-time. Don was totally intrigued by this big, underage left winger playing with the London Knights of the OHL.

I remember one night that season, Don and I went to scout Nash in a game in Plymouth, Michigan, and we kept thinking, Is there any chance we could get this kid in the 2002 draft? We loved him. And we needed him. Boydy said to me, "This is the guy who could be number one next year."

Rick grew up in Brampton, Ontario, and had a terrific minor hockey career in the Greater Toronto Hockey League with the Toronto Marlboros. He was a tall, lanky kid, a late bloomer. With the Marlies Under-15 bantam team he had sixty-one goals and

115 points in thirty-four games and was drafted fourth overall by the Knights—behind centers Patrick Jarrett from Sault Ste. Marie, who went first to Mississauga; Tim Brent from Cambridge, who went to St. Michael's; and defenseman Richard Power, who played with Rick on the Marlies. Needless to say, Rick had the better career.

During Rick's rookie season with London, he scored thirty-one goals and sixty-six points in fifty-eight games and was named Rookie of the Year. The next season, his draft year, he had thirty-two goals and seventy-two points in fifty-four games. We couldn't take our eyes off this talented six-foot-three, 210-pound left winger. It was hockey love at first sight. Rick was an easy kid to scout, too, because he seldom ever left the ice. I once asked him what line he was playing on with the Knights and he said to me, "I'm not really on a line. Coach just tells me to go on every second shift."

True enough, Knights coach Dale Hunter, who played for me the two seasons I was an assistant coach with the Washington Capitals, played Rick often during games and continually raved to us and anyone else who would listen that he would be a future NHL star. Boyd and I couldn't wait for the 2002 draft to come around. It was just our second season as an expansion team, so we had a pretty good idea that we would be bad enough on the ice to have a great chance to get Nash, and we weren't wrong.

Obviously, we spent a ton of time watching Rick. The top prospects that year were Finnish goaltender Kari Lehtonen, big defenseman Jay Bouwmeester from Medicine Hat, and Nash. Other top first-round considerations for us were Finnish defenseman Joni Pitkanen, Boston University defenseman Ryan Whitney, forwards Scottie Upshall with Kamloops and Joffrey Lupul with Medicine Hat.

We scouted all those players a lot during the 2001–02 season. In the 2001 draft, with the eighth pick overall, we had selected goaltender Pascal Leclaire, who played his final year with the Montreal Rocket of the Quebec major junior league and was selected to Canada's World Junior team. We felt comfortable that Leclaire would be our goalie of the future and he was well on his way to a great career when, after recording nine shutouts during the 2007–08 season, he suffered a serious knee injury and never really reached his full potential.

In the 2001–02 season, we finished with fifty-seven points, down from the respectable seventy-one in our first year, second worst in the league behind the Atlanta Thrashers with fifty-four. But, in what would soon become a maddening habit, the draft lottery was not kind to us. When the balls finished dropping, we had slipped to third overall, behind the Florida Panthers, who had sixty points, and Atlanta, which also dropped a spot. I was pissed.

The question we were asking was would Nash still be available at number three? I think we knew the answer.

Because we had Leclaire, we weren't going to be drafting Lehtonen. That much we knew for certain. All I could envision was Florida selecting defenseman Jay Bouwmeester, whom I knew they loved, and Atlanta taking Nash second. We wouldn't take the goalie, so we would have to move to our second group of players and miss out on the guy we desperately wanted. We really focused on the top six or so guys.

This issue was debated in our offices for a month. Who would be there for us at number three? And if Nash wasn't there, whom would we take? The second group after Nash was a good group of players, but we projected a big drop-off after Nash and

Bouwmeester. I was not overly excited about the third player on our list, who was Pitkanen.

Our staff headed to Toronto on Tuesday prior to Saturday's draft at the Air Canada Centre and set up our war room, which is a suite off the GM's hotel room where the staff convenes during the day and late evening to hold meetings to discuss the various scenarios—talking about potential trades—and also to conduct final interviews with the draft-eligible players. My mind was racing all week. The possibility of not controlling our own destiny at the top of the draft was frustrating me. Typically, during draft week you hear lots of rumors about which team likes which player, especially at the top of the draft. Whether it's scouts talking to their scouting buddies, GMs talking to each other, or hearing from agents, you always had a pretty good idea of who was picking which player ahead of you.

In 2000, our first-ever draft, I'd received a call at two thirty in the morning from Boyd informing me he had just confirmed that the New York Islanders would select goaltender Rick DiPietro, out of Boston University, with the first overall pick. That was fine by us. We would have been thrilled to get one of Wisconsin winger Dany Heatley, Slovakian winger Marian Gaborik, or Czech defenseman Rostislav Klesla. I wanted Gaborik, but I lost the coin toss between us and the Minnesota Wild, who wound up drafting ahead of us, third overall. Atlanta ended up taking Heatley second, then the Wild took Gaborik, so we got Klesla, a good defenseman who had played junior in Brampton. But at the 2002 draft, there wasn't any information leaking out of the other war rooms.

I was hearing plenty of rumors that teams were desperately trying to move up to select Nash. Washington, Philadelphia, and

Vancouver were all very active. Word came out that Flyers GM Bob Clarke had made a trade with Tampa Bay to acquire the fourth overall pick. That move by the Flyers created lots of conversation and it scared the crap out of me. Were the Flyers looking to select Pitkanen, or were they going to try to get Atlanta or Florida to move down and allow the Flyers to draft Nash? I believe Clarke really wanted Nash. That was the key reason I needed to move up in the order. But that's the sort of conversation going on in the war room, trying to figure out all the scenarios.

Our staff interviewed the top players in our war room over the final twenty-four hours prior to the draft. Typically, you bring in the top five you think could be in your range when you're making your selection. We as a staff spent time with Bouwmeester, Upshall, Lupul, and Nash. If Nash was taken in the first two picks by Florida or Atlanta we would have been drafting one of those players. We made Nash the last interview of the night, as we hoped we might get a vibe from him as to what the other teams above us were thinking. I asked Rick if he thought he would be available tomorrow when we made the third pick. A low-key kid, he was very pointed with his answer: "No, I won't be there at your pick. You better trade up if you really want me." I suspected teams told Rick they were taking him at number two if they got the pick.

I had met Rick post-game in junior when we were scouting him, just to say hello, but this was the first time I had sat down with him for an intensive interview. I had heard so much about him from our scouts, so I had a good feeling about him. I was really impressed by him—number one with how much he wanted to be a Blue Jacket—and we were blown away by his personality and character.

As soon as Rick left the room, my guys—Jim Clark, Don Boyd, and Bob Strumm—started yelling at me to make a deal. I told the staff I needed some time. I felt a ton of pressure. We really wanted Rick, but as I said, I knew George McPhee in Washington, Brian Burke in Vancouver, and Clarke in Philly were interested, too, and they had a ton of ammunition to make a deal to move up. To say I was nervous was an understatement.

But I also knew I had to make a move. There are times when a GM just has to get it done. For us, about to head into our third season, it felt like getting Nash was something we had to do. Other teams have felt that over the years, like when Burke pulled off multiple trades a couple of years earlier to get the second and third picks to draft Henrik and Daniel Sedin.

I placed a call to Panthers GM Rick Dudley, who is a great guy and not afraid to think outside the box. I asked him if he would consider flipping picks, with the Panthers moving to third and the Blue Jackets to number one. For Dudley to make the move, we agreed to flip first picks with Florida in the next year's (2003) draft. My last conversation with Dudley was at 1:30 a.m. He agreed to think on it and we would talk in morning, with the draft starting at noon. I informed my staff at 1:35 a.m. that I thought we had a good chance of making the deal.

In the morning, I was a basket case waiting. It was the longest morning of my life. Finally, at 10:30 a.m., Dudley agreed. We had a deal. When I told the staff they went nuts with excitement. The Blue Jackets get the number one pick. What a moment.

The Panthers then gave Atlanta a third-round pick (2002) and a fourth-round pick in 2003 to not select Bouwmeester. I was shocked that Dudley didn't make me pay those picks to Atlanta. But he didn't and it was fine by me. Years later, Duds explained his logic with the move. He wanted Bouwmeester and felt our 2003 pick was going to give him a better shot in that lottery and two top picks in a great draft.

After I acquired the pick, both McPhee and Burke called me looking to make a deal. Trust me, the calls didn't last long. Actually, they lasted about as long as when I called George a few years later, at the 2004 draft, when he won the lottery and had the first overall pick. I said, "Would you move the first pick for my fourth overall pick and—" He cut me off: "No, I think we will take Ovechkin." Good call, George.

As an aside, Dudley had tried to draft Ovechkin in 2003. He was born on September 17, 1985, which is two days after the eligibility date for that draft. Dudley argued that if you considered leap years he was actually draft eligible. Nice try, but the NHL said no.

It was such a great honor to stand on the stage at the then Air Canada Centre and announce Rick Nash as the Columbus Blue Jackets' number one selection and the number one overall pick in the 2002 NHL entry draft. It was a thrill for our entire staff and especially for Rick with the draft being in Toronto, his hometown.

By the way, in that 2002 draft Burke had eleven picks. Of those, just two played in the NHL, goaltender Rob McVicar, who played just one game, and defenseman Brett Skinner, who played eleven. My point being even the smartest GMs have bad drafts. That's the draft—it can be feast or famine.

As for Nash, he was everything we hoped and wound up playing nine seasons for Columbus. His first season had some growing pains, especially playing on a struggling team. He came to camp as an eighteen-year-old, and when we did our fitness testing he could only do one bench press. The big guys were doing thirty. But we still believed in him big-time. I still remember hearing a story about a young Wayne Gretzky who couldn't do any chin-ups when he first arrived on the scene. That seemed to turn out fine. That first season Nash had seventeen goals and thirty-nine points in seventy-four games. Not so bad.

But in his second year, as a nineteen-year-old, he jumped to forty-one goals and won the Rocket Richard Trophy as the leading goal scorer in the league, tied with Ilya Kovalchuk of the Atlanta Thrashers and Jarome Iginla of the Calgary Flames. After that, he continued to be a rock-solid thirty-plus goal scorer. In March 2022, the Blue Jackets retired his number 61, and I was very pleased he invited me to the ceremony. It was an amazing night. And I will never forget the kind words he had for me.

"Doug MacLean, you're the reason I am standing here today; you put your name on the line to draft me and I will never forget that," Rick said. "It's amazing to think that when Doug started here there was no arena. I'm sure there wasn't a logo or a team name. Think about the energy and excitement that Doug brought to this city and this organization to build the game of hockey. I remember one night when he brought that excitement down to the dressing room when I had my first NHL fight. There were three minutes left in the period, so after I got my five-minute major, I just went to the room to serve it. I went back into the trainer's room to watch the rest of the game. Next thing I know I was hearing doors slam—it was Doug making a straight line for me. He said, 'Nasher, never fight again. I pay guys to fight, it's not you.' I don't know how he got down [to the room] so fast. . . ."

True story! I admired his battle and compete, but the last thing we needed was him breaking his hand (or anything else) in a fight.

I remember thinking that night we were so lucky to get Rick the player, but we were also so lucky to get Rick the person. He is a better person than a hockey player and that's saying a lot. He became the face of hockey in Columbus, the guy Boydy and I talked about in 2000.

It felt then, when we made the deal to get him, and now, like we really got the first overall pick for nothing. And we kind of did, as it turned out. As with any trade with futures involved, I was concerned (but never a regret; it was the right thing to do) what the price would eventually be for acquiring the first pick from Florida. Dudley was counting on his Panthers being better than us the next season, so the swap of picks would be a win for him. But the season ended with the Blue Jackets finishing one spot below the Panthers going into the draft lottery.

The Panthers won the 2003 draft lottery, thus receiving the first overall pick, although Dudley wound up trading his first and seventy-third overall picks to Pittsburgh for the Penguins' first pick (third overall), forward Mikael Samuelsson, and the fifty-fifth overall pick. In the end, Pittsburgh got star goaltender Marc-André Fleury and winger Daniel Carcillo, while Dudley used the third overall pick to select forward Nathan Horton, who turned out to be a pretty good player, along with Samuelsson and winger Stefan Meyer, who wound up playing four games for Florida. In the end, it worked out well for Duds and me.

But with the Panthers winning the lottery, it meant the Blue Jackets didn't owe anything to Florida as compensation for

moving from third to number one to select Rick Nash, the player
we coveted, and, as I mentioned, we didn't have to give Atlanta
anything to back away from Bouwmeester. And with the fourth
pick overall we selected Russian winger Nikolai Zherdev, which
seemed like a good idea at the time but didn't end well.

I should mention, after all that wheeling and dealing to get to
Nash, we had a long, heated (at least from my end) negotiation
to get him signed, just before the signing deadline. It was a deal
worth $1.185 million U.S. per year. With bonuses, it was worth $8
to $12 million U.S. over the three years. It was the richest rookie
deal at the time.

The bonuses in the entry-level contracts drove management
crazy. Next thing you know, on the orders of my owner, I fire
Dave King as coach and I'm coaching Rick. I remember, every
time we got a power play, or a five-on-three power play, I would
put Rick out on the ice because even at eighteen he was our best
forward. My owner would cringe when he would see the bonus
checks going out, but for every power-play goal Rick got $15,000.
Those first two years, he got most of the bonus money, including
$3 million in his second year in the league. It's another example
of the push and pull a GM goes through—on one hand you want
to win; on the other hand you're worried about draft position, or
in this case the budget, as well!

After the third season, which was the lockout year, I signed
Rick to a five-year, $27 million deal. I got the owner's private jet to
fly us back to Columbus (from Toronto) once that deal was done
and I remember sitting on the plane looking at Rick thinking, I
just gave that kid twenty-seven million dollars! But it was worth
it, every cent. I fondly remember the last game of the 2003–04

season in Detroit when Rick scored to win a share of the Rocket Richard Trophy as the league's leading scorer as a nineteen-year-old. I was proud of Rick for that accomplishment and we won 4–1 that night. I was excited about the future of the Blue Jackets. Who knew how it would turn out?

When it was all said and done, no one was calling me Trader Sam Pollock for how I managed to get Rick, but I think it all worked out pretty darn well. It was my finest draft day performance!

Trades like the one I made to get Rick, and Burke made to get the Sedins, don't seem to happen anymore. You see teams move up and down in the middle or later in the first round, but you don't see the first overall pick moving. It just doesn't happen, most likely because there is so much hype around that first pick and there haven't been many busts. You feel like you owe it to your fan base to use that pick. And you'd regret forever trading down and missing out on a superstar.

I remember in 2015, when Edmonton won the lottery and Connor McDavid. I was talking with Tim Murray, who was the GM of the Buffalo Sabres at the time, and they got the second pick, who would be Jack Eichel. Buffalo had tanked that year, desperately hoping they would get the first pick and McDavid, who had been playing junior down the road in Erie, Pennsylvania.

I said to Tim, who was a friend, "You're still going to get a really good player in Eichel." Tim, who did a lot of scouting, said to me, "Doug, it's not even close." He was devastated. But that's how the first pick can be that much different from the second or third and there is a tremendous risk in moving it. That's why it hasn't happened since Dudley did it in consecutive years.

It's hard to do it to your marketplace. And it's really hard to go buy a first overall pick. Think about some of those players—Crosby, Ovechkin, Tavares, MacKinnon, McDavid, Matthews. It's hard to walk away and take that risk. For me, I just had to make it happen and was fortunate I could get Rick Nash.

CHAPTER NINE

THE WAR ROOM

DRAFT WEEK IS TRULY THE HIGHLIGHT IN A GM'S YEAR BECAUSE OF HOW IMPORTANT it is for building and improving your team, and hopefully achieving success. It's a long, exhilarating week leading up to two days of great anticipation and excitement and pressure. It's a week during which you can make great things happen for your franchise. Or get left behind.

Typically, the hockey operations staff arrive on the Tuesday of draft week, an energized and excited group. And a sizable group. The GM leads a staff of approximately thirty people, which includes the assistant GM, the director of amateur scouting and his staff (usually ten scouts), an assistant director of hockey operations, the head of the analytics department, key pro scouts in case you make a trade, the NHL coaching staff, and the head coach of your minor-league team (in case trade talks involve minor-league players). The public relations department is also part of the group, as well as the GM's executive assistant. Many teams will also have their team psychologist as part of the entourage.

The week isn't cheap, costing roughly $150,000 for travel, hotel rooms, meals, et cetera. But it's the cost of doing business.

Depending on the team, sometimes the owner will fly in for the draft (more cost), which is a royal pain in the ass because, as the GM, you have to babysit him. Teams that have a separate president of hockey operations can foist the owner off on the president and let the GM focus on the task at hand. Otherwise, the team services person often gets saddled with the unenviable job.

I remember the 2001 draft, when we took goaltender Pascal Leclaire with our first pick. Our owner in Columbus, John H. McConnell, decided he was going to come to the draft in Sunrise, Florida. Our team services guy, who was really busy booking team dinners and all sorts of other things, also had to look after Mr. McConnell and he wasn't too happy about it. Every day he had to book massages for Mr. McConnell in his hotel room. Just one more thing to do!

Upon arrival at the hotel, which is assigned to you by the league and usually has a few other teams staying there, the first order of business is to set up the war room—it's whatever room is adjoining the GM's suite. It is the hub for the week, set up to handle all the staff meetings and prospect interviews. The initial staff meetings will include the GM, the assistant GM, the director of amateur scouting, and his staff. The GM's executive assistant is available to answer all incoming calls from other GMs and team personnel regarding potential trades. Teams are constantly touching base trying to get a feel for what is happening with respect to the draft (movement of picks) and any trades that may be in the works.

Draft week is usually one of the busiest trading weeks of the season. At the 2022 Montreal draft, for instance, on day one there were seven deals involving six players and fifteen draft picks, including six first picks, one of them traded twice. On day two, there were sixteen deals involving six players and thirty-four picks. Some of the deals happen in the days, even hours, before the actual draft. Some happen while the draft is in progress. Things move quickly and you have to be ready to adapt your plans.

It is a luxury to have all your key hockey personnel together in one suite to discuss potential transactions. Essentially, the entire hockey operations department is set up to contemplate ways to improve the team. It's a busy and exciting time, and the days are long and full. I would be up at six or seven in the morning and I'd stay up until at least 2:00 a.m. every night. It's the old cliché, I suppose: You snooze, you lose.

We'd open the suite first thing in the morning and people would be in and out all day and the phone would be ringing day and night. We'd interview twenty to thirty kids, potential second- and third-round picks, whom we didn't get to meet and interview at the draft combine, which is a weeklong gathering of the top prospects who are interviewed and undergo medicals and fitness tests and is typically held in early June in Buffalo, New York. I would come and go from the suite, maybe meeting in the hotel lobby talking to other GMs. We would sit in the suite and shoot the crap. At night we'd sometimes crack open a case of beer, but there wasn't much of that for most of us before the draft. The drinking was saved for the last night when the business was done and (you hoped) you were celebrating a good draft.

Once we had everyone on the ground and the suite set up, the staff would study the final draft list and make any last-minute adjustments based on any new information the scouts had received since the final scouting meetings or the draft combine. Obviously, the kids haven't been playing for a while, since April or May, so their stock can't drop because of on-ice performance. But if the scouts have heard something bad about a kid off the ice, that he got into some sort of trouble or wasn't a good teammate, we will investigate and make adjustments. More often than not, the changes are minimal.

During the initial staff meeting, the final player interviews are set up. Team personnel contact the player agents and schedule the interviews, which for me were usually reserved for the potential first-round picks. Often, for many of the staff, it's the first time to meet our top choices. I would have seen most of the kids play, but it would be the first time that I would talk with them. During the season, my first job as GM every day was to read every report our scouts would send in from games the night before from the NHL, AHL, junior, and college teams. They would be in my computer by midnight. Some players, like Rick Nash, I might meet during the season, but not many. Otherwise, I would know everything else about them from the reports.

The player interviews can be both interesting and bizarre. The strangest one I ever attended was during the 1989 draft in Bloomington, Minnesota. I was an assistant coach with the Washington Capitals, and our assistant GM, the late Jack Button, ran the Capitals' draft for GM David Poile. Jack was as thorough as they came, but the most bizarre meetings I ever sat in usually involved Jack. Now, remember, it was 1989, so the times were definitely different.

During the final interviews Jack would ask the players to drop their pants. I'm not joking. Of course, they didn't drop their underwear. But he was checking to make sure the players' legs were developing: the calves, quadriceps, thighs. And scouts do have a model whereby if, say, a kid is five-foot-eleven today they will project him to grow at least an inch by the time we get him. And if he weighs 180, they project he'll add another 10 pounds. As a young assistant coach, I understood the process, sort of, but to say the players were shocked was an understatement. But Jack didn't leave any stone unturned. Needless to say, that would not happen in today's NHL. Scouts do see the kids in T-shirts and shorts working out at the combine, and that's good enough.

Our first pick that year, nineteenth overall, was a pretty darn good goaltender, Olaf Kolzig, from the Tri-City Americans of the WHL. But we also took a goalie in the second round, thirty-fifth overall, Byron Dafoe from the Portland Winter Hawks. It was at that point that Bryan Murray, our head coach, turned to me and said, "Typical of our team, we've lost faith in Kolzig already." Standard Bryan deadpan.

Those Caps teams were really good back then, but they never found a goaltender to help get them over the playoff hump. Goaltending was always a hot topic. I remember in the first round of the 1989 playoffs we lost to Philadelphia, a team that finished a dozen points behind us. We should have won that series but lost in six games. Afterward, Poile was devastated. Pete Peeters, our goalie, had let in the winning goal from the corner, a Rick Tocchet shot. I remember getting on the bus and we were all crushed by the loss because we were a really good team. The following week, David called us into his office to hash it all out. It was Bryan, myself, and our goaltending coach, Warren Strelow, who was sitting between us. At one point David is sitting at his desk and talking and I look over and Warren is sound asleep. David finally notices and he grabs a *Hockey News* and snaps it on his desk. Warren jumped. I thought we would all get fired for sure. We survived, but not Warren. He was actually a very good coach; he worked with some of the best and was recognized posthumously with the 2022 Lester Patrick award for outstanding service to hockey in the United States, in part for his work with the goalies on the 1980 Miracle on Ice team. But goaltending was an issue for us, which explains why we drafted a couple of them back to back.

Years ago, prior to the combine and the draft week, teams could fly players in for meetings and our fitness staff would run a battery of tests. It was a good opportunity to both see how the players measured up and get to know them more as individuals. While I was in Columbus, before the 2003 draft we flew in Eric Staal and Nathan Horton. We didn't bring in Marc-André Fleury, who turned out to be the first overall pick, because we already had Leclaire and we were not going to take a goalie.

Talk about classy young players. It's no wonder they both went on to have great NHL careers, both winning the Stanley Cup. After watching them a lot during the winter and getting to know them better I was praying we would have a chance to select one or the other. Obviously, we would need a pick in the top three to make that happen. Staal was number one to me, Horton number two.

As usual with the lottery we ended up with the fourth pick. Seriously, we never had any luck in the lottery. But we strongly felt they both had the talent and character to be franchise players. Because we were pretty certain Fleury, Staal, and Horton would go in the top three, we figured next up was CSKA Moscow winger Nikolai Zherdev. We wanted to spend a lot of time with him.

Our meeting with Nik started off with him telling us he wouldn't be available to us at number four. Based on his interviews and his agent Rolly Hedges' discussions with other teams, he was convinced he would be drafted in the top three. In fairness, Nik was rated there in the mid-season rankings and some of my staff had him there, too, so it was possible. I just didn't think so.

Our interview with Nik was challenging because of language issues, even with an interpreter. As the meeting progressed, I asked him what kind of car he owned. He said he had a Mercedes. We were not dealing with a typical draft-eligible player. Nik was an unbelievably talented guy, maybe the most pure-skilled player I ever had, but his interview should have been a warning for me—overall attitude and weirdness. He was very nonchalant compared to the Canadian kids, who are so gung ho.

Nik was convinced he wasn't going to be there at number four, and it seemed he wasn't that interested in meeting with us. Well, we got him at number four and the rest is a story for a later chapter. But those interviews happen for a reason and I should have given the red flags more weight.

Prior to the 2002 draft we interviewed Scottie Upshall, who was a top prospect. Scottie was a six-foot forward with Kamloops, a really good player, and our staff had a lot of time for him. We were focused on getting Rick Nash, but as mentioned, with the number-three pick it took a lot of work to make that happen. And I wasn't certain that deal could happen, so we had to cover all our bases. In the interview with Scottie, I asked him, "What is the difference between you and Rick Nash?" He looked me in the eye and replied, "Four inches. That's the only difference."

Scottie was right that he was six-foot, Rick was six-four. And I loved the kid. He was a terrific player and had a good personality, a really engaging kid. He was a great interview. Nashville took him at number six and he had a terrific, long career. But Nash was the better player!

Another player we liked and whom I enjoyed interviewing and spending time with was Scott Hartnell. He was a hard-nosed winger who played with the Prince Albert Raiders of the WHL. Not only did he become a good NHL player, but he was one of the great personalities in the game. He was taken sixth overall by Nashville in 2000. We took defenseman Rostislav Klesla from Brampton fourth overall. Years later, we had Scott as a guest on the *Hockey Central at Noon* radio show in Toronto. I was talking about the 2000 draft and how much I liked him as a player, but we had decided to pick Klesla instead. He quickly said to me, "And how did that work out for you?" He was pretty quick with the tongue both on and off the ice.

With the interviews you're trying to get to know the kid, get a sense of what kind of teammate he is. You ask him what he thought of the management of his junior team, the coach, his line mates. Ask about his parents. I remember, in 2005, we interviewed Medicine Hat defenseman Kris Russell. His father was a rodeo clown, the guy who runs into the ring to distract the bull after a rider has been tossed. I met both Kris' parents, the nicest people you would ever meet. We're thinking, If Kris has got guts like his father, we want him. He had as much character as any player I have ever had. We took Kris in the third round, sixty-seventh overall. He had a twin brother, Ryan, who played junior in Kootenay. I remember watching them fight each other at center ice. It showed how competitive they were and how much they wanted to win. The two actually played for part of a season together in Columbus after I was gone. The Rangers drafted Ryan, who was a center, in the seventh round (211).

There was a great article about interviews by Joe Smith in *The Athletic*. He told the story of the first time then Tampa GM Steve Yzerman met goaltender Andrei Vasilevskiy on the morning of the 2012 draft in Pittsburgh. When Steve and his scouts walked into the meeting, the big goalie was drawing something on a piece of paper. That year the Lightning had the tenth and nineteenth overall picks, but with drafting Russians, teams wanted to be extra certain the player would eventually come to the NHL so they didn't waste a top pick.

Vasilevskiy told Yzerman he wanted to play in the NHL and after two years he would be playing for the Lightning. You like a player who is confident but not too cocky. Before the interview ended, the Lightning asked Vasilevskiy to show them what he had been drawing: It was a goalie mask with the Lightning logo on the side. Al Murray, the chief scout, had seen the big goalie play for three years and was blown away by his play and the interview, as was Yzerman. They took Vasilevskiy with the nineteenth overall pick and he was, obviously, a key component in Tampa's two Stanley Cup wins.

In 2022, the Toronto Maple Leafs did an interesting thing during their interviews prior to the draft in Montreal. Sportsnet wrote that they would show NHL game videos and ask the prospects questions. The Leafs' top pick that year, Fraser Minten, said, "We'd watch a clip from a breakout or something. A significant play would happen. The screen will go black. And they wanted to hear what you thought happened next to try and test how you see the game." The Leafs were hoping to discover how well the prospects thought out the game.

The interviews are really important to get a great grasp on the kids. And that's where the analytics people have to depend on the scouts; the regional and local guys really know the players, if they have any character issues. At the meetings, you would get the team psychologist involved and you had to weigh what the prospect had to say. In 2001, we were looking at a kid named Kiel McLeod in the second round. He was a six-foot-five center out of Kelowna. Our team psychologist wondered about his committment.

Well, we went ahead and drafted him in the second round. He came to our camp that fall and I went up to Traverse City, Michigan, to watch him in the rookie tournament. I remember Ken Holland saying we (Columbus) had some unbelievable prospects. But I had heard rumbles that McLeod wasn't going to sign with us and was instead going to wait to become a free agent and go to Phoenix, where Mike Barnett, who had been Wayne Gretzky's agent back in the day, was GM. We offered McLeod a $750,000 signing bonus, but when it came time to sign he thanked me, walked out the door, and signed with Phoenix a month or two later. I called Mike and told his agent, Herb Pinder, that I had heard something funny was going on. They thought Phoenix would be a better fit and it was their right to wait until free agency, but it wasn't their right to have that settled well before. As it turned out, McLeod never played a game in the NHL. Our psychologist told us to be careful, which happened a lot. We should have listened.

Again, the final interview is usually the last of many conversations from over the season and it is another useful piece of information. But you have to keep in mind in some cases you have translators involved, other times kids are surrounded in a room and react in different ways—you have to factor all that in. I always believed in interviewing as many prospects as possible because even if you didn't draft them, at least you knew them a little better if their names ever came up in trade talks years later. And something that has changed over the years is the players have become very well briefed and prepared by their agents for the interviews, so sometimes you want to steer away from the obvious questions, and the obvious answers.

I read about one inventive question from the 2022 combine about Swedish defense prospect Calle Odelius and his interview with the Montreal Canadiens. He was reportedly asked, "Would you pick up ten dollars off the toilet seat, or fifty dollars from the toilet?" He apparently said the fifty dollars. Right answer! To me, that says he would do whatever it took, he would pay a price. And he wanted the money.

In the case of the 2022 first overall pick, the Canadiens had an interesting interview with big winger Juraj Slafkovsky from Slovakia. They talked to him about leaving home at age fourteen, having to learn to cook for himself and fend for himself, of how important his family was. As the scouts put it, they were able to learn more about his background and character and learn about him as a person, not just a player.

At the combine, the Habs took Shane Wright, who for a long time was believed to be the top pick, to dinner but not Slafkovsky. After the draft, Slafkovsky said, "The talk to me tasted better than dinner!"

Another interesting interview happened at the 1988 draft. There was a big six-three, 240-pound defenseman named Link Gaetz, who had played in Spokane and was projected to go in the first two rounds. Well, he shows up for the draft sporting two black eyes obtained in a bar fight the night before. Edmonton GM Glen Sather asked him, "Why should I draft you if that's what you're going to look like after a fight? I might as well take the guy you fought." Gaetz, who was at the bar with his brother, replied, "You'd have to use all your picks; there were nine guys we beat up!" The Minnesota North Stars drafted him in the second round, fortieth overall.

Years later, North Stars GM Lou Nanne said, "In the first round we drafted Mike Modano to protect the franchise. In the second round we drafted Link to protect Mike. In the third round we should've drafted a lawyer to protect Link." Sadly, the kid had a troubled career and a troubled life.

Another funny interview story I heard involved Ethan Moreau, who was taken fourteenth overall by Chicago in the 1994 draft and had a good sixteen-year career, mostly with Edmonton. He was interviewed by Boston, which had the twenty-first overall pick. In the interview, the Bruins asked Moreau what number he would wear if they selected him. He said number 4 or number 8. Only problem with the answer is number 4 belonged to Bobby Orr and was retired and number 8 belonged to Cam Neely, who was still playing for the Bruins.

A truly bizarre interview, which has been reported in several places, happened at the 2010 combine involving a player who had been suspended by his team for an off-ice incident. The kid got caught defecating on a car. "We didn't even have to ask," a team executive told *The Athletic*. "He walks in, very confident, sits in the chair, no hello's, no 'how are you doing?,' no breaking into [small talk]. He just said, 'Yup, it's true. I shit on my girlfriend's car.' I've never seen anything like it before and nothing like it since. It was absurd. I mean, he did handle it well for a kid who crapped on a car."

Brian Burke, when he was GM of the Maple Leafs, had an interesting interview in 2012 with top prospect Nail Yakupov. Burke recently told the podcast *Spittin' Chiclets* that after his interview with the Russian right winger there was no way he was going to draft him, even if he fell to fifth overall, which was where the Leafs were drafting. "His draft interview was the worst interview I've ever had in my life. Terrible. He was defiant, obnoxious, and sullen. John Lilley, one of the scouts, . . . almost fought him in the interview, so it was not a good interview." Yakupov went first to Edmonton and never panned out, while the Leafs took defenseman Morgan Rielly, who turned into an excellent player.

In that same 2012 draft, New York Islanders GM Garth Snow reportedly offered all seven of his picks, including fourth overall, to Columbus for the second overall pick, who turned out to be defenseman Ryan Murray of the Everett Silvertips. There has been debate as to whether Snow was hoping Yakupov would fall to second or he wanted Murray. Considering the Isles selected seven defensemen would suggest Snow had Murray in mind.

It's interesting, but recently Yzerman talked about the interview process and how it helps, but watching a player is still most important.

"We don't get to spend as much time as we'd like and I don't know the perfect way of interviewing a player, or assessing a player, his intelligence or hockey sense generally," he said. "I think you just need to watch them over and over, you'll learn a lot about them—intelligence or hockey IQ, I think that's an important part of it. . . . A challenge with the draft, interviewing the players, trying to get to know them, and assess are they smart, are they smart players, you get a lot of real street-smart guys who didn't go to school, who are tremendous hockey players."

After all the player interviews are complete, the list is finalized. The GM and director of amateur scouting will continue to talk until you get to the draft table, but very few, if any, changes are made at that point. I should mention, in all the meetings and conversations leading up to the list being made final, nothing drives a scout nuts like the GM seeing a player once and giving strong opinions after the scouts have had multiple viewings. GMs with a strong scouting background will be more involved in the process. A GM like Jarmo Kekalainen in Columbus spends almost a third of his time scouting, same with a guy like Yzerman in Detroit, who has a major rebuild on his hands. But most don't.

The idea that the GM makes the picks is a myth. But he does typically take the heat for the picks that don't turn out and obviously the boss is responsible for all aspects of the organization.

We bring our pro scouts to the draft for a reason: Their presence is important. While they aren't involved in the actual draft, they are heavily involved in constant discussions regarding trade possibilities. Draft week can be as busy as the trade deadline. To start with, teams are constantly calling the teams that own top picks about the possibility of moving up in the draft, or calling about trades. When all the teams are in the same city it is amazing how active trade talks become. Obviously, the pro scouts are heavily involved in all trade talks. It is also an opportunity to have your pro scouting staff together to meet and finalize plans for the June 30 player buyout deadline and July 1 free agency.

At the 2006 draft, we made the major decision to buy out the final year of veteran center Andrew Cassels' contract. Trust me, one of the toughest jobs as an NHL GM is trading players and notifying them, and an even worse task is telling a player that you are buying him out. I recall leaving the draft war room interviews and calling Andrew and informing him of our decision. It was one of the tougher calls in my career because Andrew was a good person and a great pro. In many cases these calls end a player's career. Andrew played thirty-one games the next season for the Washington Capitals and then his career was finished.

In Andrew's case, the buyout was $950,000 paid out over two years. We felt we could add a younger player at less money and the net difference would be the same cost to our organization. The next call was to my owner, Mr. McConnell. Another tough call. And that didn't go well. Mr. McConnell snapped. He was eighty years old at the time and didn't understand this concept and wasn't going to listen to my explanation. As far as he was concerned, I wasted $950,000 of his money. I guess you would have to agree with him.

Mr. Mac was lucky he didn't have to deal with some of the buyouts other owners did. I could only imagine telling him, for instance, what Philadelphia did in 2013, buying out goaltender Ilya Bryzgalov for a whopping $23 million, the largest buyout in NHL history. Two seasons after signing him to a nine-year, $51 million deal, they decided to part ways. I remember reading that Flyers GM Paul Holmgren called it a "very difficult decision." No kidding. The $23 million is being paid out over fourteen years. Buyouts have become pretty commonplace in today's

NHL and I shake my head when I see the media portray them as being a great way to get cap relief, versus it being a major mistake by the GM. I would absolutely hate making some of those calls— to the player and the owner.

Another whopper of a buyout involved the Toronto Maple Leafs and Columbus, after I was gone. The Leafs moved forward David Clarkson, who had five years and $27.5 million left on his deal, to the Blue Jackets in exchange for center Nathan Horton, the same Nathan Horton I was hoping to draft but who went third overall to Florida. It was widely believed that Horton's career was over because of a back injury. He had five years left with a $5.3 million cap hit annually and the contract wasn't insured. So, Columbus was paying him not to play and really couldn't afford to keep doing that. In this case, the Leafs wanted to move Clarkson and could afford to eat the Horton deal and get long-term injury cap relief. And Columbus at least got a player (briefly) for the same money they were paying. That's one of the great misses of the salary cap: There are still ways for rich teams to eat money and get around cap issues.

After all that, the interviews, the finalizing of the draft list, the strategizing and days of discussion with the scouting staff, it's go time. After working late into the night hashing out final details for the biggest day of the year, we would meet for a breakfast meeting at 9:00 a.m. The entire draft staff attends and the GM and director of amateur scouting give a pep talk to the group, talking about the thousands of miles they had traveled, thanking them for all the hard work they had put in, and that today it would all be worthwhile. This is a huge day for the team, but also for the scouts. We also remind them that today is about team first, so not every scout is going to get their guy!

We make our picks off the one hundred names on our list. Round one is typically held one night, rounds two through seven the next day. After the first round, we reconvene in the war room to focus on the next day. And there is usually lots of trade talk. With my teams, the director of amateur scouting would make the call on moving down in the draft order, I would make the call on moving up. If, say, Don Boyd said we could move down and get two extra picks, we would discuss it and make the call. And I would never move up, like we did for Rick Nash, without first having a staff discussion. I had the final say, but I wanted to know what my people were thinking. It only makes sense to use that aggregate brainpower.

Each year a big topic is always drafting by either position or best player, if a prospect isn't both. Drafting by positional need can get you in trouble. For instance, in the 2018 draft, with the third pick and in need of a center, the Montreal Canadiens selected Finnish center Jesperi Kotkaniemi, who was okay, but the Habs passed on left winger Brady Tkachuk, who went fourth to Ottawa and is the type of player every team wants. Luckily for the Habs, Carolina signed Kotkaniemi to an offer sheet; Montreal didn't match and they were able to move on from an underwhelming player, who signed a whopper of a deal with the Canes a year later. The kid struggled in Montreal and never became the number one center they had projected him to be.

As for who sits around the draft table, I've seen tables with as many as twenty people and as few as a dozen. But for sure, at one end of the table, facing the stage, you have the GM, assistant GM, director of amateur scouting, and on either side his assistant and the hockey operations manager, who works the computer, which is linked to the league's system. With the computer, you send in your pick and the league confirms the pick is valid before you head to the podium. That end of the table is where the phone is located for obvious reasons and all key trade discussions are held and draft decisions made. Most often it's the GM who will announce the first pick; subsequent picks are usually announced by the director of amateur scouting.

The next group at the table is the organization's key scouts. They are located close enough so the director and assistant director can constantly talk to them regarding decisions in their scouting region. The table also includes the team executive assistant, PR director, and head coach. The head of pro scouting is usually at the table in case there is trade talk. The remainder of the staff is located in a luxury box and available via phone for any questions. The assistant coaches are available to be used as seat fillers, just like the Oscars!

The GM's end of the table really is the hub of activity. Calls are coming in; they're tracking lists; there's a ton of talk. There are other teams' tables on either side in most cases, and lots of tables nearby, and I've been asked before, "How worried are you about being overheard, giving a secret away?" When you're on the phone, you're far enough away that no one else is going to hear the conversation. In my time in Columbus, most of the calls I got at the table were GMs looking to move up and get my pick. I remember Calgary calling with an offer of a first pick for goaltender Marc Denis. At the time I had Ron Tugnutt, who had an unbelievable year, but we thought he was starting to fade. We had drafted Pascal Leclaire. I was really nervous to make a move on Denis because he was a hot commodity and he looked like he'd be a star. I turned down the offer, but those are the sorts of decisions you have to make, often on the spot.

After two virtual drafts during the pandemic in 2020 and 2021, the league returned to in-person in Montreal in 2022. But surprisingly, there were a lot of GMs, including Yzerman, pushing for the league to go back to the virtual format. It's actually what the NFL and NBA do, with teams holed up in their home offices. It is a much more affordable, comfortable, and private arrangement. In that scenario, the top prospects would be in the same city in a banquet room, called to the stage after the picks were called in.

I understand teams preferring to be together in their home office, but I am mixed on this. I loved it when we hosted the draft in Columbus, to see how important it was to the city and how exciting it was for the fans. Being in Montreal in 2022, to see a full building and all that excitement with the Canadiens holding the first overall pick, that was special. Maybe I overvalue that, but I still like it. The drafts I was at were important to the host team and city. I always enjoyed the atmosphere in the rink and the city and it was great to see personnel from other teams face-to-face.

Sitting at the table can alternately be exhilarating and excruciating, the latter when you have your eye on a player and you are waiting, holding your breath when the picks ahead of you are announced. There can be a lot of tension at the table.

When I was with Florida, in the 1996 draft we desperately wanted to get Zdeno Chara, all six feet nine, 250 pounds of him. We had traded our second-round pick to get Ray Sheppard for our Cup run that year; otherwise we likely would have used it to select Chara. Our guys really wanted Chara and we prayed he would get to the third round, which he did. But the Islanders took him at fifty-sixth. We had the sixtieth pick and got defenseman Chris Allen, who played two NHL games. Our guys were devastated we didn't get Chara. We paid a price to get Sheppard and he was worth the price; we just couldn't do the daily double and get Chara, too.

When we were scouting Chara, who played junior in Prince George, British Columbia, he got into a fight with a tough winger from Portland named Joey Tetarenko, whom we ended up selecting in the fourth round that year. I talked to Joey after and he said he learned a valuable lesson that night fighting Chara: Never fight a guy whose arms are longer than your legs! What a career Chara went on to have.

I remember when I was an assistant coach with the St. Louis Blues, sitting at the table in 1987. Our GM, Ron Caron, had traded defenseman Ric Nattress to the Flames. Ron, who was busy at the table, had his executive assistant walk to the end of the table where I was sitting and she said, "Mr. Caron wants you to phone Ric and tell him he was just traded." Nice job for a first-year assistant coach making $35,000 a year. Obviously, I've had to make many of those calls over my twenty-two-year NHL career, but that call was without a doubt my toughest. And it doesn't get much easier.

It's amazing, as the draft unfolds, how similar other teams' lists are to yours. It's uncanny. Having said that, once in a while a bizarre pick happens to turn everything upside down. I vividly recall the 2004 draft, when the Coyotes, with the fifth overall pick, shocked the draft floor. There was a hush in the arena when Phoenix selected forward Blake Wheeler, a big winger out of a prep school in Minnesota. Blake had played in the USHL with Green Bay and scored nineteen goals and many were questioning the pick. Most teams had him rated in the second round. There was a lot of head-scratching and muttering among scouts. The

Coyotes' GM, Mike Barnett, was so livid at the reaction that he ultimately fired a number of his key scouts.

Wow, what a lesson that was about respecting other teams' selections. Blake played the next three seasons with the University of Minnesota and became a star. As it turned out, he refused to sign with Phoenix and later signed a free-agent contract with Boston. He became a really good NHL player and eventually captain of the Winnipeg Jets. Respect the opposition, and respect your scouts.

Then there is the Jarome Iginla story. He was part of the 1995 draft class, in which defenseman Bryan Berard was selected first overall by the New York Islanders. I was with the Panthers at the time, sitting at the table. With the tenth overall pick, we took Czech winger Radek Dvorak and our people were pretty pleased. He ended up playing more than twelve hundred games with a variety of teams, including ours, but he was never a star. With the eleventh pick the Dallas Stars selected Iginla out of Kamloops. That year he was a point-a-game player in junior, but he had a breakout season the next year. As it turned out, Jarome never played a minute for the Stars; he was traded five days before Christmas, along with Corey Millen, to Calgary for the rights to Joe Nieuwendyk, who was in a contract standoff with the Flames. It was a great deal for both teams. Dallas ended up winning a Stanley Cup with Joe a few seasons later and Jarome had a Hall of Fame career with the Flames.

But when the Iginla pick was made by Dallas, there were folks at our table laughing, shaking their heads. They couldn't believe Dallas took him where they did. We had him ranked twenty-eighth. Again, respect the other teams because with almost all the picks, there's no sure thing. Looking back, obviously, our guys would have liked a do-over. Several teams would have liked a do-over, because there were a lot of misses early in that first round before the Stars made their choice.

Heading into the 2003 draft, our Columbus scouts were excited about a big, raw defenseman playing with Kelowna. In seventy games, he had two goals, sixteen assists, and 167 penalty minutes. But our scouts guaranteed me we could get him in the third round and our Western scouts, Sam McMaster and John Williams, wanted assurance from me they could use that pick to select him. They were elated when I said yes. But the best-laid plans . . . In the second round, with the forty-ninth pick, Nashville selected that kid: Shea Weber. Our staff was sick when they heard. We had selected Dan Fritsche, a center out of Sarnia, with the forty-sixth pick. He was a pretty good player, but he wasn't Weber.

The draft table is an exciting place, with the selections and trade talks and quick decisions that have to be made. At the 2006 draft in Vancouver, we had the sixth pick and the Islanders had number seven. That was a terrific draft class and as usual we were picking too low to get a franchise player. Man, we needed to lose more games that year, but that's the conundrum you face as a GM: Sometimes when it comes to winning, you're damned when you do, damned when you don't. But what a group that year. With the first pick, St. Louis selected defenseman Erik Johnson. At that point, I'm praying that one of Jordan Staal, Jonathan Toews, or Nicklas Backstrom will fall to six.

I would have had a better chance of winning the lottery, any lottery, and we know what kind of luck we had with that in Columbus. Pittsburgh took Staal second (I still had hope), Chicago took Toews third (still hoping), and Washington took Backstrom fourth. I was so disappointed. We desperately needed one of those big three centers. Boston took winger Phil Kessel fifth and we wound up selecting center Derick Brassard out of Drummondville sixth. Derick was a solid pick. He had a very good career, playing more than one thousand games, and is an amazing person, but we desperately needed and missed out on a franchise player because we were picking sixth.

It's really hard to lose a lot, but it's also really hard to pick sixth and somehow be able to move forward as a team.

In that same draft, with the seventh pick, there was tremendous pressure on the Islanders to take center Peter Mueller from the Everett Silvertips. But GM Neil Smith, who had a terrific scouting résumé earlier with the Islanders and the Red Wings, instead took winger Kyle Okposo from Des Moines of the USHL. Well, the crowd in Vancouver started booing. Everett isn't far from Vancouver and there were a lot of Mueller fans present. Mueller was selected next by Phoenix.

A few picks later, Neil came over to our table and asked if we could talk. That isn't unusual, it happens all the time, but it's usually about a potential trade. When the television cameras catch you talking it starts a buzz. Well, Neil didn't want to make a trade. He told me that his owner, Charles Wang, was upset with him because of the Okposo pick and with them getting booed. Wang thought Neil had made a bad selection. Neil asked me if I could wait ten minutes or so, then walk over to his table and tell him what a great pick he had made, that we loved the kid as a player and had made a very difficult decision in not taking him. Of course, I was to make sure that Charles Wang heard the conversation. I did it. Sometimes you have to help a fellow GM with his owner. Neil certainly would have done the same for me. And Neil had made the right choice.

Obviously, all the glitz and glamour and excitement come in the first round. But at the table, we are acutely aware there are six more rounds and more often than not the seventh round is as intense as the early rounds. It's always crazy. As you get closer to the end of the draft, the regional scouts are clamoring to get one of their recommended players selected. Everyone has a voice.

There are many stories about star players who were drafted late, such as Henrik Zetterberg, taken in the seventh round, 210th overall, by Detroit in 1999. That draft was nine rounds, but you get the idea. And there was Jonathan Ericsson and Patric Hornqvist. Both were the last player selected in their respective drafts—Ericsson, 291st to Detroit in 2002; Hornqvist, 230th to Nashville in 2005. A health issue curtailed Ericsson's career, but he was a good defenseman, and Hornqvist won multiple Stanley Cups with Pittsburgh. Last overall!

You would be amazed by the panic at the table to acquire extra sixth- or even seventh-round picks. The scouts push hard because they believe in certain kids and they think we can make a steal. Take the late John Ferguson Sr. when he worked for Ottawa. At the 1994 draft, when it came to the sixth round, there was a huge argument at the Senators table, according to *Ottawa Sun* reporter Bruce Garrioch. The Senators had already taken two Europeans, Radek Bonk and Stan Neckar, and there was debate at the table about taking a third. Fergie believed in a kid and heatedly insisted that GM Randy Sexton take him. The pick wasn't a sure thing, but Daniel Alfredsson turned out to be a Hall of Famer.

"This pick was an out of the park home run," John Ferguson Jr., in management with Arizona, told Garrioch years later. "There's different ways about making those decisions and, ultimately, it does come down to the decision-maker. If you're the decision-maker, at that point of the draft, with only a few picks left, you want them to be banging the table."

I remember a couple of phone calls I made to acquire seventh-round picks because my scouts were so excited about prospects. One was to Ken Holland, when he was with Detroit, and the other was to Tim Murray, when he was with Anaheim. I knew both were avid golfers. Typically, the deal would be to exchange a seventh pick this year for a seventh next year. To twist their arms, I would offer them each a round of golf at my owner's private club, which Mr. McConnell founded—the Double Eagle Golf Club was consistently rated as one of the top one hundred courses in the United States. Both guys jumped at the offer. My scouts were thrilled; Kenny and Tim were thrilled. Win, win.

One aspect of the draft that is sometimes overlooked is that for every kid who has a dream come true that weekend, there's another whose hopes are crushed. Sitting at the table, you can't help but notice all the young players in the stands with their parents and families waiting and hoping as the picks come and go and they're not selected. The disappointment is overwhelming. Trust me, you think about those kids when you're at the table, getting deeper into the draft. You hope agents would tell kids who are not guaranteed of being selected to stay home, but that's a tough call, too.

In 2001, I remember seeing fellow NHL coach Rick Bowness sitting in the stands with his son, Ryan, who was a right winger with the Brampton Battalion. It got to the eighth round (there were nine rounds that year) and I asked our staff about Ryan and got mixed reviews. Great character, skating was an issue, but overall our guys felt that he had only a slight chance to play in the NHL. It isn't very often that the GM makes the decision after the first round, but I made the call to select Ryan with our eighth-round pick, 236th. And I was thrilled to do it.

Ryan never played in the NHL. He went to St. Mary's University and played a handful of games one season in the East Coast league. But Ryan went on to become the chief pro scout with the Penguins and in 2022 was hired as assistant GM in Ottawa, where his father once coached. Ryan is well respected around the league and, to be quite honest, I often think of that selection and hope in some small way it helped his career. You can't let emotions impact your decisions all the time, but sometimes it feels like the right thing to do. And that was one of them.

The big moment of the big day for the first-round players, but also for the GM and the staff, is the call to the podium. It's an exciting moment for the franchise. Draft day is about hope and every team is hoping they are acquiring a player who can change the fortunes of the franchise. Typically, for that first pick, the entourage onstage consists of the GM, the assistant GM, the director of amateur scouting and his assistant, the scout from the area where the first pick played, and often the head coach.

These days, the owners seem to be making more and more appearances. And in some cases, such as Edmonton, the owner will bring along one of his kids. We've watched Oilers owner Daryl Katz's son, Harrison, grow up before our eyes from draft to draft. My son, Clark, was my runner at the table. He would take our slip with the player's name to the NHL's central registry and he'd get us food and coffee, but he never made it onstage.

One detail you had to have figured out before the draft was to make sure you had several players' names on Velcro nameplates ready to put on the backs of the sweaters for the photo op on the podium. We usually had three names ready and everyone behind the scenes was told to keep quiet. I always announced the first pick at the podium. I never wrote down anything for announcing the pick, which could have been risky business. A lot of fans will recall the 2006 draft in Vancouver when Flyers president and legend Bobby Clarke was announcing their first pick. Bobby didn't have any notes and he started, "The Flyers, with the twenty-second pick of the first round, select . . ." And then there was silence. He turned to the staff and asked, "What's his name?" He'd blanked and forgotten the Flyers were selecting Claude Giroux. A great pick, by the way. We have all envisioned that scene happening to us and we all felt for Bob, but it just shows you even a great one like Bobby Clarke could get caught up in the excitement. Although a story has made the rounds that Bob was pissed off at the time because Los Angeles had made a trade to get a second selection in the first round, number seventeen overall, and used it to select center Trevor Lewis, whom the Flyers liked and hoped to get at twenty-two. Bob was pissed because he thought Ron Hextall, who a few weeks earlier had left the Flyers as assistant GM to take the same job with the Kings, had "stolen" their pick. But it turned out pretty well for the Flyers.

Walking up to the podium for the first time was definitely a career highlight for me and an experience I will always treasure. I vividly remember in 2000 in Calgary walking up with Mr. McConnell and the feeling I was experiencing being an NHL GM of an expansion team and making the first-ever selection in franchise history. After sixteen years in hockey, I was realizing that dream. And I remember that draft like it was yesterday.

The Islanders and Atlanta had the first two picks based on their finish the previous season. Minnesota and Columbus both came into the NHL together in 2000, and the league used a coin toss to determine who had the third pick. That was a big coin toss that we lost, the start of a lot of bad luck involving the draft lottery. It was disappointing to say the least. Minnesota, our biggest rival, would select ahead of us. The top four prospects in that draft were winger Dany Heatley, who was playing at Wisconsin; goalie Rick DiPietro, who was at Boston University; Slovakian forward Marian Gaborik; and defenseman Rostislav Klesla, who was with Brampton of the OHL.

Prior to the draft, we had made a trade to acquire former first-round pick and World Junior star goaltender Marc Denis from Colorado for a second-round pick. He was going to be our goalie of the future and he was projected to be a star. Because we had him, we didn't have any interest in DiPietro, so our focus was on getting one of Heatley, Gaborik, or Klesla. At 2:00 a.m. the night before the draft, chief scout Don Boyd called me to tell me a reliable source had told him the Islanders were taking DiPietro. That made me sleep a little better.

On draft day morning, we heard rumors that Atlanta with the second pick was torn between Heatley and Klesla. Boyd loved Gaborik, and after watching him a lot over the previous two years we really wanted him. As we thought, DiPietro went first to the Isles, but Heatley went second and Gaborik third. We got Rusty Klesla. Our people liked him a lot and felt he would be a great NHLer. It was disappointing not to get Gaborik, but we were pleased with getting Klesla. And he had a solid twelve-year NHL career, which was cut short by injuries. We certainly hoped he would be an NHL star. Nevertheless, walking up to the podium to make the first-ever selection in Columbus Blue Jackets history was still a very proud moment and an exciting time in my life.

The next most exciting draft moment was at the 2002 draft in Toronto when we moved from number three to first overall, finalizing the deal just hours before the draft. In one of the greatest hockey cities in the world, I announced that Rick Nash was the first overall pick of the Blue Jackets, in his hometown, in front of his family and friends. An unforgettable moment for him and for me. It was an amazing thrill for all our staff, our entire organization.

On day two, after the first round, teams don't go to the podium; they instead announce their picks from the draft table and the kids come over to get at least a team ball cap, maybe a sweater, although these days every pick gets a sweater; they just don't all get nameplates. Luc Robitaille, who was taken in the ninth round by the LA Kings in the 1984 draft (the Mario Lemieux draft), sat with his father through all those rounds and finally heard his name called. He headed from the seats high in the stands in Montreal down to the floor, but the police wouldn't let him through. An executive recognized him and cleared the way with the cops, but when he got to the Kings table he said there was no one there. Finally, the public relations guy came by, asked who he was, and looked under the table, but there weren't any hats left. So, he took a team pin off his suit and gave it to Luc—who went on to a Hall of Fame career!

Once the draft is over, the scouting staff starts working on invites to the development camp, which starts the next week. Players on the list who weren't drafted are priorities and you immediately get in touch with them and their agents.

The job of a scout has become an eleven-month grind, with long seasons and lots of travel, much of it on the road in the dead of winter, eating arena food while watching tournaments. After development camp, the scouts get a break. For the GM and staff, preparations continue for buyouts and free agency and signing season.

Once the draft is done, that final day, it is a time for all team personnel to meet the draft picks, their parents, and families in the arena suite. It's a great time, another highlight, as you get to feel the genuine excitement of the kids and their families from being drafted into the National Hockey League. A dream come true for the players, and a weekend that is vital to the future of the team, because scouting and drafting is the lifeblood of a successful team.

And, after a long week, a long season, it's time to finally enjoy a beer!

CHAPTER TEN
ANALYTICS

AN NHL HEAD SCOUT, WHO WILL REMAIN NAMELESS FOR REASONS YOU WILL SOON understand, once said to me, "Doug, the day I want to get fired is the day I will tell you the truth about analytics, because I know if I say anything, I'll get fired that afternoon."

You can't believe the number of times I have heard that same sentiment from so many different hockey people: scouts, coaches, GMs, even team presidents.

"I'll talk off the record, but I can't let my owner know what I'm really thinking."

Analytics is hockey's great divide.

I'm not overstating it. Analytics is polarizing many front offices. And that isn't discussed, at least publicly, or sometimes even within the walls of the organization. For the moment, the analytics folks have the ear of ownership in virtually every NHL city (and no doubt in the minors and juniors). It's the shiny new toy. One former NHL GM is convinced he was fired because the head of analytics had the owner's ear. It's still a relatively new tool and the owners, as we have talked about, are always looking for the quick fix to make their franchise a winner and, daresay, increase its value. Trade the first-round pick? Okay. Let's just win. Follow the analytics data? Okay. Let's just win.

Perhaps the best line about analytics and its role in the game (at least the most amusing line) came from Brian Burke, former president of hockey operations of the Pittsburgh Penguins.

"Analytics are like a lamppost to a drunk," he said. "Useful for support, but not for illumination."

When he was with the Calgary Flames for five years, starting in 2013, Burke was open about his thoughts on the subject.

"I'm not a big analytics guy," he said. "I think analytics are useful and important, but in our organization they're the third tool we use to evaluate players. The number one criterion we have is experienced scouts watching them play, and the things you see in a game that don't show up on a computer. A guy makes a mistake, comes off. You see a captain lean over and say something to him. See a coach bark at a guy. Does he slump? What's his body language? How does he warm up? Is he intense? All the stuff a computer is never going to show you. A computer just registers a blocked shot, it doesn't show you that this guy dove headfirst to get it. Our sports psychologist is really important, what can we do research-wise to find about this player as a person? We think we have the best analytics guy in hockey in Chris Snow, but we don't brag about it like some teams do and it's certainly not our primary focus in assessing player talent."

Since leaving the Flames, spending a couple of seasons in broadcasting, then joining the Penguins before departing in April

2023, Burke warmed up a little to analytics, but the pecking order hasn't changed.

"Scouts are critical, the eyeballs on the player," he said. "Research, background, siblings, school, what his family members are doing, the sketch of the person—they are all important. The regional scouts know the players well. We also include a psychological evaluation as part of the research process. Third on the list is analytics information on the players.

"If the analytics staff don't like a player, we would talk with our scouts. But they may drop the player by a round. The analytics staff relays information to the scouts during the season on players on our preliminary lists. The analytics department does not do a draft list."

There aren't a lot of hockey people willing to be so candid.

When Jimmy Rutherford got hired by the Vancouver Canucks as their president in December 2021, he was asked if he had learned anything from his signings in Pittsburgh, specifically Jack Johnson and Erik Gudbranson, signings that were panned by the analytics community.

"I use analytics a lot and I really like it," he said. "But it isn't what I make my decision on and you make hockey decisions for different reasons."

When he fortified his front office in Vancouver, Jimmy wanted to add people with different backgrounds. One of his first moves was to add to his analytics department.

Ron Francis, GM of the Seattle Kraken, made a similar move entering his team's second season on the ice. He promoted Alexandra Mandrycky, who was their director of hockey strategy and research for three seasons, to assistant GM focusing on analytics.

"I think that any tools you can use to help you become better, you'd be foolish not to use them," Francis told the *Seattle Times*. "We're trying to be the best we can be and using all the people that we have with expertise to make us better. Whether that's scouts in the field or people looking at data or a computer base, I think everyone can help."

I agree fully. Quite often you hear the phrase "it's another tool in the tool belt" and that's what it is. Or if you're making a fine meal, you need more than one ingredient to make it good. The challenge, though, for teams is to find a way for everyone to get along. There have been too many extremists on the scouting side, and too many extremists on the analytics side. Finding the middle is the key. The title for this chapter could easily be "Stats versus Scouts."

That's essentially what it has become with many teams, an internal battle between the analytics and scouting departments. In some cases, there is harmony of sorts, such as Mandrycky and the Kraken. She has managed to get the analytics and scouting departments working in harmony.

"When I reflect upon what I think has made us successful, what I consider to be a success is that nobody tries to push us out of a room," she said. "We're respected by everyone in this organization and that's the way I think it should be."

"She doesn't come in and throw the hammer down and say, 'This is how it has to be,'" said Francis. "In a lot of our discussions we don't just talk about analytics. We talk about players. We talk about things we're looking for in players. And if there's a difference of opinion—the numbers say this on Player X, but the scouts say this on Player X—it's also about going back to the research and development team to take another look. We ask the scouts to understand analytics. But we also need the research team to understand the scouts."

Of course, in some cases they only co-exist but don't mesh. One director of analytics I know said, "The scouts better buy in because if they don't they'll be washed out to sea." Strong words. He is right about having to buy in, but that has to be a two-way street. Or should be. The two sides shouldn't each feel challenged by the other.

Another person, a director of amateur scouting, told me, "Our organization's first analytics hire was an idiot. He constantly talked down to scouts and they actually hated him. Our GM said, 'Get him out.' The new guy has a hockey background, some scouting experience, and the staff respects and listen to him. The key thing is attitudes on both sides."

An assistant GM told the story of being at the draft table and when the selection was made the analytics person was pissed. It wasn't the pick he wanted. Management watched and was not pleased he was pouting at the table. The team spoke with him and said if it ever happened again he would be replaced, adding, "You will never be a final decision maker with this organization." In fairness, I've seen scouts pout as well, but you get the idea. Since then, the analytics person has developed a great delivery, is passionate but not a pouter, and is used often to present information to the staff. Attitude and delivery go a long way in getting staff to buy in.

It's clear that the analytics group is in the driver's seat with a lot of teams, whether it's about drafting, trading for players, or how the team plays and utilizes its players. In most cases, this emphasis on analytics is driven by the owner. But not everyone is buying in.

"The analytics guy would come by my office around four o'clock on a game day and have my lineup mapped out and all these stats and how we were supposed to react to different situations during the game," said one coach, who will be a Hall of Famer. "I'd say thanks and when he was out the door, I'd pitch the package in the garbage can. It was reams and reams of paper."

Another team I know hired a university student to translate the complicated analytics reports to the coaching staff and some of the scouts. In some instances, coaches didn't want the information; in others, they didn't understand it all and how it should impact their decision making.

Baseball manager Joe Maddon, who was a big proponent of analytics, once said he wanted the information, but just "give me the time, I don't want to know how to build the watch." He also didn't want analytics people in his clubhouse, dugout, or meetings.

The book *Moneyball: The Art of Winning an Unfair Game*, written by Michael Lewis about the 2002 Oakland A's and GM Billy Beane, is essentially a deep dive into the A's and their decision to adapt analytics into their approach to building a team, in this case one with a small budget. It was actually Beane's predecessor Sandy Alderson who first started using sabermetrics, the use of statistical analysis, to compare and value players. It was Beane who took it to another level.

Regarding their ability to pick talent, Beane said, "We are not very good at this. I can't walk into a high-school baseball game and say he's going to be a pro even with all my scouting experience." He said it was out of desperation that he came to use data even more. Fifty rounds of baseball drafts typically produce one player. "Could we get two players?" asked Beane. His motto became: "Can't measure, won't invest."

Despite a limited budget, from 2000 to 2003, the A's made it to the American League Division Series. They lost each year, but they got there. In 2006, they finally won a series.

"It's all about evaluating skills and putting a price on them," Beane once said. "Thirty years ago, stockbrokers used to buy stock strictly by feel. Let's put it this way, anyone can choose a fund manager who manages their retirement [money] by gut instinct, or one who chooses by research and analysis. I know which way I'd choose."

Beane became a hot commodity and in 2002 the Boston Red Sox made him a $12.5 million offer. He turned them down. Now, I would question his analytics in that particular situation! Of course, he did receive a share of the A's ownership, so maybe he had it figured out. Then again, the A's had a stretch of seasons in which they failed to make the playoffs, and never did win the World Series under Beane, which suggests to me that analytics is a piece of the pie, not the whole pie.

"Pure analytics have never won a World Series and never will in my lifetime," added Burke. "So much for *Moneyball*."

In terms of hockey, analytics is not entirely new. One of the pioneers of the use of statistics and video was the late NHL coach Roger Neilson, who was ahead of his time. Some of the stats he used, such as scoring chances and plus-minus, among others, had been around but not used by many teams. They are still used today. But the statistical areas have been enhanced: They're now known as advanced stats, which refers to metrics and theories and concepts that go beyond the traditional stats. There are things like Corsi, which counts all shots on goal, missed shots, and blocked shot attempts. And Fenwick, which is like Corsi but without the blocked shots. At first, in early analytics, Corsi and Fenwick were all we heard about, but you don't hear about them as much now. There is a new wave of analytics, categories such as expected goals, zone entries and exits, puck possession—the list goes on. And they can all be very useful.

Different teams use analytics in different ways with respect to the draft. Some include them in meetings when they're assembling their draft list; some don't. Some don't allow the analytics folks and scouts to talk to each other during the season, while others have them in communication throughout the year. Some have the two sides do separate draft lists, then compare. Some don't have the analytics people in the room when the final lists are made but still value their research. The Dallas Stars send the analytics staff out in the field from time to time to develop a feel for the "eye" test, to understand what the scouts are seeing and feeling.

Among the front-runners in analytics were the Maple Leafs with the hiring of Kyle Dubas as assistant GM in summer 2014, and in 2015 the Arizona Coyotes with John Chayka and the Carolina Hurricanes with Eric Tulsky. Tulsky was a former chemist who became a very popular advanced stats blogger. Those three hirings created a buzz in the hockey world. And the media hype that followed was out of control.

In many ways, it figured that analytics would find its way to the NHL. Everyone is always looking for an edge. And Gary Bettman's new breed of owners (many of them Wall Street millionaires or billionaires) ran businesses that relied on data; they believed the predictability that analytics brought would do the same for their new business, their hockey team.

The media, for the most part, completely endorsed this new wave of thinking: the New School of Analytics versus the Old

School of Scouting. Perhaps some members of the media were excited by dreams of following their cohorts' (analytics bloggers') footsteps in finding jobs with NHL teams. Some teams have even taken to calling their new hires "scientists."

"Analytics can be a useful tool in today's game and these people have done a good job creating a niche for themselves in the NHL, but calling themselves scientists and engineers is stretching things a bit too far," said former goaltender Tim Bernhardt, who served eighteen seasons with the Dallas Stars, a dozen as director of amateur scouting, and, ironically, seven seasons with the analytical Coyotes, five as chief scout.

As one NHL executive said to me: "Some owners want to become hockey experts and they see this [analytics] as a way to accomplish that."

The Leafs, Coyotes, and Hurricanes were front-runners in terms of setting up analytics departments, but there are mixed reviews as to the results they have produced, not that you can pin everything on them. The Leafs, for instance, improved steadily from 2016, after a couple of rock-bottom finishes. But it appears that the building of the core of the team through the draft had very little to do with analytics.

Auston Matthews was selected first overall, a huge lottery win, a no-brainer selection. Mitch Marner was taken fourth overall, William Nylander eighth (Dave Nonis was GM), and Morgan Rielly fifth. The other key core piece is captain John Tavares, acquired via free agency ($77 million).

How much did analytics influence those moves, or were they obvious to a scout's eyes? Those top picks were all pretty much obvious choices, although there was debate as to whether to take Marner or defenseman Noah Hanifin, who went fifth to

Carolina. And was that call made by former assistant GM Mark Hunter? Most think so because he drafted Marner in junior, in London. Hunter left the Leafs when Dubas was named GM. There was a debate of sorts as well in 2014, when the Leafs took Nylander ahead of tough forward Nick Ritchie, who went tenth to Anaheim. Again, they made the right choice and even went so far as to sign Ritchie as a free agent a few years later, although that didn't work out. In fairness, the Leafs and Hurricanes have used analytics to help improve their depth lines via signings and trades and have strong teams. Alex Kerfoot is an example, with his numbers thought to be a perfect fit with the bottom six with the Leafs.

With respect to the Coyotes, well, the jury is still out, I suppose. The team never made the playoffs until Chayka's final season before departing. Bill Armstrong has taken over and while employed by the St. Louis Blues, where he rose to assistant GM and director of scouting for their Stanley Cup–winning team, Armstrong utilized analytics and felt it was a valuable tool paired with scouts' knowledge. With Arizona, Armstrong stockpiled picks. Heading into the 2023 draft, he had a total of twenty-one picks in the first three rounds of that draft and the two to follow: four first-rounders, nine seconds, and eight thirds.

The Hurricanes have made the playoffs from 2019 through 2023 with a combination of good, young talent maturing and a world-class coach in Rod Brind'Amour, who was offered an amazing deal by the Seattle Kraken, from former Canes GM Ron Francis, but he chose to stay. Under Tulsky, the Canes analytics department are key decision makers in all parts of the organization. No deals are made without the approval of Tulsky's department. For instance, the acquisition of defenseman Dougie

Hamilton was heavily weighted by numbers (he left as an unrestricted free agent to New Jersey).

With respect to drafting, Tulsky was asked by the blog site Canes & Coffee if the draft strategy was to opt for "high upside-skill players at every stage and avoid safe low ceiling picks."

"In the NFL, a team will be looking at a twenty-three-year-old who's going to play for them next year, the scout's job is mostly about projecting how his skills will translate," said Tulsky. "But in the NHL, we're drafting an eighteen-year-old—in addition to estimating how his skills will translate, our amateur scouting group has the daunting task of projecting what he will look like after five years of development. Even the top pick in the draft isn't safe. It might be a reasonably safe bet that he'll play in the NHL, but he has a long way to go to become the player you need him to be. There's a huge range of possible outcomes for every player in the draft and the goal isn't to pick a player with a high floor or a high ceiling, it's to think about all of a player's possible outcomes and pick someone who would be a good bet."

You certainly can't blame analytics for the issues these three teams have dealt with and you also can't say analytics alone made them contenders—through drafts, signings, or trades.

"I'm someone who doesn't really like the term 'analytics,'" said Montreal Canadiens assistant GM John Sedgwick. "I think if you replaced it with 'information' it wouldn't ever be viewed in a negtive way."

Sedgwick was promoted in February 2022 and part of his responsibility was to grow an analytics department. The Canadiens hired Chris Boucher, who had been with the sports analytics company Sportlogiq and had been a pro scout with San Jose for two seasons, as their first-ever director of hockey analytics. Chris is a bright, sensible, solid guy. The Canadiens scouts will tell you that Chris can explain the mathematics in hockey language and is a believer that the numbers can confirm what the eyes are seeing. Like many, he believes the math can help define the draft list and is an important tool. It appears the Canadiens' analytics and scouting staffs are in lockstep. One wonders how much the eyeballs and the numbers people came together to make Juraj Slafkovsky the first overall pick in the 2022 draft, bypassing the much-heralded Shane Wright.

One team that has a small analytics staff, just a couple of people, is the Ottawa Senators, yet they have one of the best prospect pools in the league. They have a part-time person who reports to GM Pierre Dorion, who receives the daily Sportlogiq reports, but no one else in the organization sees them and no one else in the Sens organization talks to that person. Most NHL teams have departments consisting of two or three analysts. I know of a team that added three more analysts to give them six. The Leafs have had eight or so staff involved with research and development, but money is no object in Toronto. There is no salary cap in the front office, just a budget.

The departments produce their own information, but most also receive data from Sportlogiq and InStat at a cost of up to $100,000 per team. Sportlogiq, as of 2022, serviced all thirty-two teams. With the additional data, teams modify and add to their existing team models depending on their individual needs.

So, how much of a role does analytics play in the building of an organization, in particular with amateur scouting? Obviously, I'm not an analytics expert. When I was a GM analytics wasn't out there at that time; it was just barely coming in. Or, as some would tell you, analytics in its simplest and earliest form had always existed, just with different name tags. Put it this way, I remember Jim Corsi when he was just a goalie coach in Buffalo, not an advanced stats guru! So, I have simply been relaying what team personnel are saying with respect to the role of analytics in their hockey operations departments. Several prominent, veteran scouts (and I know they may have an old-time bias or resentment) insist that analytics has maybe a 5 percent involvement in the creation of the final draft list and ultimately the selections.

Another chief scout said once the draft list is together, then the analytics folks weigh in, adding, "The best thing a scout can do is listen to what others have to say, whether it's analytics, or another scout. But they have very, very little say with the draft. If there is a big discrepancy between the analytics group and our scouts on the ground we will look further into the player, dive deeper and see what the problem is."

It seems, in talking to many organizations, that analytics has become a filter of sorts in the draft process, red flagging certain players and giving the scouting department a chance to further look into a situation. And what if there is a stalemate? With most teams I've spoken to, management will look at both sides and it may take the GM to step in, look at some video, and make the call. That pertains mostly to pro scouting but sometimes the kids, too. At the very least, if there is a stalemate or a question raised by the analytics staff, the scouts will go back and watch tons of video to confirm or deny.

How do teams incorporate analytics into their amateur scouting? Every GM and chief scout wants information. The more information the better. Describe, decipher, distribute is the mantra. Some teams will have the analytics department do a mock draft, using their team model plus information from Sportlogiq and InStat. It's a mock draft using only numbers and data, no eyeballs! Mock drafts like this are often out of whack with the scouts' findings. One mock draft had a five-foot-six Swedish kid going number one—the numbers clearly favored point production way over everything else!

As the amount of data improves, so too will the relevance of the analytics. Regional scouts will still be the key, along with the head scout and crossover scouts. But as for today, teams are still nervous to say there is little analytics involvement because, as one director of amateur scouting said, there is some serious ass-kissing in the organization because of that great divide.

It's fair to say the gap between the analytics department and the scouts is shrinking gradually in most cases, as it needs to. Scouts are starting to understand the data and are slowly buying in. This will only increase as analytics becomes more ingrained as management encourages scouts to learn and grow.

"With our club, it's not adversarial between the scouts and our two analytics people," said Burke. "We won't let it be. We would like to add a third person. We use Sportlogiq and league information, but we're trying to get data to suit our team needs. I find a lot of the stats are arbitrary—like fifty-fifty puck battles, blocked shots, scoring chances. . . . We want it custom made to suit the Penguins."

The bottom line is analytics is here to stay and there are plenty of hockey people excited about it and its future. It's still a distant third in player evaluation behind what the scouts see and background evaluation, and it is a solid third. The teams that figure out how to get analytics and traditional scouting working in harmony will no doubt succeed the quickest. And know this: The day is fast approaching, if it hasn't already come in some organizations, where the analytics department will be evaluated like everyone else in the organization, like the GM and the scouts. And that's the way it should be.

"Analytics tell you a lot," said former GM Pierre Page. "They tell you about scoring, who scores the first goal, who scores the third goal, who scores the important goals, who scores from the slot, who scores on rebounds. They give you a lot of more pertinent information that helps you make a better decision for sure.

"One of my good friends in Switzerland is an astrophysics guy and he keeps telling me analytics is fine, but astrophysics is another level. We have to keep thinking, What's even better than analytics? You have to do something different if you want to be different and better. The Liverpool soccer team hired an astrophysics guy to do scouting. He had never watched a football game. In a short time, they started to find the right players. Boston Red Sox did the same thing. The Red Sox own the Liverpool team [and the Pittsburgh Penguins].

"A lot of analytics people haven't figured out how to win; it's going to take a few years to find out who the analytics people are who know how to win."

Detroit GM Steve Yzerman thinks teams are still figuring everything out.

"I think hockey is still in the infancy stages of analytics," he told the *Agent Provocateur* podcast. "I think we're all still trying to figure out what's really important, what has value, what doesn't have value. I do think it's important we look with our eyes and our experiences. You look at it from an analytics perspective and it forces you to re-evaluate, what does the data tell us, is it supporting what we're seeing, is it contradicting what we're seeing, if so, why? We're still trying to figure out what it's telling us and what we do with it."

The final thought on the state of analytics and old-time scouting goes to my pal Brian Burke.

"We try to take a commonsense approach here," said Burke, while he was with the Penguins. "Take horse racing. You have all the stats on the horses, splits, and how they finished. I would rather talk to the jockey or the trainer. Analytics is good information and our organization respects the process."

But there are still others who prefer to remain quiet until they're ready to be fired or retire.

CHAPTER ELEVEN

THE PITTSBURGH MODEL

THE 2005 DRAFT WILL BE REMEMBERED FOR A LOT OF REASONS. FOR MOST, ESPE-cially the Pittsburgh Penguins, it will be remembered as the Sidney Crosby draft. For me, it will always be the draft that eventually cost me my job and probably about $30 million.

Back in 2004–05, there wasn't a worse team in the NHL than Pittsburgh, at least not officially. That's because there wasn't an NHL season. The entire season, all 1,230 games, was canceled because of a labor dispute, the owners and the league locking out the players in their pursuit of a hard salary cap. I understand the issues that were involved and what commissioner Gary Bettman and the owners wanted to achieve for what they believed was the long-term good of the business. But what ultimately happened, in my opinion, was wrong, with the owners and players sharing equal blame: On February 16, 2005, the season was officially spiked.

It was only the second time in professional sports that a season was canceled. The other was in Major League Baseball, when in mid-August the players' strike killed the remainder of the 1994 season. Without a season, there wasn't a Stanley Cup final, the first time that had happened in the NHL since 1919 when the Spanish flu pandemic forced the league to cancel the final. For that 2004–05 season, the words "Season Not Played" are engraved on the Stanley Cup.

Just prior to the season officially being canceled, Bettman convened a meeting of the thirty team owners. My owner in Columbus, Mr. John H. McConnell, was not well, so I attended in his place to take that vote. Bettman said to us we were voting on whether or not to stay the course and keep the players out until we got a hard cap. Of course I had spoken with Mr. McConnell and our vote was to stay the course. When it came to Detroit, Mike Ilitch stepped up and said stay the course. But at the same time, Bill Davidson, who owned Tampa, yelled out his "stay the course" vote. He was at the buffet table getting lunch, making noise with the dishes. Bettman said, "No, Bill, this is Detroit's vote." Davidson said, "I know, stay the course." Well, he was confused to say the least. You see, Davidson also owned the NBA's Detroit Pistons! When it came time for Tampa to vote, there was silence. Bettman said, "Bill, what is your vote?" He hollered back, "I've already voted!"

Well, the owners unanimously agreed (including Toronto, which didn't want a lockout because of all the money they were losing) and without a season there were no standings—and no traditional draft order. Another first. Now, every draft is important to a team, but there was an added significance to the 2005 draft because of Crosby, the consensus number one pick, a generational player, a franchise changer, the next greatest since Wayne Gretzky in the eyes of many. Gretzky himself had said Crosby was the best player to come along since Mario Lemieux. Heady praise, indeed. There were other very good players in that draft, but Sid was number one. No question.

And whether he was the next Gretzky, or Lemieux, or even Eric Lindros, pretty much everyone was certain he was not going to be the next Alexandre Daigle, the Victoriaville center taken first overall by the tanking Ottawa Senators in 1993. Daigle was pegged by many to be the "next one," but he turned out to be the "big one" as in the big bust. That season, Ottawa and San Jose went toe-to-toe trying to finish last, with the Senators getting the nod because their ten wins were one fewer than the Sharks'.

Funny how that draft turned out. Ottawa took Daigle first, but the Sharks traded the second pick to Hartford for Sergei Makarov and a package of picks, dropping to the sixth pick, who turned out to be Viktor Kozlov, a decent player at best. With the second pick, the Whalers took defenseman Chris Pronger, who went on to win the Norris Trophy, the Hart Trophy, and a Stanley Cup and was inducted into the Hall of Fame.

After that draft Daigle famously stated: "I'm glad I got drafted first because no one remembers number two." Ouch. To which, years later, Pronger replied, "No one remembers number two— guess who ate the shit sandwich on that one?"

Because of the canceled season, the forty-third NHL draft was unique in many ways. First, it was pushed back from June 25 to July 30, eight days after the lockout ended, after the owners had gained their salary cap. And instead of taking place in Ottawa's home rink, then called the Corel Centre, with fans and the draft-eligible kids and their families in the building, it was held at the Westin Hotel in downtown Ottawa, in large part because the arena couldn't be set up with such a short turnaround time. For the first time since 1980, the public wasn't invited and only the top twenty prospects on the Central Scouting list were invited to attend. The teams were given a table that seated five, not the usual dozen or more. It was crazy different. And the confines were tight. It was tough to work the room. It's too bad for the players that one of the greatest days of their careers wasn't what it should have been, either.

With no final standings to determine the draft order, instead there was the ultimate draft lottery involving all thirty teams, held the same day the lockout officially ended. The lottery was weighted and was fairly complex in how they set it all up. It was based on playoff appearances from the previous three seasons and first overall picks in the previous four drafts. My Columbus team, the Buffalo Sabres, the New York Rangers, and the Pittsburgh Penguins were all given three lottery balls because none of us had made the playoffs for those years and we didn't have the first pick in that time. Ten teams—Anaheim, Atlanta, Calgary, Carolina, Chicago, Edmonton, Los Angeles, Minnesota, Nashville, and Phoenix—were given two lottery balls because they had either one playoff appearance or a first overall pick. The remaining sixteen teams got one ball each.

So, we had a 6.3 percent chance of winning. And, of course, we didn't. When the balls dropped, the big winner was Pittsburgh. What a franchise-changing moment that was for them, and in a way for a lot of us that didn't win.

I wasn't happy from the start that all thirty teams were involved in the lottery because we were one of the lower teams the previous season. We had the fourth-worst record with 62 points, behind Pittsburgh (58), Chicago (59), and Washington (59). I also felt as a relatively new franchise to have everybody, including the Stanley Cup champions (Tampa Bay), have a chance of winning was just not right. I didn't like the top ten teams having a chance at all, but because it was Crosby there was a lot of serious debate about how the lottery should work. Everyone thought their team deserved a shot at Sid. I remember being pissed at the GM meetings because it was tough to muster any support to change the process.

I thought the bottom group from the previous season should have been involved for the first overall pick, then do another lottery draw to sort out the rest. Why everyone was included was beyond me. The league said because we didn't play they didn't know how we would have finished, so everyone should get a chance at a generational player. The lottery at the best of times is a crapshoot; even though we had three balls it didn't feel like a huge advantage. We would have had to be unbelievably lucky to get that top pick. In the history of the Blue Jackets, just four seasons then, and through 2023, they've never won a lottery and the team was near the bottom for a lot of years.

Brian Burke, who was GM of Anaheim at the time, has been outspoken about how he didn't think the format was fair then, and even now—and he ended up picking second, having had the ninth-worst record that previous season. So, he did well. And Pittsburgh did have the worst record the year before, but still. Understandably, there was no way to make every team happy, but I just know how I felt at the time.

What that lottery and draft did for Pittsburgh, as we all know, was unbelievable. In his third season, Sid led the Penguins to the Stanley Cup final where they lost in six games to Detroit. The following spring they beat the Red Wings in seven games to win the Cup, and they have won three Cups in total with Number 87. What amazing good fortune for the Penguins, as the franchise not only tanked the year before but was in dire straits off the ice, too.

Something similar happened in 1984 when they tanked to get Mario Lemieux, then the next generational player. Lemieux made the club profitable again then, just as Sid did after his arrival. What Sid has accomplished and means to that franchise, the money he has made for the owners, including Mario— unbelievable.

I remember one day, long before that draft, I was driving to Syracuse to scout when Bettman phoned me. It was ten o'clock at night, and because I was our alternate governor he asked if Columbus would vote for Pittsburgh to be allowed to move to Portland, Oregon. It was a straw vote. As always, Gary tested the waters and wanted to know what the votes would be, which he always did, before he took anything to the full board of governors. I said I had to speak with my owner, Mr. McConnell, and I'd get back to him right away. We decided we would vote for them to move. They were a disaster, on the brink of bankruptcy. Sid's arrival helped keep the team in Pittsburgh and turned things around. There were a lot of people who thought the fix was in with the '05 lottery, because the Pittsburgh franchise was teetering again. As the team with the worst record going into that lottery, maybe it adds up that Pittsburgh won, but a lot of bottom teams got burned.

There was actually a lot of wild movement in that draft lottery. Based on the previous season standings, we fell from fourth to sixth in the lottery. Chicago moved from second to seventh.

Washington dropped from third to fourteenth. Maybe I didn't do so bad! Some of the winners were Anaheim, from ninth to second, Carolina eighth to third, Minnesota twelfth to fourth, Montreal eighteenth to fifth! See why I didn't like how that lottery was structured?

One of my favorite stories that stems from that draft came years later when Brian Burke was the president and GM of the Toronto Maple Leafs. Back in 2005, Burkie was hired as GM of the Ducks just before the lottery, and they "won" the lottery in many ways by getting the second pick, though as I mentioned, he wasn't happy. Instead of getting Sid, the Ducks ended up drafting a pretty good player in Bobby Ryan, although Brian worked hard to try to trade down because he believed they had Ryan rated higher than other teams and the draft was deep enough that he thought he could still get him later.

But when Burkie was running the Leafs and they were struggling, he was asked by a reporter if the Leafs should be patient and build a winner the way the Penguins did—the Pittsburgh Model, they called it. The Penguins did suffer for many years, which allowed them to draft top picks such as goaltender Marc-Andre Fleury, center Evgeni Malkin, defenseman Ryan Whitney, and, of course, Sid. Whitney was a fifth overall pick in 2002, Fleury was a first overall pick the next year, and Malkin was second overall when they lost the lottery in 2004 to Washington, who got Alexander Ovechkin. Pretty good second prize!

"Pittsburgh Model my ass," Burkie told the reporters. "They won a goddamn lottery and they got the best player in the game. Is that available to me? Should we do that? Should we ask the league to have a lottery this year and maybe we pick first? The Pittsburgh Model? My ass. Ray Shero [the GM at the time] has done a good job. He's an excellent GM and he's a friend of mine. But I love when people talk about the Pittsburgh Model. The simple fact is that they got the best player. We came in second that year in Anaheim. We got Bobby Ryan. Impact player, good player. They got Sidney Crosby in the lottery."

Vintage Burkie. He has long been an advocate for revamping the lottery system.

"The teams that need the most help, get the most help," he has said. "That's the theory of inverse order of finish. Now you've got teams that openly talk about tanking, teams that clearly tanked, so we have to put in a lottery. I agree. I get it. But we've got all the non-playoff teams in the lottery and I think that's a joke. I think it should be five teams in the lottery. The second tweak is we shouldn't reward sustained failure. So, if you pick number one overall you cannot pick number one overall for three years. The best you can pick is four, you cannot pick in the top three, and if you pick twice in the top three you are relegated to no better than fourth for the next three years."

Had that plan been in place, had there been a cap on how often a team could pick first, Edmonton might not have gotten Connor McDavid in 2015 because they picked first in 2010 (Taylor Hall), 2011 (Ryan Nugent-Hopkins), and 2012 (Nail Yakupov). Interesting idea. Of course, as I said, Pittsburgh drafted first overall in 2003, selecting Fleury, had the second pick in 2004, taking Malkin (losing the lottery to Washington and Alex Ovechkin), then got Crosby.

There were a lot of good players in that 2005 draft, the likes of Crosby, Ryan, Jack Johnson, Benoit Pouliot, Gilbert Brule, Anze Kopitar. We didn't bother to interview Sid. I would have loved to talk with him, but it would have been a waste of time, his and mine. We didn't interview Carey Price, either, because we had him ranked twelfth and we weren't taking a goalie. We did interview Ryan, Johnson, Pouliot, Kopitar, and Brule. We had actually invited Brule to come to Columbus for an interview earlier, the way we had with Nathan Horton and Eric Staal a couple of years before, but he never made it. He said his flight was canceled, or something. That bothered some of my staff and maybe should have been a red flag.

It's surprising now, but that whole year there was a controversy about Sid and Brule, who was considered by some to be the Sid of the West. The Vancouver Canucks' chief scout at the time, former player Ron Delorme, said, "Crosby is a known because he's in his own league at this stage of development. That separates him from Brule for the moment. Brule will play in the NHL, though, because he has the qualities you look for. He can skate and he's got grit. He can score."

I remember going to the prospects game in January in Vancouver. Sid didn't play in that game because he was injured, although the Westerners didn't believe it. Don Cherry and John Davidson were the honorary head coaches, with the legendary Brian Kilrea (Ottawa 67's) and Don Hay (Vancouver Giants) the assistant coaches.

At the time, Brule was ranked sixth by NHL Central Scouting, but a lot of people had him ranked right behind Sid. Some compared him to a young Steve Yzerman, whom I knew well. In that prospects game without Sid, who was fresh off World Junior gold and was playing in the Quebec league with Rimouski, it was the Gilbert Brule show. He was a center with the Giants, five feet ten, 185 pounds, WHL Rookie of the Year in 2004, and that night he had three goals and one assist to lead Team Cherry to an 8–4 win. He put on an unbelievable show in his home building.

I remember reading in the newspaper the next day Cherry saying he was surprised Brule was ranked sixth. "I don't think he'll be number six after this game," he said.

Within our organization there was controversy all year. Our guys really liked some of the other players: Pouliot, Ryan, Johnson, and Kopitar. All year long it was a vicious battle. Our guys in the West (scouts John Williams and Sam McMaster) loved Brule. He was so damned good that year. There was tension at almost every scouts' meeting we had. It was the Western guys for Brule versus the guys from the East. I really liked Brule from what I had seen of him. I also loved Kopitar. All our guys really liked Kopitar, including my head scout, Don Boyd.

Kopitar was a left shot center from Slovenia. I went to Europe to meet with him and his dad, who was a quality guy and a coach. Anze was playing in the World Championships as a kid. He was a classy guy. I was told years later he was really disappointed he wasn't drafted by us. But at the time a couple of things came up. One was the issue of us selecting Nikolai Zherdev the previous year and the issues we had with him and his behavior and drinking. He was a headache. We started to wonder about Kopitar, even though there was no other reason to worry than what we were going through with Zherdev. We wondered, Okay, he's from Slovenia; will there be similar issues? It should have never entered my mind, but it did.

Boydy loved Brule, too. There wasn't much of a battle about Brule. And after the headache since drafting Zherdev from Russia, I asked Boydy, "How do we take the European kid ahead of the North American kid?" Boydy never said a word. Truth is, I thought Brule was going to Montreal at number five, so our decision would have been made for us. I would have taken Kopitar number six. And what a career he has had.

The draft unfolded in part the way we thought, although we wondered if Pouliot might slide. But Sid, of course, went number one to Pittsburgh. Ryan went number two to Anaheim. Then Johnson, a defenseman with the U.S. National junior team, went third to Carolina, and Pouliot, a left winger with Sudbury, went fourth to Minnesota. The surprise came with the fifth pick, which belonged to Montreal. Pierre Dorion, who was a scout with the Habs then, is sitting at their table and he leans over to Boydy and me and says they're *not* taking Brule—"we're taking the goalie." It was Carey Price, who was playing with the Tri-City Americans. We had him rated twelfth. Most had him in the second round; they were taking him fifth overall.

Analyst Pierre McGuire, who was working on the TSN broadcast, said what a lot of us were thinking when the Canadiens selected Price, reciting the list of goaltending they already had: "Jose Theodore, Cristobal Huet, they traded Mathieu Garon, they have Yann Danis, who they signed as an unrestricted free agent coming out of Brown University—this is not a fit for Montreal; they have so many other needs."

Years later, Price said he had a feeling he might end up with us, which wasn't going to happen, but he had also talked with Minnesota and Atlanta. For the Habs, it sure turned out to be a great pick! On the broadcast they mentioned some of the players the Canadiens passed on—Marc Staal, Brule, Kopitar. Boydy turned to me after Dorion shared the news and said, "Oh, no. Here we go."

We had Kopitar rated ahead of Brule, and he was, amazingly, still available. But we ended up going off our draft list and took Brule. The only two people who could stray from that list were Boydy and me. And the only way Boydy could stray from the list was if I said so. And the only way I would stray was if I talked it out with Boydy. We took Brule and I never thought a thing of it. We were excited to get him. In my mind, there was not a chance Brule was going past number six. He was in the top six or so of every team. Some may have had him higher.

The amazing thing that happened after we made the pick is how the next few picks unfolded. With the seventh pick, Chicago took winger Jack Skille from the U.S. National junior team. San Jose then traded up (with Atlanta) to select winger Devin Setoguchi from Saskatoon. I thought for sure Sharks GM Doug Wilson was moving up to take Kopitar. Ottawa had the next pick and took Brian Lee out of the USHL, who never panned out. At number ten, Vancouver took defenseman Luc Bourdon out of Quebec, who tragically died at age twenty-one in a motorcycle accident. Then, at number eleven, the Los Angeles Kings took Kopitar, who watched the draft online in Sweden with a few of his teammates. He became the highest-picked Slovenian player ever. I read an article a few years ago in which Kopitar said he "had a somewhat strong feeling or somewhat of an idea that I was going to Columbus. I had met with their GM a few times. All those meetings were very productive so I figured that was it. They were pretty straightforward by saying that if I was still available that they would pick me. It didn't happen." Staal, who said he interviewed with twenty-nine teams, went next to the New York Rangers. We had spent a lot of time with Marc Staal.

Years later, working on television, Burkie said to me not one team in the league had Kopitar in the top ten, so get over it. Well, one team did and we didn't take him. And I'm still not over it. If you did that draft over, it would be Sid first, either Price or Kopitar second and third.

As for Brule, he came to camp in the fall and made the team. We signed him to a three-year entry-level deal on the eve of the season. He started out well enough, but in his second game he suffered a fractured sternum, forcing him to miss seventeen games. A week or so after he got back playing, he broke his leg in a game against Minnesota. He wound up playing seven games, had two goals and two assists, but he looked like he would be a pretty good player. We never had any problems with him off the ice.

We had Brule stay with one of our players, Luke Richardson, and his family that first year in Columbus. The Richardsons loved him. But he was eighteen, away from home, and with the injuries it was tough. We sent him back to the Vancouver Giants in January, in part because he had been through so much and needed to play and build up his confidence and in part because I had acquired Sergei Fedorov in a trade, in part to mentor Zherdev which didn't work out, so Brule's playing time would have been limited. Back in junior, he had thirty-eight points in twenty-seven games, played really well, and led them to the Memorial Cup. I went to the Memorial Cup in Moncton to watch him and I had every hockey person in the building tell me what a future superstar I had. He was so good in that tournament, with twelve points in five games, the leading scorer. I remember thinking what a good player I had.

The following year he made our team, played seventy-eight games and had nine goals, nineteen points, and was minus 21. The next season he played sixty-one games, had a goal and eight assists, then wound up in the minors. It's tough. He had had injuries. He was a good player. I often wonder, Was it our expansion situation that held him back? Would he have been different somewhere else? He was just so darn good. After I was let go, he got traded to Edmonton, which is where he was born, then wound up in Phoenix and later played in the Russian league. He wound up playing 299 NHL games. We still exchange text messages.

Had we stuck to our draft list and taken Kopitar, who knows how things might have turned out for me in Columbus. To this day, the writers in Columbus talk about Kopitar versus Brule. They never mention the other players taken before and after. Everyone seemed quite excited about Brule. It wasn't until I left the organization that I kept reading and hearing about how all the hockey people wanted Kopitar. Funny, but I don't remember any of those conversations.

That's the tough part of the draft and it can haunt you. It certainly haunted me. When you are a young franchise and it doesn't pan out, it really hurts, especially when you think he's a can't-miss guy. But you also have to keep it all in perspective. When you think about it, other than Sid, who really hit home runs early in that draft? Other than Sid, Kopitar, and Price, there were ultimately a lot of average players in that grouping. There's not a GM who hasn't had a similar story and that was mine. Lots of people took hits in that draft.

We actually had a pretty good draft otherwise, taking Adam McQuaid 55th, Kris Russell 67th, and Jared Boll 101st. With Brule, that was four NHL players, three of them having long careers. There were several gems later in that draft, too. Toronto (though they traded him) got goalie Tuuka Rask 21st, Dallas got forward James Neal 33rd, Pittsburgh got defenseman Kris Letang 62nd, LA got goalie Jonathan Quick 72nd, and with the 230th and final pick of the draft Nashville got winger Patric Hornqvist. Not bad.

Over the years, the NHL has made multiple tweaks to the draft lottery to not reward teams that finish too high in the standings and not reward teams that finish too low, too often. Meaning, they didn't want a repeat of what happened to Detroit in 2020, when they finished dead last and slipped to the fourth pick, while the Rangers, who played in a playoff qualifier round, drafted first overall.

That lottery might have been the closest to 2005 in that the lottery and the draft all happened during the COVID-19 pandemic, which cut short the 2019–20 season. A special playoff format was put forth, including a qualifying round. But the lottery occurred before everyone had qualified. It got complicated and there were phases to the lottery with placeholders involved for teams still playing, which meant multiple lotteries. The long and short of it was the Wings fell to fourth and the Rangers moved nine spots to first and selected top prospect Alexis Lafreniere. As it turned out, with the fourth pick the Wings leaned on their Swedish scouting system and selected winger Lucas Raymond, a really good player. But after that, there was another tweak to the lottery so that the worst-finishing team could only drop to three.

The lottery, of course, was brought in because teams were perceived to be tanking, the way the Penguins and New Jersey did in 1984, trying to get Mario. Of course, now teams are often quite up-front about their plans, telling fans and media they are in a "rebuild" phase, which could easily be just another word for tanking! But at the end of the day, wherever you pick, you still have to get it right. Not every draft is a sure thing, like Mario and Sid, and in recent times Auston Matthews and Connor McDavid.

I remember a few years ago, when I was working at Sportsnet, my friend and former NHLer Nick Kypreos asked me on our radio show, "What do you think that decision to take Brule ahead of Kopitar cost you?" I said, "It probably cost me about thirty million dollars personally, which is what I might have earned if I had made the right pick and kept my job! If I had made that decision to take Kopitar, he and Rick Nash would have been un-believable together in Columbus. If only I could do it over again, but you don't get those chances.

CHAPTER TWELVE

NIKOLAI THE (NOT SO) GREAT

IN BETWEEN HITTING DRAFT DAY HOME RUNS WITH RICK NASH IN 2002 AND STEVE Mason in 2006, there was the curious case of Nikolai Zherdev.

The 2003 NHL draft in Nashville will go down as being one of the strongest and deepest teenage talent pools in league history, a hugely successful day for a lot of teams. Me? I wound up with a giant-sized Russian headache.

Don't get me wrong; Zherdev was an immense talent. All you have to do is go on YouTube to view his incredible highlights. In Zherdev's rookie year he set up Nash for his club-record forty-first goal, in the season finale. That was Nash's second year and he tied for the Rocket Richard Trophy with Jarome Iginla and Ilya Kovalchuk.

The *Hockey News* once put Nash and Zherdev on its cover, calling them the "Rick and Nik Show" and comparing them to the Atlanta Thrashers' dynamic duo of Kovalchuk and Dany Heatley.

One of my favorite Zherdev moments was his end-to-end game-tying goal with twenty-four seconds remaining against the Chicago Blackhawks on Boxing Day, 2005. We won the game in overtime, but getting there was an amazing display of talent. Zherdev took possession of a short pass from Ron Hainsey in front of our empty net. Zherdev then whistled past Chicago's Martin Lapointe behind our goal and with a burst of speed he was at the Blackhawks' blue line, heading down the left side.

He skated between Chicago's Matthew Barnaby and Jim Dowd just inside the blue line, but Dowd stayed with Zherdev. He then split Dowd and defenseman Jim Vandermeer, slipping the puck through the latter's legs. With future Norris Trophy winner Duncan Keith closing in from his right, Zherdev fired a low glove-side shot past goaltender Nikolai Khabibulin. It was an incredible goal—and the easiest assist of Hainsey's career.

The Blue Jackets finished twenty-eighth out of thirty teams in 2002–03. That meant we entered the draft lottery with the third-best odds to land the first overall selection. But, of course, we did not improve our standing. Instead, we slid a spot to fourth. My old buddy and trading partner from the 2002 draft, Florida Panthers GM Rick Dudley, ruled the day again. The lottery pushed him from the fourth seed to the front of the line of an amazing draft.

Take a glance at the first-round talent: Marc-Andre Fleury (1st), Eric Staal (2nd), Nathan Horton (3rd), Nikolai Zherdev (4th), Thomas Vanek (5th), Ryan Suter (7th), Braydon Coburn (8th), Dion Phaneuf (9th), Jeff Carter (11th), Dustin Brown (13th), Brent Seabrook (14th), Zach Parise (17th), Ryan Getzlaf (19th), Ryan Kesler (23rd), and Mike Richards (24th).

But the hits didn't stop there. Later rounds produced Patrice Bergeron (45th), Shea Weber (49th), Corey Crawford (52nd), David

Backes (62ⁿᵈ), our pick Marc Methot (168ᵗʰ), Joe Pavelski (205ᵗʰ), Tobias Enstrom (239ᵗʰ), Dustin Byfuglien (245ᵗʰ), Matt Moulson (263ʳᵈ), Jaroslav Halak (271ˢᵗ), and Brian Elliott (291ˢᵗ), the second last selection. That collection of players contains so many Stanley Cup champions, captains, and stars.

The final NHL Central Scouting list had Staal, Brown, Vanek, Horton, and Getzlaf as the top five North American skaters. Fleury was the top-ranked goalie. Zherdev, Milan Michalek, and Andrei Kostitsyn were one, two, and three on the European skaters list. Dudley traded the first overall selection for the second year in a row. This time, he swapped picks with the Pittsburgh Penguins. The seventy-third overall selection (Carcillo) also went to Pittsburgh in exchange for the third choice (Horton), the fifty-fifth pick (Stefan Meyer), and veteran forward Mikael Samuelsson.

If Dudley didn't make those first overall swaps, the Panthers could have had Nash in 2002 and Staal in 2003. But they did okay with Bouwmeester and Horton.

Yes, we loved Fleury, but we drafted Leclaire eighth overall in 2001, and he was developing in the AHL with the Syracuse Crunch. Denis was the Blue Jackets' number one, so we weren't going to take another netminder.

I liked both Staal and Zherdev, but Staal was the guy I desperately desired. He was a number one center and, combined with Nash, would be a franchise maker. Our chief scout, Don Boyd, and his staff, however, had Zherdev at the top of our list, followed by Staal, Horton, Vanek, and Fleury.

When we mapped who would likely go where, we felt our fourth slot would come down to either Zherdev or Vanek.

We interviewed Zherdev at the draft. He was born in Kiev, Ukraine, but had a Russian passport because he left Ukraine to play in Russia's lower leagues as a fifteen-year-old. In his draft year, he played for CSKA Moscow, otherwise known as Red Army. He was six-foot-one, 186 pounds, and possessed a prodigious amount of skill. He was a right-shot forward who could play either wing. He was mentioned in the same breath as Staal at Christmastime as the potential first overall pick. Don Boyd said Zherdev might be in the top 5 percent of the skilled guys he had watched in his forty years in the game. Zherdev was that good.

He played for Russia at the World Junior Championship in Halifax in late December 2002 and early January 2003. Led by a seventeen-year-old Alex Ovechkin, Russia defeated Canada in the gold medal final, 3–2, but Zherdev checked in with only one assist in six games.

In Nashville, six months later, Zherdev arrived for his interview with our team wearing a black suit. Most guys are neatly dressed but not quite like that. But so far, so good. But he couldn't speak a lick of English, so he needed an interpreter. We learned about his challenging upbringing. His family was impoverished. His father suffered from poor health.

One of the first things he uttered in his interview, through the interpreter, was that the Blue Jackets were wasting their time talking to him because he wouldn't be there when we made our selection at number four.

I'm thinking, I hope so, because that means someone like Staal or Horton will fall to us.

In the interview, Zherdev didn't come across as a bad person, just cocky. I asked him what kind of car he owned. He said a Mercedes SL sports model. Different kid, for sure.

Draft day comes. The Penguins chose Fleury first, followed by Staal to the Carolina Hurricanes and Horton to the Panthers.

For us, we continued to mull over Zherdev or Vanek. We absolutely loved Vanek. He was Austrian, a quality kid. He played in the USHL for the Sioux Falls Stampede, scored forty-six goals in fifty-three games, and scored another thirty-one goals in forty-six games in his freshman season at the University of Minnesota.

But our Russian scout, Artyom Telepin, drove me crazy and convinced our staff to go with Zherdev. Boyd and Blue Jackets assistant director of amateur scouting Paul Castron also were smitten with Zherdev.

On TSN's draft broadcast, Bob McKenzie called Zherdev "a poor man's Ilya Kovalchuk." But here was McKenzie's description after I announced Zherdev was our selection: "Great speed. Great skill. Great goal-scoring ability. Quick hands. Quick feet. He's a little bit temperamental. He sometimes doesn't use his teammates as much as he should. [The Blue Jackets] weren't the only team in the National Hockey League that believes Nikolai Zherdev was the number one talent. Of the four players who have been taken so far each of the four have received some consideration from their scouts as the number one overall pick. It was spread across the board."

I felt pretty good about the selection because as I walked off the stage after announcing Zherdev as our pick I passed by Sabres GM Darcy Regier. He was approaching the stage to take Vanek with the fifth overall selection. "We were taking [Zherdev] if you didn't," Regier told me.

But now, almost two decades later, all I can do is shake my head. There was so much talent in the 2003 draft and I wound up with a problem.

Among the top ten picks that June, nobody played fewer combined regular-season and playoff games in the NHL than

Zherdev. Even the tenth overall choice, Andrei Kostitsyn of the Montreal Canadiens, played in 447 regular-season and playoff games to Zherdev's 436. But the problem began before he even stepped foot on the ice.

In July, we signed Zherdev to a three-year entry-level contract and sent a $100,000 US check to CSKA Moscow as a transfer fee. The word was out that Zherdev was going to spend a second season with Red Army, but that was fine with me. An extra year in Russia would help him develop as a player and mature as a person. Besides, the coach at CSKA Moscow was the legendary Viktor Tikhonov.

But in September, we received word from Zherdev's agents, Rolly Hedges and Sasha Tyjnych, that the kid wanted to play in the NHL right away. It was a murky situation because there were claims Zherdev had commitments to serve in the Russian army and therefore would be forced to stay put with CSKA Moscow.

Tyjnych and Hedges informed us that was fake news. So, we started to pursue the possibility of Zherdev joining us in the fall of 2003. We contacted the NHL head office and the IIHF and kept in touch with his agents to follow the proper procedures. The big question remained: Did Zherdev have Russian military commitments or not? We decided to go to the Mother Country to meet with CSKA Moscow officials to hear them out.

I didn't go to Russia because of my frightening experience with a Russian contingent when I was with the Red Wings at the 1993 IIHF World Junior Championship in Ostrava, Czech Republic. I had been back to Russia, almost every year, scouting, but I didn't feel comfortable going to a meeting like that in this type of negotiation with the Russian military. Instead, our assistant GM, Jim Clark, traveled to Moscow in late October. Clark watched Zherdev play for CSKA Moscow before the meeting took place in a warehouse-type building beside the CSKA soccer stadium. It was barren. Clark arrived with Telepin, Zherdev, and the two agents. The entrance to the building was a sliding steel door. They were met inside by two armed security guards in suits.

"They had their suit jackets open and you could see their guns," Clark recalled.

After checking in with the receptionist, there was an hour delay. The entire CSKA sports empire was owned by Russian oligarch Roman Abramovich, who also owned the famed soccer club Chelsea, of the English Premier League. Clark and Co. were waiting for CSKA president Evgeny Giner to arrive from London. Although Giner spoke English, the meeting was conducted in Russian. Periodically, Tyjnych would provide translation for Clark.

The disagreement continued to be whether or not Zherdev had a two-year military commitment. It became a good old-fashioned Cold War episode. The kid was labeled a deserter. Zherdev made sure we knew through his agents that not only had he never shot a gun, but he also didn't own one. Zherdev was trying to tell us the army story was fiction.

Clark watched Zherdev play in another game before returning home. Nothing was resolved at that point. The NHL then stepped in and started dealing with the touchy situation. NHL vice-president Bill Daly (now deputy commissioner) was a big help.

"At this point, we've not been provided with sufficient evidence to establish either A, that he has a compulsory military service obligation or B, that he's conscripted in the Russian military," Daly said.

It was apparent the Russians were trying to hold us hostage. With the league picking up a portion of the expense, about $1.2 million was spent in legal fees to free Zherdev from his Russian shackles. We talked about the possibility of some exhibition games against CSKA and possibly holding part of our training camp there. But it became a point-of-no-return situation that fall. We had to get Zherdev out of Russia. His team and Russian officials could have made life difficult if he had stayed. He already had gone from playing among the top six on CSKA to the fourth line.

Clark and Boyd traveled to Helsinki, where Zherdev was competing for Russia in the annual Four Nations under-20 tournament against Finland, Sweden, and Czech Republic, or Czechia as the country is now known.

"Back then, Russian hockey players carried two passports," Clark said. "They had a passport to travel within Russia and were given a passport for international travel that they had to turn back in after the trip."

On the last day of the tournament, Boyd and Clark met Zherdev outside the rink before he boarded the team bus. They presented the Russian with a plane ticket from Moscow to Toronto via Frankfurt, Germany. When Zherdev returned home to Moscow, he held on to his international passport and went to the airport the next morning to begin his journey to North America on November 24. After arriving in Toronto, he then traveled to Ottawa to meet Boyd and his agents to obtain a work visa at the U.S. Consulate.

Mr. McConnell's private jet helped the cause. It flew Zherdev from Ottawa to Columbus in the cover of the night on Monday, December 1, 2003, and he played his first game for the Blue Jackets the following evening.

The IIHF wasn't much help in the matter. Even after he started playing for the Blue Jackets, hockey's international governing body and CSKA took the issue before arbitrator Stephan Netzle of the Court of Arbitration for Sport in Zurich, Switzerland. In early March 2004, a few months after Zherdev began playing for Columbus, Netzle ruled in favor of the Blue Jackets. The arbitrator stated we had followed all of the rules of the then agreement between the IIHF and NHL and had the paperwork to prove it. The arbitrator further ruled there was no evidence Zherdev was a member of the Russian military at the time he left CSKA Moscow for Columbus.

"I'll never forget the strange scene after the ruling in our favor," Clark said. "There were the CSKA officials hugging Zherdev like nothing happened."

I'll never forget the excitement generated by our nineteen-year-old Russian that first day in Columbus. My son, Clark, was twelve, and he took the morning off from school to watch our morning skate.

I was coaching at the time, and from the moment I stepped on the ice I could not believe how scary good this kid was, watching him skate and handle the puck. I also remember respected veteran Tyler Wright skating over to me at the morning skate and saying, "Holy shit, how good is this guy?"

I'm not trying to justify the pick, but Zherdev was one of the best pure talents I've seen in my life. In Zherdev's debut, the Blue Jackets defeated the Anaheim Ducks 2–1 at home. He didn't register any points in that first outing. But in our next game, two nights later, he scored twice and assisted on another.

The only problem was his first goal didn't count against the Nashville Predators. The situation room in Toronto deemed the net came off its moorings before the puck crossed the line. He didn't like it. Our fans didn't like it and I wasn't too fond of the decision, either. We'd fallen behind 3–0 when he scored his first goal for real, with 5:32 remaining in the third period. He then set up Nash with 21 seconds left. The Predators scored into the empty net for a 4–2 victory, but the crowd left the building buzzing over Zherdev's promising start. At one point, on his way to the bench during a stoppage, the crowd gave him a standing ovation.

To watch his first few games was a treat. But it was apparent this was a kid with some real challenges. He was a strange guy. He didn't speak English and had zero interest in learning a new language. When we had Sergei Fedorov in Detroit, he struggled with his English at first. But he took his time and eventually grasped the language.

Despite the language barrier, Zherdev finished that first season with thirteen goals and thirty-four points in fifty-seven games. He was invited to play for the West in the YoungStars game all-star weekend in St. Paul, Minnesota, and scored a goal in his team's 7–3 victory. All signs indicated this nineteen-year-old kid was on his way to becoming a superstar.

After his rookie year, Zherdev returned to Russia for the offseason. Shortly after his departure, I got a call from Nationwide Insurance. He lived in an apartment set up by the Blue Jackets next to the rink, and Nationwide asked me if I had time to examine his living quarters.

The place was a disaster. There were wine stains everywhere. The locks had to be changed seven times because he kept damaging them. Now I'm wondering, What sort of character do I have here? What was he doing, sitting around his apartment drinking the night away? I'd heard rumblings about him, but not enough to be alarmed. This was a wake-up call. He had big-time off-ice issues.

But there wasn't an opportunity to straighten him out the following year because the lockout canceled the entire 2004–05 season. Zherdev spent the year back with CSKA Moscow. Apparently, he was no longer a deserter. I was worried sick about how he was acting back home. Unfortunately, the timing of the lockout could not have been worse for the Blue Jackets and Zherdev.

He arrived back in Columbus for training camp in September 2005 with a thirty-five-year-old girlfriend on his arm. He was two months shy of his twenty-first birthday. That development just added to the concern for our bad actor. I hired a private investigator to follow him around for a week. He reported back that Zherdev was drinking, partying. Yes, there are plenty of young people who follow this path. But Zherdev's after-dark frolics were nonstop. He eventually became aware that he was being tailed, so he would slip out the side door of his condo building on his way to his night on the town. The investigator was convinced we had a serious problem on our hands.

English was still an issue, especially after spending a whole season playing in Russia, so I decided to bring in Sergei Kharin, who played seven games for the Winnipeg Jets in 1990–91 and spent several seasons in the minors. I hoped Kharin would be a good influence, help him learn English, and essentially be a babysitter.

I also tried Sergei Fedorov. On November 15, 2005, I traded for Fedorov and a fifth-round 2006 selection (Maxime Frechette) from the Anaheim Ducks for Wright and defenseman Francois Beauchemin.

A month earlier, I had blown my stack at Zherdev after a 4–3 loss to the Anaheim Ducks on the road. Finally, after another half-hearted effort, I'd had enough. I watched from the press box and was angered by the complete lack of respect he showed for his teammates. I stormed the dressing room and unloaded a tirade fit for a drill sergeant on the twenty-year-old, right in front of his teammates. My discourse was so loud the two Columbus reporters could hear me from outside the dressing room.

When Fedorov arrived for his stint in Columbus, he wasn't the same player who dominated with the Detroit Red Wings and won three Stanley Cups. But I did the deal with Ducks GM Brian Burke because I felt Fedorov could help Zherdev move to the next stage of his career. After all, Zherdev idolized Fedorov. Maybe that was what the youngster needed. But within weeks of Sergei's arrival in Columbus, he came to my office and told me he couldn't help him. Fedorov was frustrated. He couldn't get through to Zherdev and couldn't believe his disrespect for others.

There were other concerns in the way he treated people. One day, Jim Clark witnessed Zherdev treating our strength coach, Barry Brennan, in a shoddy manner after they worked on a knee ailment. Barry was trying to get him to work harder in the gym, but the kid just laughed at him, didn't show him any respect. Well, Jim heard about it and went down and gave Zherdev shit while he was riding a stationary bike. I went down a little while later and Zherdev asked me, "Who was that curly-headed guy giving me shit?"

"He's the assistant GM," I said. "He's the guy who spent all that time with you and got you out of Russia."

We sent Zherdev to Syracuse in early December for a two-game stint. But it wasn't a punishment or anything for his off-ice behavior. The Blue Jackets had a week off, and we didn't want some of our young players to be out of action for that long. So Zherdev, rookie Dan Fritsche, and some others went down to the AHL. Zherdev managed to finish his sophomore NHL season with twenty-seven goals and fifty-four points in seventy-three games, tied for second in team scoring with Nash and only behind David Vyborny's sixty-five points.

There was nothing to be concerned about regarding Zherdev's on-ice performance. He still was a treat to watch. But whatever good vibrations we felt for him about his future and development as a player were quelled in summer 2006. Because of the canceled season, his entry-level contract had expired. The local media was all over the organization, all over me, to open the owner's wallet and sign Zherdev to a long-term deal.

I had no problem with his skill, his production. What he exhibited with his on-ice performance should have resulted in a hefty second contract. But I had significant concerns about his off-ice behavior and I didn't feel right about giving him a long-term deal. He threatened to stay in Russia to resume his career. I started to check around the league with other GMs to see if there was any trade interest in Zherdev.

Dallas Stars GM Doug Armstrong also faced a complex negotiation for a contract extension with forward Brenden Morrow. Doug and I started down the road of a potential trade. I liked Morrow. Who didn't? He was twenty-seven, a tough Western Canadian kid, coming off twenty-three-goal and twenty-five-goal seasons. He was a future captain.

We were in Traverse City, Michigan, for our rookie camp before the main training camp. Doug and I had a basic agreement for a trade, a simple Zherdev for Morrow swap. But I needed approval from our ownership. I flew back to Columbus to present the trade to Mr. McConnell. He knew about our off-ice concerns with Zherdev. Local media and fans continued to clamor for us to fork out big dollars to sign the Russian, but still, we decided to go through with the trade for Morrow. My staff was on board, too. We agreed Morrow was a perfect fit for the Blue Jackets.

I was on the verge of unloading a massive aggravation. But when I called Armstrong back, he delivered distressing news: The Stars were close to a new six-year, $24.6 million extension. Morrow signed that extension on September 21. I wanted to cry.

Zherdev would play in eight games for Mytishchi Khimik in suburban Moscow. But Zherdev knew he couldn't play a shift for his new Russian league team after October 5, a day before the Blue Jackets' opener. Otherwise, he had to spend the entire year in Russia. Our initial offer was for two seasons at $3.8 million total. Then we expanded the proposal to $6.9 million for three years. His agent countered with a ludicrous three-year, $8.5 million ask. Eventually, we finally agreed on a three-year, $7.5 million deal on September 28, 2006.

But Zherdev returned to Columbus looking like a doughboy— terribly out of shape. He never got on track that season, finishing with a paltry ten goals and thirty-two points in seventy-one games. Two goals came in his season debut.

After another missed playoffs in 2006–07, I was dismissed less than seven months after Zherdev showed up grossly out of shape.

My replacement, Scott Howson, did his best to give Zherdev a fresh start. He checked in with twenty-six goals, sixty-one points, in eighty-two games the next season, but the Blue Jackets unloaded him the following summer. On July 2, 2008, he was dealt with Fritsche to the New York Rangers for defensemen Christian Backman and Fedor Tyutin.

Zherdev put up decent numbers in his only season on Broadway with twenty-three goals and fifty-eight points in eighty-two games. But another contract dispute ensued after the 2008–09 season. He took the club to arbitration and won. He was awarded a $3.9 million salary. The Rangers, however, decided to walk away from the decision.

Zherdev went back to Russia, only to return for one final NHL season with the 2010–11 Philadelphia Flyers, signing a one-year free-agent deal worth $2 million. He averaged less than thirteen minutes of ice time with the Flyers but scored sixteen goals and twenty-two points in fifty-six games. This, however, was the end to his time in the NHL. He spent the next seven seasons bouncing around Russia with nine different teams. He then sat out three years before returning to play for the Bratislava Capitals in the Austrian league and then Merano HC in Italy in 2021–22.

He was a disaster. He had no respect for teammates, management, or the coaches. And he had no parental support; he'd left his home in Ukraine at fourteen to play in Moscow. His parents were good people, but he was on his own from an early age. And Fedorov couldn't help him. It still haunts me to this day, selecting him fourth overall in 2003. I liked him as a kid. I felt sorry for him. He never got remotely close to reaching his potential.

It was a sad career for one of the most talented players I've ever seen play. When I run into scouts and other hockey executives from that time, we still talk about his demise.

Did the Zherdev experience change the way I drafted? Yes. After this, I was more cautious of drafting players from Europe and Russia. Rightly or not, I didn't trust my assessment of their character.

Obviously, I got unlucky with Zherdev. But Europeans have had such a tremendous impact on the NHL. And it's hard to think of what the league would look like without them. You certainly wouldn't have thirty-two teams of the caliber that exists without them filling roughly a third of the player pool in the NHL.

It was back in 1972, after the incredible Canada–Soviet Union Summit Series, that we started thinking differently about the Soviets and Europeans and the skill sets they possessed. It took some time, and some heartache, but the Europeans started making inroads, with the likes of the late Borje Salming starring with the Toronto Maple Leafs and dispelling the "Chicken Swede" myth.

The WHA, which was born in 1972, opened the door for more Europeans with the likes of Swedes Anders Hedberg and Ulf Nilsson coming over to star in Winnipeg with Bobby Hull. But the real turning point in European drafting probably didn't occur until 1989. That year eighteen-year-old Swedish center Mats Sundin was the first overall pick, the first time a European was taken first. Meanwhile, in the real world, the Iron Curtain was beginning to fall in the Soviet Union, East and West Germany were starting to unite, the Cold War was ending, which led to not just Europeans being drafted but more players from the Eastern Bloc countries, especially the Soviets. Players would soon no longer have to defect from their country to play in the NHL, but that was still a couple of years away.

In that 1989 draft, the Detroit Red Wings made a bold statement. After taking center Mike Sillinger eleventh overall, then defenseman Bob Boughner thirty-second, with their third-round pick, number fifty-three, they took defenseman Nicklas Lidstrom, who became one of the best ever. In the next round they took Fedorov, another star in the making. And in the eleventh round, 221st overall, defenseman Vladimir Konstantinov, a key component in a championship team. That was the start of a Russian invasion in Detroit during the nineties, which is when I joined the team, and it was led by GM Jimmy Devellano and a scouting staff that included Neil Smith, Ken Holland, and European chief scout Christer Rockström. During that time, the Wings stockpiled European talent.

But perhaps the most shocking pick in that 1989 draft was high-flying Soviet right winger Pavel Bure, who wasn't expected to be selected too early because he still would have had to defect to play right away. There was also a huge debate over his draft eligibility. Put simply, teams didn't think the eighteen-year-old was draft eligible until the following year, but the Vancouver Canucks thought otherwise and selected him in the sixth round, 113th overall. Had teams known what the Canucks knew, he would have been taken higher, likely the second round, though some thought he was the best player.

It was believed because he was eighteen Bure had to be selected in the first three rounds. If taken later, he had to play two seasons (a minimum eleven games in each) with his Central Red Army team. The Canucks, in particular head scout Mike Penny, believed he had already played those games and was eligible. Detroit had been planning to take Bure but was told he wasn't eligible. Vancouver took him three picks ahead of Detroit. The selection was ruled illegal by NHL president John Ziegler, but the Canucks appealed, produced the evidence, and just prior to the 1990 draft, when he would have been "eligible," the Canucks won the battle. It wasn't until early November 1991, after the court proceedings and a bunch of money had been paid to the Soviets, that Bure made his debut. He might have been a head-ache for the Canucks, but not after he arrived!

In subsequent years, of course, the drafting of Russians with top picks became the norm, such as in 2004 when Alexander Ovechkin and Evgeni Malkin were taken first and second. Fast-forward to 2022, the sixtieth NHL draft, when the Canadiens selected Slovakian left winger Juraj Slafkovsky first overall. The New Jersey Devils followed, taking fellow Slovak defenseman Simon Nemec. It was the second time two players from the same European country were drafted one-two.

A total of eighty-eight players, 39.1 percent of the players drafted, were from ten different European countries, ranging from Sweden, Russia, and Finland at the top to Germany, Switzerland, and Belarus. How the times have changed, and for the better. I only wish Zherdev had been more like Bure.

CHAPTER THIRTEEN
LAST WORDS

"FORTY-SEVEN YEARS. IT TOOK ME FORTY-SEVEN YEARS TO FINALLY BE AT MY FIRST draft, and it was worth the wait. These last two days, the energy in this city has been awesome. . . . Congratulations to all the players who are going to hear their name over the next two days. Understand that it's just the beginning and probably the easy part. What's ahead of you is even harder. And for the guys who don't hear their name, it's okay. It's not the end. You just keep pushing. If you match work ethic with will, you can accomplish anything."

Those words, spoken by Montreal Canadiens coach Martin St. Louis, were the opening remarks at the 2022 NHL draft in Montreal. They're not only inspiring but the best piece of advice for anybody, chasing any dream.

He should know. Despite many disappointments and all the odds that were stacked against him, St. Louis kept pushing. His size was considered a liability, but the five-foot-eight, 175-pound right winger ultimately became the patron saint of the small player. He went from being undrafted to the Hockey Hall of Fame in 2018 after a brilliant career that saw him win two Art Ross trophies as the NHL scoring champion, a Stanley Cup with the 2003–04 Tampa Bay Lightning to go along with a Hart Trophy and Pearson Award that same season, a 2004 World Cup title with Canada, and Olympic gold with Canada in 2014.

St. Louis is a prime example of how imperfect the draft can be. For every Connor McDavid can't-miss pick, there is a St. Louis how-did-we-miss-him pick.

St. Louis slipped through the cracks of three NHL drafts. But it's not like he was an unheralded talent. He was the ECAC conference player of the year in his second of four seasons at the University of Vermont. He was named captain of the team for his junior and senior seasons, helping Vermont capture its first ECAC championship and advance all the way to the 1996 Frozen Four—with teammates goaltender Tim Thomas and forward Éric Perrin—only to lose 4–3 to Colorado College in double overtime in the national semifinals.

The Laval, Quebec, native was a finalist for the Hobey Baker Award in three of his four seasons at Vermont. The Ottawa Senators offered St. Louis a tryout after his college career concluded. But the Senators eventually cut him loose. So, he signed with the Cleveland Lumberjacks of the IHL and continued his high-scoring ways with 50 points in 56 games, which was good enough to catch the eye of the Calgary Flames.

Give credit to Flames coach Brian Sutter for bringing St. Louis to the NHL and to Flames developmental coach Tom Watt for helping St. Louis blossom. Sutter was coaching the Boston Bruins in the early to mid-1990s when he watched St. Louis play for Vermont and immediately liked how the pint-sized forward played.

In the late 1990s, Sutter found himself behind the Flames bench. He couldn't believe St. Louis was in Cleveland, so Sutter told Flames GM Al Coates about the talented offensive forward. Coates asked director of player personnel Nick Polano to check out St. Louis.

Polano, who I worked with in Detroit, watched St. Louis score a hat trick in the IHL all-star game in Orlando. The Flames' assistant GM immediately recommended to his boss that they lock up St. Louis. Nine days later, on February 18, 1998, Calgary signed St. Louis and assigned him to the AHL Saint John Flames. He finished the season with twenty-six points in twenty-five regular-season games and another twenty points in twenty playoff games as Saint John advanced to the Calder Cup final, but they lost in six games to the Philadelphia Phantoms.

St. Louis was twenty-three years old when he made his debut in Calgary for the 1998–99 season opener. He scored his first goal in his fifth game but was back in the AHL by mid-December for the rest of the season. He started the next season back in Saint John but was promoted in late November and finished the season in Calgary. But new management came in that summer when Craig Button was hired away from the Stanley Cup–champion Dallas Stars. One of the new GM's first moves was to cut loose St. Louis.

Button often admitted his regret about that decision, but we've all made calls we regret. Tampa Bay GM Rick Dudley, who did a lot of scouting, signed St. Louis, and he became a full-time NHL player, the start of fourteen years with the Lightning. He suffered a fractured leg in his second season with the Lightning but enjoyed a breakout year in 2002–03 with thirty-three goals and seventy points in eighty-two games and added another seven goals and twelve points in eleven playoff games. He was on his way to a remarkable career with 1,241 combined regular-season and playoff games and was named five times to the NHL all-star team, despite his undrafted status.

As St. Louis discovered, the trek to the top was not easy. But he was committed, impassioned, and determined. The competition for NHL jobs is fierce. There are only 736 roster spots among the thirty-two teams, and about 225 players are drafted each year, depending on the number of compensatory selections awarded. But as St. Louis and many others also have discovered, there are several paths you can take to the NHL and a lengthy pro career.

As a coach, St. Louis continues to be the patron saint of undrafted players, but in a new way. He's proud of his Canadiens defenseman Arber Xhekaj. The Hamilton, Ontario, player was twice passed over in the OHL draft, the first time one of just two eligible players on his minor hockey team not selected. But with the support of his parents, he persevered and was eventually signed by Kitchener. In his second season, he was traded to the Hamilton Bulldogs and played in the Memorial Cup. But he was twice passed over in the NHL draft. The Habs invited him to training camp in 2021 and he impressed, earning a contract. After another season in junior, he returned to the Habs training camp in 2022. He expected to be headed to the minors, but the team had suffered injuries and his determined play awarded him a spot on the big team. He quickly became a fan favorite.

Xhekaj is hardly the only one to get a second chance. "To all the guys leaving the draft or sitting at home undrafted: put your head down and go to work. All you need is your belief in yourself to make something special happen," Los Angeles Kings defenseman Sean Durzi wrote on his Twitter account after the 2022 draft.

Durzi knows. He was a second-round (fifty-second overall) selection of the Toronto Maple Leafs in 2018 after being over-looked as an eighteen-year-old in 2017. He played four seasons of major junior in Owen Sound and Guelph, winning the league championship and a trip to the 2019 Memorial Cup tournament with the latter. The Maple Leafs traded Durzi as part of the deal to acquire veteran defenseman Jake Muzzin from the Kings in January 2019. Durzi spent two full seasons with the AHL Ontario Reign and thirteen more games to begin 2021–22 before being promoted to the Kings for the rest of the season. He scored his first goal in his first NHL game, which just happened to be against Toronto. But being a second-round selection did not guarantee Durzi an NHL roster spot. So, he kept his eye on the prize.

While Durzi, Xhekaj, and St. Louis traveled the path most taken by future NHLers by developing in major junior and the U.S. College ranks, there are other routes. Cale Makar was drafted after his second full season with the Brooks Bandits of the Alberta Junior Hockey League, a Tier II loop, though he did play two more years at UMass-Amherst. The Colorado Avalanche defenseman won the Calder Trophy, Norris Trophy, Conn Smythe Trophy, and Stanley Cup before his twenty-fourth birthday and, as I have said earlier, he might be the next Nick Lidström. Pretty heady praise indeed.

Auston Matthews of the Maple Leafs departed for Switzer-land in his draft year to play for Zurich SC and head coach Marc Crawford. There have been plenty of U.S.-born talents who have been drafted out of the U.S. national team development program, players such as Brady Tkachuk and Quinn Hughes, or drafted straight from the USHL, such as Boston Bruins goaltender Jeremy Swayman and center Ross Colton, a Stanley Cup winner with Tampa Bay.

Part of finding the right path is finding the right agent or family advisor, someone with a feel for laying out the options and guiding you to take the correct route. This should occur at age thirteen or fourteen, because decisions are made regarding whether to enroll in prep school or AAA programs with an eye on the next step after that. A lot depends on how much the player has developed to this point. For example, St. Louis won a league scoring championship in his midget year in Laval and decided the next step should be with the Hawkesbury Hawks (near Ottawa) in the Central Junior Hockey League. He scored thirty-seven goals and eighty-seven points in thirty-one games in his only season there before he went off to Vermont.

I also would advise you to turn a blind eye to all the ranking lists. History has proven these lists aren't the be-all and end-all. There are one thousand different ways to make it to The Show, and you must keep believing you're on the right track. You can't read too much into what others say.

Parental advice, however, is another matter. Hockey is a game of instincts, or on-ice smarts. Obstacles or distractions thrown at a player interfere with performance. It's tricky to walk that line of offering your kids support in their hockey endeavors but letting them find their own way and their own reasons to chase success.

Is it any wonder the well-known hockey fathers in this world—Doug Orr, Walter Gretzky, the less-well-known Jean-Guy Lemieux—were not overbearing but rather were encouraging and supportive people. It boggles my mind that hockey parents have not learned this lesson. I've seen too many talented kids not work out because of domineering dads or moms.

I remember when Wayne Gretzky retired he was asked what his greatest day in hockey was. Surprisingly, to me and many others, he said it was his final game. Not the game itself, but that day he drove to the rink with Walter and they talked hockey, just like Wayne did as a six- or seven-year-old and for years after. He said his hockey life had come full circle. Those are memories you want to have as a kid and a parent.

My friend Brian Burke once told me when he was a teenager he had a rule with his dad. After the game, driving home, he couldn't talk about the game unless Brian said he wanted to talk about what happened. That's a good rule for parents. Everyone take a deep breath and a little time and calm down.

I have to admit, I have had my moments in the rink watching my son, Clark, play over the years. When I was president and GM in Columbus, I remember coming off the road one day and racing to see Clark play in a really competitive high-school game. I get into the rink and my wife, Jill, is standing there with friends and is quite agitated. She says to me a gentleman just told her she was full of shit. I looked at him and said, "Did you just tell my wife that?" He said he did, that Jill had said a goal should have counted against his son's team and he disagreed. I told him he was an idiot. Two weeks later, the same two teams are playing in our practice facility at Nationwide Arena. The guy was a dentist. At the end of the first period, he was standing over the alleyway leading to our kid's dressing room and he's screaming at our players. I went over and kicked him out of the rink, barred him from the Ice House. As president of the Blue Jackets, and as it was our rink, I could do that.

Now I've gotten caught up in it myself. My first year in Columbus, when we were putting the team together, Clark was eight or nine, playing atom hockey. I helped out the coach and we were in a tournament in Cincinnati. I'm on the bench—I had been fifteen years in the NHL as a coach and assistant coach—and the officiating was awful. I called the referee over and I told him he had to get in the game. He told me if I said one more word he would throw me out of the game. I said two more words: "You're awful." He threw me out. When we were driving back to Columbus, I asked Clark if he'd noticed what happened and he said, "Yes, you got kicked out." I said, "Maybe we should keep that between us and not tell Mom." Well, a week later I was on my radio show and some guy called in and said, "I see you got tossed out of an atom game." Jill just happened to be listening.

Was I right? I think so. Did it help or make a positive difference? No, not really. The bottom line, parents have to strive for two things: Number one, make sure your kid enjoys the game. Number two, remember the best evaluation of yourself is if at the end of the season the kids say, "I learned a lot and want to play for that coach again." If that happens it has been a successful year. I used to say this to coaches in minor hockey.

It's not just in minor hockey where parents can get too involved. It happens in the NHL. I put Danny Fritsche in the NHL as an eighteen-year-old in Columbus. He was a second-round pick, a Memorial Cup most valuable player in London going head-to-head with Sidney Crosby. Danny made our team in training camp and he played a few games to start the season. He was a great kid.

Five or six games into the season my phone rings and it's his father, Jim, who was also a great guy, though he could be a bit intense. Well, he starts yelling at me that Danny's not getting enough ice time. I said, "Jim, you're phoning me to complain about the ice time an eighteen-year-old is getting. Are you serious? I just put him in the NHL; he's making four hundred and fifty thousand dollars." After that we had a good relationship.

The problem with parents—and I was the same—is no matter what age their kids are, parents live vicariously through them. I say to Clark, who is now a player agent, that if you're recruiting a player, if the parents are crazy, run from them, even if you love the kid.

The great Connor McDavid of the Edmonton Oilers was a phenom from a young age. He credits family and friends for his personal development over the years. "I look back at my childhood with really, really, great memories," he told NHL.com. "When you have a really tight circle around you and a close-knit kind of family and friend group, I really feel that it's a great escape from whatever is going on. I think back to minor hockey days and I've nothing but amazing memories. I remember being a kid and playing street hockey, going to the pond with my brother. All these amazing things and great memories."

Ultimately, it's about an individual chasing a dream with hard work and passion. But having a dream is not enough. So many talented people think they're outworking their competition. But that shouldn't be the focus.

You have to embrace the journey. You have to want to push through that early-morning workout when you don't feel like it, or push through to stay late when everyone else has gone home. In many cases, it's about proving the naysayers wrong and grinding it out.

"When you're touted to be this certain guy, there's a lot of pressure that comes along with that," said McDavid. "How do you deal with that? I think I dealt with it, you know, by working harder. It really pushed me to work harder."

Luc Robitaille beat the odds, too. He scored thirty-two goals in his rookie QMJHL season with the Hull Olympiques. Yet it was determined his skating wasn't up to NHL standards, and so he fell all the way to the ninth round in his draft, 170 selections after Lemieux was taken by the Pittsburgh Penguins first overall in 1984.

Despite that, Robitaille checked in with fifty-five- and sixty-eight-goal seasons to complete his junior career and never had to play a single game in the minors. He won the 1987 Calder Trophy with a brilliant forty-five-goal rookie season with the Los Angeles Kings. He went on to have a Hall of Fame career, winning the 1991 Canada Cup and 1994 IIHF World Championship with Canada, and finally a Stanley Cup with the 2002 Detroit Red Wings. Robitaille would claim two more league titles as a member of the Kings' front office in 2012 and 2014.

Robitaille had a belief in himself. So did Alex Smart—the Kings scout who pestered rookie Los Angeles GM Rogie Vachon to take a late-round chance on Robitaille. In his playing days, Smart became the first NHLer to score a hat trick in his first game but only played eight games with the Montreal Canadiens, scoring five times. He finished his playing career in the Quebec senior league with Montreal and Ottawa, winning an Allan Cup with the 1949 Senators. Smart worked four decades with the Goodyear tire company as he scouted. He had faith in Robitaille. Number 20 never forgot that faith and made sure to thank Smart in his Hall of Fame acceptance speech in 2009.

"He was the one person who believed in me. I owe my career to Alex Smart," Robitaille said. "He was the only scout who ever talked to me. I was on one [team's scouting] list."

There are a ton of stories like St. Louis and Robitaille, who persevered and prevailed. And a guy like Andrew Mangiapane, who sat through seven rounds of the 2014 draft in Philadelphia and didn't get his name called. The following year, convinced by his father, he attended again in Florida and sat through six rounds before the Flames finally called his name, 166th overall. Since then, he has had a pretty darn good career.

"It doesn't matter what round you're drafted," he said years later. "I just wanted to go play hockey and do the best that I can . . . work hard and train and give it my all."

A terrific message. Don't get bothered or overexcited about scouting lists and draft positions. Work hard and have faith. And to the parents, be supportive of your kids and let them discover their work ethic and passion. You don't have to buy your way to the big time, whatever level that is. If the system misses you, as it happened with St. Louis and others, trust me that the system will find you. The scouts don't miss very often at any level—pee-wee, bantam, midget, junior, or pro, they will find you.

I remember being in rinks hearing parents complain their kid was playing with a lesser player and that would ruin his chances of getting drafted. No, it won't. It doesn't matter if you are a top center playing with a fourth-line winger; the scouts know what to watch for. They look for the character of the kid, an ability to adapt; they want to see how valuable a teammate the better player is. Play your game, be a good teammate, and the scouts will notice. They won't look away if you don't score or get scored upon. They know.

If a player doesn't passionately love the game, he will not play in the NHL. It's hard to play the game at any level if you don't love it. And it's really hard to get to the top. There is no shame if you don't.

As for Martin St. Louis, his hockey career has, in a way, come full circle. Undrafted, he persevered to become a Hall of Famer. But now, like Juraj Slafkovsky, the player the Habs selected first overall a few minutes after St. Louis offered his sage advice to the Bell Centre audience, he has to persevere again and win in a hockey-mad Montreal market, where hockey is a religion. The same goes for GM Kent Hughes, who along with his staff made the bold move to pass over Shane Wright in the first slot.

And don't forget the words Wright's dad, Simon, told him during the draft as he slipped to fourth overall after being pro- jected as number one by many: "I know it's easy to say, it's not when you go, it's what you do. It's never been about when. Where and what you do." Terrific advice to players at any level, and people anywhere in their careers.

Kent Hughes made a very big decision. That's the draft and the realities of the NHL. The hope is always that the first pick, and all that follow, will help turn things around, and in a hurry.

The odds of making the NHL are minuscule. Every level you go up in that pursuit, from minor hockey to junior or college, to pro, to the NHL, every step narrows. It is very, very difficult and if you're one of the lucky ones to get there, it's often even tougher to stay there. But all the hard work, discipline, passion, and char- acter that goes into it, whatever level you are trying to get to, the experience will stay with you and will serve you well on and off the ice for all your life.

I've had very few players I coached, or managed, who I didn't like as a person. Yes, there were a lot of times when I didn't approve of how they played, or maybe how they behaved, but I liked almost all of them as people. What does that tell you? Being a good person means a lot in the pursuit of the dream.

ACKNOWLEDGMENTS

THERE ARE SO MANY PEOPLE I WOULD LIKE TO THANK. I HAVE MENTIONED MY WIFE, Jill, and children, Clark and MacKenzie. They have sacrificed a lot over the years, moving from city to city, job to job. At last count, from when Jill and I married and I began coaching, we have lived in twenty-nine different houses. Sometimes we would rent, then buy. Almost always we would sell!

Thanks for all the people who impacted my career as a player, then as an assistant coach, assistant GM, head coach, GM, and president. And broadcaster. There are far too many to mention, but I couldn't have done it without them and many of the stories that appear in this book are because of those people and our relationships. The hockey community is the best.

A very special thanks to Jim Clark and Don Boyd, who have worked with me for so many years and have been a big part of my life. I would also like to thank the many club presidents, GMs and assistant GMs, coaches, and scouts who contributed their stories and expertise to this book. Their input was invaluable and greatly appreciated. In particular I would like to thank former Quebec Nordiques GM Pierre Page for all the insights and behind-the-scenes information he provided us for the Eric Lindros chapter, sharing stories never told before.

This was my first attempt at writing a book and I quickly realized that, just like hockey, it takes a team to make it happen and, hopefully, be successful. To that end, I would like to thank my coauthor, Scott Morrison, for all his efforts, as well as Tim Wharnsby, another longtime hockey reporter and author, who helped in so many invaluable ways. We also tapped into many books, websites, podcasts, and publications for details and anecdotes. Hopefully all were credited sufficiently in the text.

Thank you to our editor, the unflappable Justin Stoller, senior editor of nonfiction with Simon & Schuster Canada. Scott worked with Justin previously and he told me all was good, that we were in steady, calming hands, and he was right. Justin kept us pointed in the right direction from start to finish. And thanks also to copyeditor Barbara Wild, who did a fabulous job making sure everything was just right; and to Lloyd Davis, whose hockey knowledge was invaluable. Thanks also to Kevin Hanson, president and publisher of Simon & Schuster Canada, who guided us through this journey, along with literary agent Brian Wood.

Heading into this project, I wasn't sure what to expect, or whether the insights, inside looks, and the stories would make for a good book. We hope they have. Like draft day, you just give it your best.

INDEX